# The Educator's Guide
# to Substance Abuse Prevention

# The Educator's Guide
# to Substance Abuse Prevention

## Sanford Weinstein
*New York University*

**LEA** LAWRENCE ERLBAUM ASSOCIATES, PUBLISHERS
1999  Mahwah, New Jersey  London

Lawrence Erlbaum Associates, Inc., Publishers
10 Industrial Avenue
Mahwah, NJ  07430

Cover design by Kathryn Houghtaling Lacey

**Library of Congress Cataloging-in-Publication Data**

Weinstein, Sanford.
The educator's guide to substance abuse prevention / by Sanford Weinstein.
     p.    cm.
    Includes bibliographical references and index.
ISBN 0-8058-2594-0 (cloth : alk. paper). — ISBN 0-8058-2595-9 (pbk. : alk. paper)
    1. Drug abuse—Prevention—Study and teaching (Elementary and Secondary)  2. Substance abuse—Prevention—Study and teaching (Elementary and Secondary)  I. Title.
HV5808.W45    1999
372.3'7—dc21

               99-22619
               CIP

Books published by Lawrence Erlbaum Associates are printed on acid-free paper, and their bindings are chosen for strength and durability.

Printed in the United States of America
10  9  8  7  6  5  4  3  2  1

# Contents

# Preface

This book is a guide for teachers in preparation, practicing teachers, and other school personnel whose present and future students may raise issues about drug education, substance abuse prevention, and drug control. Students usually raise these issues in response to community events, because of personal or family experiences, to challenge the teacher and the curriculum, or because of their own drug use or that of peers. This book was written so that teachers can help children cope with drug-related events and experiences that relate to these issues.

Therefore, the primary goal of this book is to help educators work effectively within their classroom management practices, the school curriculum, and the provision of pupil–personnel services. In these ways, teachers of all school subjects may rely on their own interests and capabilities to help students in need and especially those who are at risk.

The book addresses teachers' concerns in several ways. It provides a guide through which teachers may resolve personal and professional concerns about the commitments and limits and boundaries of their working relationships with students. Also, it describes tasks that teachers can perform and mental hygiene issues they can address in creating policies, procedures, and rules to promote healthful learning activity in the classroom. And, it summarizes past and present theory about substance abuse prevention to integrate all the preceding concerns into professional teaching practice.

Furthermore, this book helps teachers explore drug-related issues from within the context of their own curricular specialties. These curricular contexts, which are subsumed under the broad themes of policy and culture, include art, music, language arts, literature, social studies, history, government, economics, science, technology, and culture. The narrative refers teachers to relevant biography, historical events, and social issues, and it suggests ways that teachers can respond to problems such as disillusionment, alienation, and dangerous trends and fads of popular culture as they relate to the problem of drug use. In these ways, this book guides teachers to better use what they already do, know, and are in order to respond competently, responsibly, and with sensitivity to the needs of their students.

Part I of this book forewarns readers about the challenging, and at times frustrating, undertaking of substance abuse prevention in the schools. Chapter 1 addresses teachers' personal and professional concerns about substance abuse prevention and drug education. Chapter 2 explores classroom management issues, the concept of children at risk, and the teacher's role as surrogate parent. Chapter 3 examines the very serious problem of school violence in relation to drug use.

Part II familiarizes the reader with theory and practice in drug education and substance abuse prevention. Chapter 4 summarizes historical efforts and failures of moralistic and propagandistic approaches. Chapter 5 examines modern theory and guidelines for teachers. Chapter 6 describes social influences on drug-using behavior.

Part III addresses historical and political curricular contexts for drug education and substance abuse prevention. Chapters 7 through 10 examine social and drug policy, and social and political disillusionment.

Part IV presents curricular contexts of art and culture. Chapter 11 identifies cultural influences on drug use and chapter 12 presents content related to popular and youth culture. Chapter 13 addresses cross-cultural and international comparison.

I thank Naomi Silverman, education editor at Lawrence Erlbaum Associates, Publishers for her enthusiastic support and wonderful assistance throughout the duration of this project. Also, I acknowledge the contributions of Dr. Peggy Ishler of the University of Northern Iowa. Her review and suggestions regarding the initial prospectus shaped its development in many important ways. I express gratitude to Dr. Norma Wilkerson of the University of Wyoming School of Nursing for her very thorough review of the initial draft of this book. Her comments and suggestions added elegance and polish to the final product. And finally, I thank Dr. John Sumerlin of Medgar Evers College–CUNY for his excellent review and editing suggestions. These were the finishing touches of this project.

—*Sanford Weinstein*

# Introduction

This textbook is about substance abuse prevention in the schools. It is primarily a guide for teachers who do this educational work, but it also may be of interest to researchers and scholars who study prevention. Therefore, this volume emphasizes the inspiration and intuition of teaching, and the teacher's clinical proximity to children. However, it also seeks to strengthen the teacher's art with the scientist's clinical distance, objectivity, and theories.

A clinical emphasis is important to substance abuse prevention because teachers practice in complex and fluid environments, and teaching is action-oriented work. Teachers must manage the processes of education as they occur and respond to many unexpected events. Recurrently, circumstance forces teachers to make quick judgments and take immediate action with little time for forethought or planning. The seamless transitions and subtle responses of skillful and sensitive teaching are the most important elements of substance abuse prevention in the schools.

Furthermore, teachers work in diverse settings. Many teach in classrooms, but many others teach in rehearsal rooms and auditoriums, art studios and technology facilities, laboratories and kitchens, and in gymnasiums and on playing fields. Some educators work in school health clinics, and in counselor, social worker, or administrator offices. Therefore, this book presents theories, ideas, and strategies that teachers can use to perform the formidable tasks related to substance abuse prevention in these many differing settings.

Although the narrative contains vernacular and slang to capture the clinical feel of good teaching, it offers precise language and definitions, too. The definitions guide the reader's understanding and help educational curriculum developers, policymakers, and researchers who decide to test this book's theories and strategies.

Generally, the definitions reflect perspectives of adversaries in the drug debate because of the fierce policy and moral conflict that forever surrounds the drug issue. The drug debate includes the *drug control* perspective, *diagnostic* or *functional* perspective, and the *drug education* perspective. From the perspective of drug control, *substance abuse* is any illicit or illegal use of a controlled substance. Therefore, drug control advocates aim *substance abuse prevention* at influencing people to abstain from illicit drug use, or inducing young people to postpone use of substances to which age restrictions apply, such as alcohol or tobacco. The prevention goal of drug control advocates is to stop nonusers from trying drugs (*primary prevention*), to stop noncompulsive users from continuing to use drugs (*secondary prevention*), and to force compulsive users into recovery (*tertiary prevention*).

Drug control activities attempt to suppress the supply side of drug use by banning production and distribution of certain substances, and to suppress the demand side by constraining potential users. The major actors are the police, the courts, and at times, the schools. Their mission is to eradicate illicit recreational drug-taking behavior.

*Suppressive tactics* include coercion through fines, imprisonment, confiscation of private property, and denial of public entitlements (welfare benefits, student loans, school expulsion, driver's licenses), and *deceptive practices*, such as misrepresentation and propaganda. Teachers and other prevention workers often implement the latter two under the guise of drug education. Drug control advocates justify all these tactics as weapons of the "war on drugs." Thus, to drug control advocates, substance abuse prevention is a moral battle between the forces of good and evil.

In contrast, from the *functional perspective of diagnosis and treatment*, human service providers and mental health practitioners define substance abuse as episodes of dangerous misuse, or the development of dangerous patterns of licit or illicit drug use. To be dangerous, these episodes and patterns must create excessive risk of compulsive use (habituation, addiction) or health, social, psychological, behavioral, and legal problems. Thus, the treatment community focuses on these problems as a function or outcome of the misuse or abuse of drugs and other druglike substances.

In accordance with the functional perspective, substance abuse prevention is activity aimed at reducing or eliminating dangerous episodes and patterns of drug use and addresses only the demand side of drug use. Abstinence and postponement or primary prevention for nonusers are appropriate goals, in some instances, but they are not the only goals of prevention activities. Secondary prevention, or inducing drug users to modify drug-taking behavior to reduce risk, is yet another goal. The major actors are parents, teachers, churches, and other social and human service providers. Their mission is to eradicate the problems and liabilities caused by drug misuse and abuse rather than to altogether eliminate drug use.

From the functional perspective, tertiary prevention is aimed at preventing relapse among addicted individuals who are in the process of recovery. The major players are hospitals, treatment programs, and other victims in self-help groups. Teachers rarely, if ever, provide tertiary prevention services.

However, teachers can and do provide primary and secondary prevention services that include disseminating information and implementing various psychosocial education interventions. In these activities, teachers help students consider the risks of drug use and reduce needs and social pressures that drive dangerous forms of drug use. These, too, are types of drug education. It is from the functional perspective that this book defines substance abuse prevention by teachers.

However, *drug education* goes far beyond the limits of drug control and substance abuse prevention. This book portrays drugs as one more arena of technological innovation that serves many useful purposes in society. As with other technological developments, misuse and abuse are certainly possible. But, so, too, are many benefits that drugs provide as medicines, social lubricants, spiritual facilitators, performance enhancers, and sources of pleasure, soothing, and emotional relief. From this perspective *drug education* is defined here as preparation for the safe use of drugs and druglike substances that provide these benefits.

With these definitions in mind, one can reasonably conclude that despite America's 100 years of drug control and other substance abuse prevention efforts, the problem of substance misuse and abuse is not a dead issue. Unlike ancient civilizations, about which new discoveries shed light on objects and events long past, drug use remains a very active moral and political battlefront. Consequently, new objects and events emerge from it incessantly.

Clearly, the struggle is dynamically alive, changing, and continually reborn in both new and old forms. Therefore, this book relies, to a degree, on the work of journalists and reporters. Their reports of interviews and on-the-scene observations in newspapers and magazines often are the most up-to-date and only primary source materials about the emerging history of the drug world. Scholarly reports in professional journals and books are often a step behind.

It is true that some journalists and reporters distort, exaggerate, and sensationalize to sell their medium to readers, viewers, and listeners. However, so do other scientific and presumably more reliable observers who are caught up in the moral and political struggle associated with our drug policies. Therefore, this book, while summarizing the divergent claims of observers of the drug world, emphasizes issues raised by the great variety of their reports rather than their veracity. More important, the narrative offers guidelines to teachers so that they may investigate issues of drug use and abuse together with students in the schools. In providing these guidelines, the central and organizing theses of this book, and therefore its biases, are as follow:

1. The development and use of intoxicating and performance-enhancing substances have a very long history and are a permanent part of all human cultures.
2. Drug use is not always equivalent to substance abuse.
3. When society restricts the individual's freedom of choice about using drugs, it violates its own democratic values and beliefs.
4. The rhetoric of prohibition and of liberalization of drug laws each contain valid and invalid arguments.
5. Although drug prohibition is the dominant social policy at this time in history, prohibition has probably caused more problems than it has solved.
6. Americans should reexamine current drug policies and assiduously monitor new ones as they evolve.
7. Teachers are in a central position to influence knowledge, attitudes, behavior, and values about abstinence, use, misuse, and abuse of drugs.
8. By effectively educating today's students, teachers can influence future drug laws and policies.
9. Teachers must separate drug education from substance abuse prevention and drug control, and establish a rapprochement about the conflicts and differences between these three activities.
10. Teachers can use many elements of the academic curriculum to implement substance abuse prevention and drug education goals.
11. Teachers should use their social positions as surrogate parents, role models, and educators to implement substance abuse prevention strategies.

These central and organizing theses are important because substance abuse prevention and drug education lead to a moral and political battlefront that raises many issues for teachers. Teachers must prepare for challenging encounters when parents, students, and colleagues raise these issues.

# I

# Substance Abuse Prevention and Drug Education: Professional Issues and Concerns of Teachers

# 1

# Teachers as Agents
# of Substance Abuse Prevention

The goals for this chapter are:

1. To explain how a teacher's place in the life of children presents many opportunities for substance abuse prevention.
2. To show how separation between the academic curriculum and traditional approaches to drug education have excluded teachers from substance abuse prevention.
3. To summarize new thinking that recognizes the value of teachers as agents of prevention.
4. To explain how substance abuse prevention fits within standard practices of good teaching.
5. To alert teachers about the relevance of drugs to many significant people, places, events, and activities that are studied in the academic curriculum.
6. To warn teachers about conflicts and contradictions between democratic values of teaching and undemocratic tactics and strategies associated with drug control.
7. To help teachers develop realistic expectations about substance abuse prevention in the schools.

Substance abuse prevention offers rewarding opportunities to teachers, but also presents them with frustrating dilemmas. Therefore, teachers who accept its challenges should carefully consider their choices and define the limits of their efforts.

For example, substance abuse prevention requires teachers to balance their commitments. To be effective, teachers should not do this work as a minor or occasional activity. However, teachers must also avoid excessive involvement that distracts them from the school cur-

**3**

riculum or drains them of resources. Therefore, this book describes how teachers may achieve a satisfactory balance by integrating substance abuse prevention strategies with daily teaching practice and the school curriculum.

In addition, substance abuse prevention obliges teachers to be organized and methodical in their work and requires an orderly process of teaching and learning. Because chaotic life circumstances are a major risk factor in substance abuse, teachers must avoid becoming an unnecessary additional stressor for children at risk. This book offers teachers suggestions and ideas about how to create stable and consistent learning environments in classrooms and other school settings.

Furthermore, teachers have their own personal concerns about doing substance abuse prevention work. These questions are straightforward: "Why me?" "Why bother?" "Is it really my business, anyway?" "Am I just asking for a lot of extra work?" "Will it divert my attention and energies from what I really like in teaching?" and "Am I setting myself up for disappointment and trouble?"

These "me, myself, and I" questions are important because teachers must be thoughtful about how to use their potential to help. They can easily waste it by neglecting their own self-care, disregarding their professional obligations, or failing to derive personal gratification from teaching. Physical and emotional exhaustion, loss of professional status, and burnout are the consequences of these mistakes. Such risks are stern reminders that teachers must be balanced, organized, and disciplined about substance abuse prevention.

Finally, substance abuse prevention demands that teachers carefully negotiate perilous social and political terrain. This source of peril can distort substance abuse prevention and threaten teachers because:

1. Teachers' efforts in drug education and substance abuse prevention have an historical context that has meaning in the classroom.
2. Culture and social policies regarding drugs and drug use define the teacher's role in prevention.
3. Teachers who do prevention work must contend with abhorrent motives and events associated with U.S. drug policy and drug control practices.
4. Drug policy and drug control clash violently with important social and educational values.
5. Teachers' exposure and vulnerability to community pressures to violate these values is a problem in drug education and substance abuse prevention.

## WHY SHOULD TEACHERS BE CONCERNED
## ABOUT SUBSTANCE ABUSE?

With regard to drugs, teachers often find themselves in the position of people who are first to arrive at the scene of an accident. This happens because teachers usually are the primary adults who participate in a child's daily life outside of the family. Consequently, teachers may, at times, prevent serious problems in which a child's own behavior is a source of peril.

Substance abuse is just one such problem. Although teachers are helpful and some provide instruction in drug education, they most often assist children on an ad hoc basis. Usually, a teacher's help is extemporaneous and intuitive, and a humane response to an immediate crisis.

At such times, teachers may refer children to other adults for assistance, but a teacher's own crisis management efforts may be helpful, too. However, because they often are reactions to the unexpected, a teacher's interventions usually are unsystematic, isolated from any organized larger effort, and fail to address concerns about preventing future crises. Even when they manage future considerations effectively, teachers may be unaware of this good work (Weinstein, 1995c).

Consequently, schools overlook the classroom teacher's opportunities to prevent substance abuse and underutilize his or her capacities to help with this problem. Therefore, one purpose of this book is to inform teachers that, despite many problems, exciting possibilities exist in substance abuse prevention. This is so for all classroom teachers, regardless of their curricular interests.

In fact, teachers can be key to prevention because of their position in the schools and in the life of children. Teachers are a valuable resource because schools have captive audiences of an age appropriate to early prevention, and have larger numbers of this age group than any other community agency. Most important, schools offer almost limitless opportunities for face-to-face social interaction between teachers and children (Ellickson, 1995).

## ARE CLASSROOM TEACHERS ISOLATED
## FROM SUBSTANCE ABUSE PREVENTION?

Teachers may expect the schools to continue to shoulder the bulk of the prevention effort, just as schools have in the past (Ellickson, 1995). Despite this, schools isolate most teachers from organized substance abuse prevention efforts. In part, this happens because teachers focus their attention primarily on subjects in the academic curriculum and strive to help children master them.

In preparing to be educators, teachers choose an academic major such as mathematics, art, history, music, health, foreign language, or science, and seek professional education to teach that as a school subject. State certification requirements usually mandate teacher education experiences. In general, teacher education includes college courses in child development, educational psychology, educational history and philosophy, child abuse identification, teaching methods, and student teaching.

Many teachers use this preparation to define the boundaries of their work in the schools. Despite conditions that increasingly push classroom teachers to be social service providers, administrators expect health or physical education teachers to teach drug education and do substance abuse prevention work. They also expect pupil personnel services staff members to help children with substance abuse problems. Pupil personnel staff include school psychologists, social workers, nurses, and guidance counselors.

This is consistent with the fact that only 11 states require instruction in substance abuse education to be a teacher certification requirement (Office of Educational Research and Improvement, 1988). Although 40 states mandate drug education classes for school children and 32 have minimum standards for drug education curricula, only 17 have adopted or designed these curricula. Furthermore, only 10 states require that schools provide drug education classes outside of health or driver education.

Consequently, few teachers other than health or physical educators expect to participate in formal substance abuse prevention programs, or teach the drug education curriculum. Even though many teachers think substance abuse prevention is a legitimate concern of the schools, most see it to be peripheral to their own teaching responsibilities.

## WHY DOES THE CLASSROOM TEACHER HAVE A MARGINAL ROLE IN SUBSTANCE ABUSE PREVENTION?

The focus on the academic curriculum is important to contractual arrangements between school districts and teachers. However, the very nature of teaching contracts may unwittingly contribute to the isolation of teachers from substance abuse prevention efforts. Hopefully, this and other perplexing problems will not discourage teachers interested in substance abuse prevention, but whose first love is to teach reading, history, or art.

Some problems emanate from preservice teacher education, as described previously. However, turf struggles in the education community, social and educational policies about substance use and abuse, economic constraints, and the attitudes of teachers are problems, too. These problems have pushed teachers to the fringes of substance abuse prevention.

Turf struggles between various teaching and pupil personnel service specialties are particularly troublesome. These struggles impact school policy, funding, and hiring practices, and affect job availability, job security, and the status of teachers. For example, despite intense effort, school health is a low priority, has poor visibility, and receives little emphasis in efforts to reform and improve education in the United States (Miller & Telljohan, 1992). As a result, health educators work self-protectively to promote their proprietary interest in substance abuse prevention and drug education, and a variety of other curricular areas related to health.

Their professional organizations are continually involved in expanding and promoting the Comprehensive School Health Program (CSHP). The American School Health Association (Allensworth & Kolbe, 1987) and the federal government's Centers for Disease Control and Prevention (CDC) are principal advocates of the CSHP. Because the CSHP places substance abuse prevention within the domain of comprehensive school health, the teacher of other school subjects has marginal status by de facto nonassignment.

The CSHP identifies health education and physical education teachers as the primary instructional staff for health in middle and secondary schools. Other nonteaching health and pupil personnel services staff are included too, but as part of the school health program's nonteaching components.

However, the classroom teacher of other school subjects, particularly in secondary schools, has an insignificant position relative to any subject matter connected with health. The exception is elementary school teachers who teach all subjects in self-contained classrooms in most school districts. Nevertheless, the rhetoric of the ongoing turf war argues that classroom teachers are ill prepared, boring, disinterested, repetitive, and ineffective when they teach about health-related matters, including substance abuse.

In addition to these struggles, broader social and educational policies have pushed teachers to the margins of substance abuse prevention, too. These policies have blurred the boundaries between drug control, drug education, and substance abuse prevention. Consequently, substance abuse prevention has become drug education's preeminent goal, and both are subject to increasing intrusion by the policy agenda of drug control.

Because of this, teachers who openly explore and are truthful about drug use tread dangerous ground. For example, thoughtful teachers might suggest to students that, as the facts indicate, substance "use" and substance "abuse" differ, or that responsible use is a viable alternative to abstinence. However, these teachers face vindictive reactions from some parents, administrators, other teachers, and community members. The net result is that the validity of drug education, in its broad and most meaningful sense, is seriously compromised. To teach truth about drugs places teachers at risk of being labeled traitors in the war on drugs.

This problem may lead some teachers to argue that if prevention has a place in the schools, it is not within classroom teaching. This is not my position, but the issue is worthy of consideration by policymakers and the professional community of educators.

Also, prevention experts now advocate comprehensive strategies that enlist parents, business leaders, law enforcement, and other segments of the community. However, the place of the classroom teacher in the mix is unclear. This is particularly so because dwindling resources and austere budgets have forced school personnel to acknowledge limitations in capability and motivation.

Furthermore, teachers' own lack of interest in, if not aversion to, drug education and substance abuse prevention may contribute to their marginal status. Because of this disinterest, many publishers do not see teachers as constituting a market for methods books on the subject. In fact, not a single current, comprehensive, nationally distributed textbook about teaching drug education or substance abuse prevention existed at the time of this writing (L. Akers, personal communication, January, 1994).

Eisman and Eisman (1997) wrote a small guide to drug education and substance abuse prevention in schools. This guide offers discussion topics that may be useful in the classroom, but its focus is narrow and superficial. It presents some drug-related content, but is biased about issues, and does not consider teaching–learning processes. These limitations, and its brevity (80 pages in length), restrict its usefulness to teachers.

The two most substantial books on this topic are out of date, and have been for some time. One is an edited volume by Eisman, Wingard, and Huba (1984) that first appeared in 1971, with later printings updated into the early 1980s. The other is a coauthored text by Cornacchia, Smith, and Bentel (1978), which is directed toward health educators. The second and last edition of this book was written in the mid-1970s. No subsequent updated editions are available for either book.

This is sad because researchers studying substance abuse and addiction have produced important new insights that are of value to teachers. Such knowledge often pertains to school children exposed to the dangers of substance abuse.

The distillation of this new information that more recent writing could provide is sorely needed. As Goode (1993) suggested, the flood of information about drugs and drug use is now so enormous that even the most diligent reader must ignore most of it, and narrow his or her field of view to a limited segment. Furthermore, in studying alcohol abuse, Levin (1995) described the research literature as difficult for clinicians and teachers to use, even when delimited. He suggested that an overemphasis on research technique, arcane statistical analysis, and researchers' clinically remote perspective inhibits useful interpretation. Levin concluded that addiction researchers have reached a point where they appear to be discovering more and more about less and less.

Despite these observations, many current texts focus on drugs, alcohol, and substance abuse from a wide variety of perspectives. Although these texts provide a wealth of curricular content in drug education, their authors provide little direct guidance for integrating that content into teaching and learning processes. Texts on health education teaching methods usually address drug education, but do so as one small part of the larger health education curriculum. Consequently, books about drugs and books about teaching methods limit their content about drug education teaching and substance abuse prevention to one relatively brief chapter.

Therefore, colleges and school districts rely primarily on locally produced guidebooks and writings for teacher preparation in substance abuse prevention. Although many of these materials may be of high quality, few, if any, are exposed to expert review and dissemination beyond the locality in which they are produced. As a result, these materials offer no guarantee of conformity to any evolving national consensus about the teacher's role in drug education or school-based prevention.

Such materials, regardless of their excellence or shortcomings, represent the current "catch as catch can" approach to teacher preparation in substance abuse prevention and drug education. Teacher certification requirements in drug education are a hodgepodge of legislation and state education department regulations. As few as eight states require a college course in teacher education pertaining to drug, alcohol, and tobacco abuse. Others require more limited instruction as part of other teacher training classes. Given these conditions, the fact that drug education and substance abuse prevention are minor concerns for most teachers is not surprising.

This may account for Botvin's (1995) observation that, too often, teachers of drug education classes have little expertise in the subject area. Where researchers conducted controlled experiments to evaluate educational innovations in substance abuse prevention, they frequently attributed negative findings to faulty or uninspired teaching (Ellickson, 1995).

This is a problem because, to be implemented meaningfully, the content and methods of drug education curricula demand more than vague familiarity with pertinent skills and knowledge. Modern prevention programs in particular demand that enthusiastic teachers exercise sophisticated social skills and possess an understanding of risk factors for substance abuse.

This is evident in Botvin's (1987) finding that quality of implementation is related to outcome in his Life Skills Training substance abuse prevention program. No doubt, teaching and other educational work in prevention often requires high motivation, some special training, and extra preparation by teachers. This is so even though information about drugs has become much less important to substance abuse prevention.

## CAN CLASSROOM TEACHERS DO SUBSTANCE ABUSE PREVENTION?

New understandings about risk and resistance factors in substance abuse reveal that classroom teachers have many good opportunities to pursue prevention goals. This is true for teachers who are interested in substance abuse prevention and for teachers who feel otherwise. In part, prevention experts discovered these opportunities because recent understandings have led substance abuse prevention away from information-oriented strategies of the past.

Information-based approaches presume that children accept certain social and health values, are ignorant of risk, and will be rational when informed about the dangers of substance abuse (Goodstadt, 1978; Steuart, 1969). These presumptions may be valid.

However, in view of the fact that the dangers of many drugs are too equivocal, and information sources too untrustworthy to dissuade adventurous young souls, one must question who is being rational. Is it the teacher who passionately advocates abstinence, a position that is not entirely supported by the evidence? Or, is it the recreational drug user who carefully and responsibly seeks the pleasures of his or her drug of choice?

New thinking makes this question a secondary issue. Furthermore, newer prevention approaches and reduced emphasis on dissemination of drug information lessen the demand that teachers possess broad general knowledge about pharmacology, human neuroanatomy and physiology, law, health and social impacts, and culture as they relate to drugs and substance abuse.

Newer thinking also minimizes troubling issues raised by strategies founded on "personal deficit" explanations of drug use. Deficit-oriented strategies presume that "affective" intervention bolsters weaknesses in mental health and social adjustment, and deters "self-medication" as a motive for substance abuse. In some ways, deficit-oriented programs place teachers in the position of providing mental health services. This is no longer a serious concern because affective approaches have receded after a 15-year period of prominence in substance abuse prevention.

Obviously, the preparation needed to satisfy these many demands and requirements is extensive. The breadth of knowledge required for information-oriented teaching can be an eclectic specialty in itself. Competent implementation of affective programs to some degree relies on skills in counseling, human relations, and group dynamics. Teachers rarely develop such a broad personal background of skills and knowledge when it is tangential to their primary interests.

Now, more than ever, such skills and knowledge are far less prominent as requirements for modern substance abuse prevention activity. As this book explains, many traditional skills, understandings, practices, and commitments of good teaching apply to substance abuse prevention in the classroom.

## HOW DOES THE CONCEPT OF "CHILDREN AT RISK" INCLUDE CLASSROOM TEACHERS IN SUBSTANCE ABUSE PREVENTION?

In a pragmatic way, new theory emphasizes resistance and susceptibility to substance abuse social pressures, especially to assist children thought to be in danger of becoming victims (Anthony, 1987; Brown & Mills, 1987). Accordingly, language that identifies and describes newer methods as "social inoculation" or "social influence" reflects the direction of this thinking.

Essentially, risk and resistance factors associated with life circumstance, popular culture, peer influences, and legal prohibition are now the focus of substance abuse prevention strategy. This has produced strategy that emphasizes social skill development, interpersonal relationships, social processes in the peer group, and desensitization to media influences. The first three of these are important to skilled teaching in any subject area, and have been teachers' traditional windows of opportunity as helpers to children.

To scientifically validate this theory, researchers have identified life circumstances that contribute to risk of and resistance to substance abuse. For example, children who repeatedly fail in school, suffer lowered social status, and endure other serious personal struggles are prominent among those who are in peril (Ackerman, 1983; Brown & Mills, 1987; Jewett, 1982). Alternatively, children who have adequate adult support, protection, and supervision are less vulnerable.

These are a few of many circumstances that fall within the themes of susceptibility and resistance. A more general concept that identifies a child's susceptibility is a life that is excessively disorganized and beset by stressful events (Savage-Supernaw, 1991; Wills, 1991). A second general concept is a social environment that promotes and supports drug use. Clearly, these concepts address a child's struggles with self-care, failures by adult caretakers, problems grasping positive social opportunities and resisting negative ones, and in basic terms, not having much fun.

On the other hand, stable life circumstances, and protection from extremely aversive experiences appear to enhance resistance. So do social environments that oppose drug use.

Thus, teachers may best direct their efforts toward:

1. Helping to bring order to chaotic lives.
2. Protecting children from assaults with which they cannot effectively cope.
3. Helping children gain positive social support and resist negative social pressures.
4. Teaching skills that children may use to manage and defuse stressful challenges.
5. Helping children find joy in healthy living.

Teachers can, in many ways, support a child's own striving in these areas. They can create safe and trustworthy learning environments, serve as resource persons and leaders for classroom discussion about life issues, create alternative learning strategies for children with learning difficulties, and help children gain access to resources and opportunities in the community. In so doing, teachers will attack directly those life circumstances implicated in substance abuse.

As managers of classroom learning environments, teachers can shape school experience to make it orderly and to minimize stress. School may then offer a respite and haven to children for whom disorganization and stress are endemic to home and community (Weinstein, 1991). In so doing, bonding or attachment to school, an important resistance factor in substance abuse, may be strengthened.

As discussion leaders and resource persons, teachers can help children explore life issues. Children confront many such issues in the academic curriculum, as observers of events in the community, and through personal experience. In these roles, teachers can mobilize the positive potential of the peer group, help children examine cultural definitions, identify community resources, and foster introspection.

In so doing, teachers can promote positive and constructive social interaction among peers in the classroom. Similarly, teachers can promote a shared vision of the purposes of school and learning, an emphasis on children's strengths and opportunities rather than their weaknesses and inadequacies, and a sense of belonging (Allen & Allen, 1990).

Success here supports exploration and dialogue with trustworthy adults and peers about many personal, social, cultural, and health concerns. Often, these concerns are disorganizing influences and sources of stress for children. Knowledge and sensitivity about the nature and causes of drug abuse, and a teacher's readiness to help are important to this as a substance abuse prevention tool.

By devising alternative learning strategies, teachers may circumvent reading problems that can short circuit learning in critical areas of the curriculum. Although the importance of reading cannot be minimized, children can study historic events such as Custer's Last Stand through means other than reading and writing. The arts and other creative activities (Crawford, 1981; Metcalf, 1987) provide many such opportunities. Consequently, reading deficits need not be an insurmountable liability or guarantee of failure in all areas of the academic curriculum.

Arts activities as alternatives for learning have particular relevance to special education students. These children often are limited by poor skills in reading and writing, suffer diminished social status as a result of special education placement, and struggle with a variety of social difficulties.

By helping children gain access to opportunities and resources in the community, teachers can intervene directly into risk associated with isolation and alienation. Although teachers can do this in many ways, the field trip is an underused opportunity for linking children with the community. Teachers can expand this even further by finding service learning opportunities in which students participate at community sites, do volunteer work, or provide assistance to individuals, groups, and organizations outside of the school.

Field trips and service-learning experiences allow children to see, firsthand, success and achievement in business, industry, the arts, health care, and culture at sites in the community (Central Park Historical Society, 1989). Such sites provide children with first-hand exposure to positive social values, rich cultural traditions, multicultural understanding, and valuable opportunities for substance abuse prevention.

More important, the teacher can provide children with knowledge and skills to return to such sites independently or with parents and friends. That such places exist, how one may travel to them and gain access, and how to behave within them may be startling discoveries for children at risk of substance abuse. Often, the life circumstances of these children have deprived them of opportunities for such important learning.

## DO DRUG EDUCATION AND SUBSTANCE ABUSE PREVENTION FIT WITHIN THE ACADEMIC CURRICULUM?

As discussed previously, policymakers' linkage of drug control with substance abuse prevention and drug education creates curriculum problems for teachers. However, whether we like it or not, drugs and alcohol are an integral part of U.S. cultural, economic, social, and political life and history. Nevertheless, the rhetoric of drug control insists that drug education and substance abuse prevention espouse zero tolerance for anything other than unequivocal condemnation of drug use.

This is a difficult bind because the place and meaning of drugs and alcohol in community life and our cultural heritage is as valid to social studies, science, health, and arts curricula as is Custer's Last Stand to the U.S. history curriculum. Because the world in which we live is painted in shades of gray rather than black or white, the curriculum must present many perspectives, interpretations, and opposing arguments on all topics and issues.

For example, was General Custer a brave soldier who died a hero's death in the line of duty? Or, as some argue, was he a pompous and arrogant fool who underestimated his enemy at the cost of his own life and the life of the troops in his command? Debate about this question is certainly legitimate learning activity in the classroom.

Similarly, the history of drug use's influence on the events and destiny of people in politics, business, industry, the arts, and the professions has curricular validity, too. However, class discussion about drugs' positive effects or even their irrelevance violates mandates that teachers remain stalwart soldiers of the war on drugs. As soldiers in this war, teachers must be strident communicators of antidrug rhetoric.

For some community members, teachers are the only accessible and trustworthy source of information about many controversial issues, despite teachers tenuous hold on academic freedom and frequently embattled commitment to truth. The availability, utility, and dangers of drugs and medications in the legitimate and illegitimate marketplace are among such issues. Children, and, at times, their parents turn to teachers for knowledge and understanding about such matters.

Information poses an interesting dilemma for substance abuse prevention because it does not deter substance abuse. Nevertheless, knowledge about the dangers and uses of drugs is at the heart of sound judgment and informed decisions about them.

For example, to know that improper use of antibacterial drugs breeds drug-resistant infections is as educationally valid as knowing the dangers of alcohol consumption during pregnancy. In becoming drug resistant, some bacteria evolve to produce an enzyme called beta-lactamase that breaks down penicillin and similar drugs, thus making them ineffective. And, alcohol may not only damage fetuses, but may be dangerous to mothers by raising risks of breast cancer, even at moderate levels of consumption.

Similarly, to know that hyperactivity, attention deficit disorder, and some depression can be controlled with medically supervised drug use is of equal importance to knowing that smoking tobacco causes fatal respiratory and circulatory disease. Even the fact that many foods and beverages contain drugs or druglike substances and that one can overdose on some nutritional supplements has relevance to everyday life in U.S. communities. This is particularly true now because of the large number of drugs that are legally available either through medical prescription or over the counter.

U.S. history reveals that this was not always the case. Before 1900, physicians had little medication of benefit to offer patients beside morphine (Sandor, 1995). However, since then, the practice of medicine has become more scientifically based, and the pharmaceutical industry has been prolific in its discovery and production of useful new drugs.

Now, for conditions from "A to Z," there are drugs to treat or control acne, addiction, arthritis, appetite, anxiety, bacterial infection, baldness, blood pressure, bowel movement, cancer, cholesterol, cold sores, depression, fertility, impotence, mania, menopause, pain, viral infection, seasickness, sleeplessness, wakefulness, and zoophobia. Consequently, in pursuit of health and happiness, Prozac is on the tip of the tongue today just as were penicillin and laudanum, the "wonder" drugs of earlier eras.

In fact, so ubiquitous are drugs from "A for aspirin" to "Z for Zoloft," that Americans constantly face a dizzying array of possibilities and dangers. Recently, scandals in connection with Halcion, a sleep medication, and Prozac, an antidepressant, have shaken public confidence in drug companies and the Food and Drug Administration (FDA). That the drug industry has been dishonest in reporting clinical safety tests, and the FDA has been remiss in performing its duties, are frightening possibilities for a society that relies so heavily on drugs and medications.

Furthermore, drug choices have become increasingly confusing because generic and brand names obscure the legal drug landscape just as street names have proliferated in the world of illegal drugs. "A for Acyclovir" and "Z for Zovirax," which are the same herpes medication, is a case in point among legal drugs. Worse yet, the name of an illegal drug sold on the street often has nothing to do with its true content.

Also, increasingly active participation in medical treatment decisions by patients and consumerism in health care provide new benefits, but impose new responsibilities, too. As if to emphasize this last point, drug companies now promote and advertise psychiatric drugs directly to patients, rather than to physicians, as they did in the past (Freudenheim, 1998).

What is more, the poor among immigrant populations whose countries of origin have few controls seek and obtain, without a doctor's prescription, prescription drugs and medications from pharmacies (Fisher, 1998). In some cases, they do so to keep their health care costs down, and in others they do so out of ignorance of U.S. laws. The problem is that some unscrupulous pharmacists illegally dispense these drugs and medications.

Physicians and public health officials are concerned about many risks associated with promotional efforts of drug companies and pharmacists' illegal sales. Among these concerns are manipulation and exploitation of mentally ill patients and invasion of their privacy (Freudenheim, 1998), the development of antibiotic-resistant strains of bacteria, dangerous allergic reactions, and bad treatment and a worsening of illness for very sick individuals (Fisher, 1998). Thus, the observation that every new solution to old miseries confronts us with new problems and miseries is particularly vivid in the world of drugs.

With regard to drugs and medications, sound judgment and informed decisions are complex. Nevertheless, they are important to childrearing, self-care, civic responsibility, and personal happiness in modern society. Therefore, if the schools' mission is to prepare the citizenry for community life, drug education has a place in the academic curriculum that is both independent of and important to substance abuse prevention.

## HOW DOES GOOD TEACHING CONTRIBUTE TO SUBSTANCE ABUSE PREVENTION?

Despite blurring of differences between them, important distinctions exist between drug education and substance abuse prevention. These distinctions enhance the teacher's potential as an agent of prevention. That they are not the same thing means that teachers' potential may be realized without teachers ever participating in a formal program or preparing a lesson on substance abuse. This is so even though education can be part of larger prevention efforts.

Opportunities for substance abuse prevention exist within the roles and tasks inherent to teaching. Some of these roles and tasks are simple and easy and others are more subtle, complex, and difficult. But, they address core issues at the heart of risk factors in substance abuse and represent central concepts of this writing.

If a unifying theme is present in these concepts, it is a theory about interpersonal relationships (Rogers, 1962) in the context of the academic curriculum. For teachers, such relationships offer opportunities to support the efforts of capable parents and to minimize or repair damage that may result when parents are irresponsible or inept (Weinstein, 1995c).

These opportunities exist because of, rather than despite, teachers' focus on the academic curriculum in guiding educational activity. The curriculum and children's mastery of school subjects represent a central mission of the schools, but a good teacher's working relationship with children often produces many benefits beyond academic success.

Among these benefits is the shaping of behavior so that, with the onrush of adulthood, children may more capably exercise self-care, meet social obligations of community life, and find joy in existence. A child's substance abuse may be indicative of impeded progress toward these goals, and poses a serious threat to hard won development of such essential elements of healthy maturity.

## WHAT DISAPPOINTMENTS ABOUT SUBSTANCE ABUSE PREVENTION CONFRONT TEACHERS?

Many educational approaches to substance abuse prevention, old and new, are problematic for uninitiated and unwary teachers (Fields, 1992). In part, this is a problem because ineffective or unproven prevention approaches often appear to make such good sense, and many seem to offer deceptively easy solutions. Furthermore, parents, other community members, and some teachers have unrealistic expectations about how much influence the schools can exert in preventing substance abuse (Goode, 1993).

These are serious concerns because hundreds of drug education programs aimed at substance abuse prevention now exist. Unfortunately, evaluators have subjected only a small number to rigorous testing, and most evaluated programs have shown little promise as prevention strategies (Ellickson, 1995).

The prevention mission of education programs often is outrageously seductive because it appeals to a common human desire to feel heroic and powerful (McLelland, Davis, Kalin, & Wanner, 1972). In the past, some approaches offered sincere but naive teachers opportunities to direct others' behavior, to preach and admonish, to exhort, persuade and convince, and to frighten young onlookers in a grand effort to rescue them from drug use (Fields, 1992). Later, "affective" approaches provided opportunities for teachers to become healers and therapists in helping to mend deficits in self-esteem, assertiveness, and communication. Such strategies were inappropriate and unrealistic.

These substance abuse prevention approaches, just as drug abuse itself, satisfy Blachly's (1970) criteria for his concept of *seduction*. According to Blachly, seductive attractions offer users some short-term rewards, but cause much long-term disappointment. Substance abusers, at some level of consciousness, recognize the shortsightedness and futility of their actions. So do teachers engaged in ineffective substance abuse prevention activities. Just as addicts may perpetuate their addiction through denial, teachers find comfort in often quoted rationalizations such as: "If I reach just one child, the effort is worth it!"

The cost of such efforts raises serious questions about this justification. Available evidence indicates that most educational strategies have been ineffective or even counterproductive to prevention. Furthermore, their troubling potential to waste time (Goode, 1993) and other resources, and to distract teachers and students from the academic curriculum adds to long-term disappointment. Although some methods appear to hold promise, drug education as a means of prevention has produced many failed efforts, ineffective strategies, and much frustrating reappraisal (Avis, 1990; Goodstadt, 1978).

The most recent of such disappointments is Project DARE (Drug Abuse Resistance Education). Project DARE, created by the Los Angeles Unified School District and the Los Angeles Police Department in 1983, is the most widely used school-based substance abuse prevention program in the United States. A distinguishing characteristic of Project DARE is that police officers come into the schools to provide drug education experiences for children. Outlays of school time and finances represent large expenditures of resources.

To examine the effectiveness of Project DARE, researchers used sophisticated statistical methods to combine and analyze evaluation data from eight separate locations in North America and Hawaii. This meta-analysis revealed that the program's effectiveness is meager and it is less effective than many other prevention programs, particularly programs in which social interaction is a prominent feature (Ennett, Tobler, Ringwalt, & Flewelling, 1994).

In part, this explains drug education's and substance abuse prevention's status as orphans of current U.S. drug policy (Haaga & Reuter, 1995). Ironically, many people view prevention as the best hope for combating substance abuse, but drug control, law enforcement, and interdiction of drug imports continue to receive the lion's share of funding. Prevention has long been at the bottom of the food chain of resources that fuel drug policy, and typically receives between 9% and 16% of total Federal drug-related expenditures.

## WHAT DANGERS ARE INHERENT TO SUBSTANCE ABUSE PREVENTION BY TEACHERS?

The distinctions between drug control, drug education, and substance abuse prevention that create opportunity also create danger for teachers. In troublesome ways, these distinctions confront teachers with seriously conflicting values.

For example, U.S. educational tradition and teacher education institutions advocate democracy, dialogue, choice, personal responsibility, humanitarianism, enlightenment, and free will. However, policymakers increasingly have made substance abuse prevention an extension of drug control rather than an application of drug education. Consequently, prevention is tainted by the moralism, tyranny, coercion, corruption, and propaganda associated with prohibitionist drug policy.

Drug policy appears to swing between periods of calm and times of panic. About every 20 years, youth and popular culture attract renewed attention to some form of drug involvement. Various segments of the community react with fear and moral outrage, and politicians and policymakers tighten the screws a bit on drug prohibition. Since 1950, U.S. communities have experienced these swings with marijuana, LSD, amphetamines, and cocaine. In early 1999 America is emerging from its most recent panic about crack cocaine, but heroin has become the latest threat. Consequently, drug policy and substance abuse prevention focus most intently on recreational use of illegal psychoactive drugs. Alcohol and tobacco are legal for adults, but they are not for children, who are the primary targets of prevention efforts.

Although substance abuse prevention programs pay lip service to proper use of over-the-counter medications and medically supervised prescription drugs, programs place major emphasis on illicit drug use, particularly alcohol, tobacco, and marijuana. Policymakers and drug control advocates claim that these substances are "gateway drugs" and first steps on a slippery slope to more dangerous drugs and drug fads.

These policies and perspectives exert great pressure on teachers, who are prevention's agents in the schools. Teachers must parrot strong abstinence and drug control messages. Implicitly and explicitly, these messages assert that all drug users inevitably become enslaved by demonic forces, and that all drugs and drug use are invariably evil, dangerous, and inherently damaging (Goode, 1993). Just as in the days of the alcohol prohibition movement, the cry is that the Devil is in our midst and must be eradicated.

Teachers, as purveyors of truth, often find themselves in an untenable position. They discover that the facts about recreational drug use do not support the mandate to forcefully convey this strident message to children. Despite some very real risks and horrors, most people experience no harm whatsoever during any single episode of use, and most users are not ever harmed by the drugs they use. Furthermore, most people who experiment with drugs do not slide inexorably down a slippery slope into stuporous oblivion and abject misery.

These inconsistencies, and actions such as the Drug Enforcement Administration's continuing refusal to legalize marijuana to treat glaucoma, wasting caused by AIDS, and nausea caused by cancer chemotherapy create problems for teachers. Policymakers' refusal to make sterile hypodermic needles available to intravenous drug users during the current AIDS epidemic raises questions, too. They make drug policy and substance abuse prevention look very bad to reasonable people, especially from the perspective of traditional educational and health values.

Accordingly, when drug policy intrudes on the curriculum and academic freedom, teachers have reason to be frightened. For example, teachers must advocate abstinence and "zero tolerance" for fear that parents and school officials may accuse them of promoting drug use among children. They must teach that drug use is wrong, dangerous, and will not be tolerated (U.S. Department of Education, 1992). These demands are not to be mitigated in any way by the validity of facts to the contrary, counterarguments, and alternative opinions about drug use (Office of Educational Research and Improvement, 1988). The distinctions between drug control, drug education, and substance abuse prevention have become casualties of the war on drugs.

Therefore, teachers assume serious risks if they address drug use as a debatable issue, or pursue goals of responsible drug use with children who are determined to try legal or illegal drugs (Office of Educational Research and Improvement, 1988). Furthermore, teachers are reluctant to acknowledge that, for better or worse, the United States is a drug-using culture (Gitlin, 1990), that all drugs are not equally harmful, and that drugs have the same potential for use or abuse as other technical innovations (Sandor, 1995). Consequently, the social control represented by intrusion of drug control into the curriculum violates a basic tenet that U.S. education is an arm of democracy.

To protect themselves, many teachers resist any association with drug issues. They conscientiously avoid discussion about drugs in the classroom or exposure to situations in which drugs or alcohol may become an issue (Ellickson, 1995). This self-protective insularity may be a product of fears about accusation (Weinstein, 1995b), as mentioned previously. However, loss of credibility among students, or an aversion to values implicit within prohibitionist social policy are concerns, too.

Such problems are clear in the 1995 case of Long Island, New York, high school teacher, Andrea Lund (McQuiston, 1997). Lund, a foreign language teacher, was fined $39,000 by the New York State Education Department when students accused her of allowing them to drink alcohol on a 10-day school trip to Italy. The students' accusations emerged following disciplinary actions for their rude and insubordinate behavior on the last day of the trip. Lund claims that she had done her best to prohibit drinking on the 1995 trip, and has coordinated 10 such trips without incident during her 22 years in her school district. She had led trips to Mexico, China, and Spain without pay and on her own vacation time. According to Lund, the trip to Italy "has cured me" of risking further exposure to problems such as these.

## WHAT ARE THE LIMITS OF SUBSTANCE ABUSE PREVENTION IN THE SCHOOLS?

As the preceding narrative indicates, teachers must always temper their enthusiasm about substance abuse prevention. The potential effectiveness of the best conceived school-based educational programs, and teachers' ad hoc efforts have inherent limitations as stand-alone strategies. To date, the effects of the most promising prevention programs erode fairly rapidly, especially in the absence of ongoing or repeated exposures.

Goode's (1993) summary of the forces that impose these limitations is succinct. According to Goode, most of the social influences that contribute to substance abuse operate outside of school, and children's time in school is limited, as is the school time that can be spent on substance abuse prevention activities. Furthermore, those children most likely to become involved in substance abuse are most alienated from school and hardest for teachers and other school personnel to reach.

Nevertheless, classroom teachers may be these children's last best hope. To reach such children, teachers must invariably work with skill and sensitivity. They must accept the fact that the task is quite similar to catching a very large fish with a flimsy fishing pole and light fishing line; a few wrong moves and child and fish are lost.

However, a teacher's careful applications of patience, gentleness, and trust may succeed. This book is intended to help teachers find their way through the morass of obstacles so that they may more effectively use these tools with all children and especially those at greatest risk.

## SUMMARY OF KEY POINTS

This chapter presents several important messages in orienting teachers toward substance abuse prevention in the classroom and other school settings. First, teachers should view prevention as a serious commitment to be integrated in reasonable ways with broader teaching responsibilities. In so doing, teachers may become prominent among the few helpful adults available to children endangered by chaotic and stressful lives.

However, the prevention arena presents teachers with many difficult challenges. These include the following:

1. Personal concerns about the limits and boundaries of professional responsibility.
2. Limited preparation.
3. Pressures within the education community that have pushed classroom teachers to the fringes of substance abuse prevention.
4. Conflict between democratic values of teaching and drug policies.

On the other hand, new thinking about children at risk has made the classroom teacher visible as an agent of prevention.

Teachers can fill this role by:

1. Creating an orderly and safe learning environment for children.
2. Providing children with an appropriate forum for discussing life issues.
3. Teaching social and other skills for coping with peer relations and stress.
4. Helping children gain access to community resources outside of the school.
5. Devising alternative learning strategies for children with reading deficits.
6. Correlating relevant drug-related material with the curriculum.

However, teachers must accept important limits and potential disappointments in substance abuse prevention. Principle among these is that children at greatest risk may be the most difficult to reach. However, much of the remainder of this book addresses this serious problem. A teacher's skill, sensitivity, and enthusiasm, when shared with all children, may save those in greatest peril.

# 2

# Helping At-Risk Children in the Classroom: The Teacher as Surrogate Parent

The goals of this chapter are to help teachers to:

1. Understand the concept of *students at risk*.
2. Recognize opportunities to help students at risk.
3. Become responsive and helpful to disengaged and alienated students in the classroom.
4. Understand the role of teacher as "surrogate parent" in the life of needy students.
5. Define the priorities, goals, and limits of the surrogate parent in the classroom.
6. Apply the principles of surrogate parenting in the context of teaching.

From time to time, most teachers in elementary, middle, and high schools have had to manage the repeatedly disruptive behavior of a troubled child. Some of these students aggressively act out their unhappiness in class, but teachers also witness other unhappy children who quietly withdraw from peers and adults. Troubled children can frustrate even the best teacher, although the quiet ones create fewer problems and are not disruptive in the classroom.

Consequently, a teacher who is drained and exhausted may seek relief from the annoyance and despair that such students can provoke. In response to aggressive students, the teacher's thinking may be: "I've tried everything I can think of, but this or that student is still self-defeating and disruptive. The student is capable enough, but I'm probably going to have to kick him or her out of class." The same teacher may simply ignore withdrawn students, thus granting them their wish to hide.

Aggressive children in particular frustrate teachers because their behavior toward adults and peers sours the class atmosphere or disrupts learning activities, or both. What is more, the problems these children create are contagious and are likely to escalate as they reverberate among other students in class (Weinstein, 1995c). This troublesome behavior always exhibits one or more of the following characteristics:

1. Hostility and abuse.
2. Carelessness and neglect.
3. Deviousness and deceit.
4. Exploitation of others and selfishness.
5. Passive and active resistance to obligations and commitments of class membership.

Teachers who contend with such problems often feel helpless because they recognize that these children are not merely "cutting up," or mischievous and the quiet ones are not just shy and retiring. Such disengaged students do the minimum to get by academically, attribute little importance to education, and probably are among the 20% of all students who are alienated from school (Steinberg, 1996).

However, sensitivity to forces that underlie troublesome student behavior enables a teacher to recognize children whose actions are saying: "I am at risk." *At risk* means that for these students, life is chaotic, and stressful, and something is wrong in their "relations with adult society and the messages and priorities they are learning from their elders" (Steinberg, 1996, pp. 16–17).

Students who are disengaged and alienated from school are more likely to use drugs and alcohol, participate in risky sexual behavior, and commit acts of crime and delinquency (Steinberg, 1996). These students are openly hostile and defiant toward teachers and school.

In fact, such students, as a pretense of independence, turn away from adults, even though they need adults, just as do all children. Consequently, they become increasingly dependent on peers for social support. Peers whose life circumstances parallel their own are especially attractive to them. Together, these problem children display behavior that is increasingly nihilistic and hedonistic. They withdraw from adults, and their very identities become linked with drug and alcohol use, defiance and rebellion, and violence (Steinberg, 1996).

In some cases, teachers know about a child's emotional problems or troubled family circumstances. In these instances, teachers may feel that such a student is hopeless because of the seeming intractability of emotional difficulties and disrupted homes. As a result, many teachers feel that managing the problems these students exhibit in class is beyond their training and understanding.

At other times, teachers find such information puzzling because some problem students come from ideal homes. Of course, both terrific and troublesome students come from capable as well as impaired families. Accordingly, mental health professionals long have pondered the question of why some people who emerge from good circumstances do poorly and others who come from horrendous circumstances seem to thrive. In the first instance, children emerge from good homes but fall victim to a myriad of social and emotional problems. In the second, children emerge, apparently unscathed, from profoundly disrupted families. Unfortunately, we have yet to resolve either of these troubling quandaries with broad, universally applicable understandings.

## CAN TEACHERS HELP WHEN HOME
## AND COMMUNITY FAIL CHILDREN?

Ejecting a destructive child is always an option, but doing so prior to trying some of the suggestions that follow may create one more missed or destroyed opportunity for a child at risk. Many capable teachers, especially in activity-oriented subjects such as the visual arts, performing arts, athletics, and technologies, are in an advantaged position to help, but these teachers often underestimate their capabilities to do so.

That teachers may be very good helpers is evident in important clues provided by children who thrive in the face of adversity. One clue is that even very troubled children have a remarkable ability to amplify and benefit from the smallest emotional support available in their surroundings (Miller, 1981). A second is that, for children struggling with personal problems, an important difference between those who flourish and those who do not is the former's ability to establish meaningful relationships with adults outside of the family (Ackerman, 1983).

No doubt, parents who become alcoholic, drug-addicted, mentally ill, or lost in marital conflict can behave in ways that are damaging to the integrity of the family and destructive to their children. These extreme cases are the exception rather than the rule of troubled parenting.

More commonly, troubled parents display inadequate ways of coping that are less obvious, although destructive, to their children. For example, some parents are so overwhelmed with responsibility and personal needs that they have few emotional, physical, and economic reserves to share with their children. Other parents may unwittingly pass on to the next generation the troubled parenting they received.

Regardless of the source of impairment to parents' ability to support, protect, and supervise their children, the observations described previously suggest that parental inadequacy need not cause irreparable damage. Many wounds inflicted by troubled parenting can be fixed.

To prevent emotional hemorrhage, such wounds require, at least, the trustworthy presence and attention of appropriately caring parental surrogates. This is important to teachers because the potential for emotional support and a good relationship with an adult is present in the classroom, the rehearsal room, the art studio, the gymnasium, the school library, and the industrial arts and technology shop. For the educator who realizes this potential, troublesome behavior need not be indicative of unsolvable problems, even if a child's behavior, at times, is frustrating and provocative.

A miraculous and complete reversal in a troubled child's behavior is a rare event. But, effective adult help can reduce this behavior to levels that are far less disruptive to learning activities, and less damaging to children.

## HOW DOES THE SURROGATE PARENT
## REDUCE RISK FOR CHILDREN?

Even children of grossly destructive parents may seek and find alternative sources of support from other adults with whom they have regular contact. To some degree, to be valued by a few special adults outside of the family is important to all children, regardless of life circumstance (Kagan, 1986). Accordingly, children who are musically inclined may find the school band, choral, or orchestra director to be a good alternative among adults to whom they can turn. The same may be said for athletic coaches, other arts instructors, shop teachers, teachers of academic subjects, teachers who serve as students club sponsors, and adult advisors to special programs that attract students.

These teachers are in positions to offer attractive possibilities to children from difficult homes and communities. Troubled students' interests and talents may draw them to various activities, but they also can use these activities to find emotionally supportive and protective care. In this way, school activity enables socially skillful teachers to contribute positively to success and help some students avert disaster.

However, teachers should be forewarned that their best efforts and those of other sympathetic school personnel may fail. Some children suffer such emotional damage at so tender an age that they never can have meaningful relationships with adults within or outside the family. In other instances, life circumstance may block children's participation in regular or special programs and activities, and thus alternative resources are unavailable to them.

Some children are simply unlucky because chance factors such as being in the wrong place at the wrong time deny them access to adults. Even when adult support is available, adults may fail to notice a child in need. Some children may be victimized by the adults from whom they have sought assistance.

## What Happens to Students Who Miss the School Safety Net?

Although no means exist to reliably predict the future for troubled children, that they are recognized as "at risk" means that the odds of negative life outcomes are greater for them than for other children. There is much at stake for such children who some overburdened teachers would rather forget. Hopefully, the negative life outcomes described in the following paragraph will sensitize the reader to the urgency of these children's needs.

In the most serious cases, children who are unable to find suitably caring adults may be irretrievably lost to institutional care in mental hospitals, residential treatment facilities, and juvenile detention centers. Still others, from abusive or negligent families, may pass from one foster care setting to another without forming an attachment with any trustworthy adult.

Such children eventually may join the estimated 250,000 to 1 million runaways who live as homeless street kids (Office of the Inspector General, 1983). They support themselves emotionally through gang membership and addiction, and materially as thieves, prostitutes, and drug dealers (Lundy, 1992). Their future leads to impoverishment, imprisonment, violence, and death.

The process leading to these tragic outcomes begins in the family. However, opportunities for rescue outside the family are encountered by many such children before this process becomes irreversible. Often, a patient and sensitive teacher is a final chance and last hope. Therefore, the opportunity for help is a precious one to these children.

Such an opportunity may be lost or wasted. Through acts of commission or omission, some teachers and other adults contribute to children's deteriorating life circumstances. Tragically, these children emerge from untrustworthy families only to discover an untrustworthy world beyond the family.

## WHAT PRIORITIES ARE IMPORTANT TO MANAGING BEHAVIOR PROBLEMS IN THE CLASSROOM?

Trust between children and their caretakers is the emotional raw material of healthy growing up. Trust is important at birth and remains so throughout the developing years. For this reason, teachers are more than a just a guide to academic achievement. They are caretakers of children and must, by design, establish and maintain trust in their work with them.

To establish trust, a teacher not only must provide appropriate support, protection, and supervision for children in his or her charge, but must do so in a stable and consistent fashion. In this way, teachers may awaken and strengthen a child's internal capacity to trust. This is important because the capacity to trust is jeopardized when a child is deeply disappointed by irresponsible parents or other inept and uncaring adults. The damage that begins in the home is only worsened when further disappointment is experienced at the hands of others outside of the family.

As mentioned earlier, damaged trust causes a child to behave in ways that express a kind of "pretend independence" regarding adults, and to become overly reliant on the peer group for emotional support (Kohut, 1971). The child's emotional life may lose its vitality. As a result, such children reject adult support they so desperately need, and seek the drama of high-impact experience to feel emotionally alive. Relationships with others become troublesome as these children use drugs, violent activities, and risky adventures to create transient illusions of emotional excitement. For such unfortunate children, a "Who cares?" attitude, pleasure-seeking behavior, and self-destructive acts contribute to increasing personal failure.

School offers many enticing stages for children to enact the drama of such negative impulses. The resulting behavior can, no doubt, drive a conscientious teacher to distraction. For these children, ambiguity and uncertainty about the nature of adult expectations and responses evokes strong emotions that drive negative behavior. The distrustful child's own anxiety and anger are more than he or she can manage. Therefore, a safe and predictable learning environment prevents or even reverses many of these problems before they generate an explosive head of steam in the classroom.

## WHAT IS THE PLIGHT OF CHILDREN IN NEED OF SURROGATE PARENTS?

Adults who observe destructive children often wonder about the destructive events to which such children may have been subjected. Certainly, some of these children experience extremes of mistreatment, but most were victims of a steady rain of more subtle difficulties. They were left alone too often, or parents rarely helped with homework and showed little interest in school activities. Parents may have forced a child, at too young an age, to take too much responsibility for his or her own care.

Some children are passively victimized, being deprived of opportunities to participate in important school or community activities because of a lack of help from parents. For others, the mess of a chaotic and tense home or the slovenliness of a frequently inebriated parent may be too embarrassing to risk inviting friends to visit.

This small sample of potentially damaging experiences are but a few of the many that destroy trust and lead to disillusionment among children. These and others are really examples of adult failure to provide adequate support, protection, or supervision to children. These three areas of parental responsibility address most directly the vulnerabilities of dependent children.

When children, frequently and for long periods of time, are inadequately served in these areas, bad things begin to happen. Children may first protest, but in the face of continuing disappointment, they may give up, and eventually, they withdraw. They may act out their despair and withdrawal by passively fading into the woodwork or aggressively lashing out at anyone who comes near. Over time, very deep disappointment about the reality, meaning, and value of parental love becomes a final agony.

A child's immediate experience of this disappointment is basic and direct. Not surprisingly, he or she feels pain, fear, sadness, and anger. Because human beings have evolved to be tough and resilient, occasional disappointments usually cause no damage. For this reason, parents and other adult caretakers, such as teachers, need not be perfect, but only good enough.

However, if children's negative experiences at the hands of parental figures are extreme and frequent, the feelings associated with them continue beyond the moment of their occurrence. This is so even though the pain that defines a bad experience may pass relatively quickly. Consequently, these children's sensitivity to potential threat is heightened to hair trigger levels, while curiosity and interest are dampened because the unknown is too scary.

Worse yet, children find themselves on the horns of a terrible dilemma. Although they want very much to understand why bad things happen to them, they also want to see their parents and other significant adults in positive ways, regardless of the truth. Because this dilemma is unresolvable, disappointed and traumatized children may direct anger and blame for painful experiences at self rather than at irresponsible parental figures. The child views self as unlovable and unworthy, and begins a process leading to failure.

In this process, children often deny, but are energized by, their unexpressed anger (Milburn & Conrad, 1996). They use this energy to strive mightily for their parents' love. Such children do this by attempting to grant their parents and other adults that which problem kids believe grown-ups want most: a good excuse to be rid of them (Farberow, 1980).

Innocence, naivete, and desperate need for parents' love blind children to the truth of what is happening. This truth is that the child's parents, if not purposely victimizing the child, are dangerously incompetent and irresponsible.

In the adult world, too, victims, at times, identify with and excuse aggressors who have harmed them. However, maturity provides many tools for coping with others' hostility, incompetence, and irresponsibility. Adult victims do not blame self so readily and more easily point the finger of blame at guilty parties. They also apply negative labels that describe the manner in which these parties violated the person and domain of others. These labels have powerful meaning and are therefore painful for children to apply to even the worst of parental misconduct.

The violations to which some children are regularly subjected would lead an adult victim to label perpetrators as "brutes and bullies" for the abusive acts they commit, or to deride them as "cowards" for inflicting these acts on defenseless individuals. Adults would call perpetrators "rats" for abandoning others at a difficult time of need. An adult victim's contempt would be clearly evident in branding perpetrators as "users" or even "rapists" for their exploitative ways. Guilty parties would be disdained as traitors for their broken promises and violated commitments. And finally, they would be reviled as "screw ups" and "goof offs" for their negligence. These labels and their extremely negative meanings are bitter pills for children to swallow in connection with their own parents.

Nevertheless, these are the objective facts and social meanings that define the victimization of children by their caretakers. Some children are victimized and experience disillusionment because they are repeatedly abused. That is, they are assaulted physically, verbally, or psychologically. Some are exploited to satisfy the needs of caretakers with no regard for the consequences of such exploitation. Other children are neglected because they are left to do without that which they need but cannot provide for themselves. Some are betrayed repeatedly in a deluge of broken promises, confidences, allegiances, and agreements. And finally, some are abandoned to fend for themselves at times when they most need parental support and protection.

## What Are the Limits of Surrogate Parenthood?

Troubled children can become skillful at acting out self-hatred and re-confirming their distrust of adults. By creating troublesome situations and crises wherever they go, these children provide adults with perfect excuses to be rid of them. As a result, teachers throw them out of classes, recreation leaders eject them from community activities, coaches kick them off of athletic teams, arts instructors dismiss them from performance ensembles, and unfortunately this list can grow *ad infinitum*.

Clearly, to be a surrogate parent to someone else's child is a trouble-some proposition to sensible adults. The possibilities for intrusion into the private family life of other people and becoming engulfed in the difficulties of a troubled child are not attractive. The wish to achieve glory in a heroic rescue or the desire to adopt and take home a needy but lovable child are usually impossible dreams. These are but a few of many legitimate concerns about helping children in need.

Teachers and others on the front lines of the schools need not fall victim to these dangers, and can be surrogate parents at little risk and small cost. Teachers can minimize risks and costs by behaving in ways that are beneficial to all children with whom they work, not just those with special needs. In so doing, neither the efforts of the teacher nor the problems of the child become conspicuous. It is interesting that, for children on the brink, teachers can contribute to the most miraculous rescues and important emotional healing while neither they nor the children they help are aware of their heroism.

## How Does a Teacher Become a Surrogate Parent?

The teacher's first task in becoming a surrogate parent is to be a visible target for attachment and bonding within the context of teaching. Teachers do this by visibly acting as competent and responsible persons and displaying a genuine readiness to fuss over children who show an interest in the teaching–learning activities at hand (Weinstein, 1987). This does not imply that a teacher must heap special attention on children who are needy or in jeopardy. Except in cases of suspected physical abuse or neglect, teachers need not even recognize such children or differentiate between them and other children who are in class (Weinstein, 1995b).

The teacher's second task is to create an awareness of his or her adult authority that is consistent with the principles of good parenting. Both of these tasks define behavior that is necessary to foster and promote trust between parents and children, and between people generally, regardless of age or social context.

The goals discussed here highlight the universal mission of parental relationships with children:

1. Help children grow to take care of themselves.
2. Help children learn to meet the social obligations of community life.
3. Help children learn how to enjoy life.

To achieve these goals, adults help children learn to exercise control over their own lives and recognize the connection between behavior and outcome; they help children become socially integrated with their peer group and the larger community; and they help children to develop and maintain open minds, be alert to new information, and risk experimentation in comprehending and mastering present and future challenges.

In addition, adults help children enjoy living by helping them appreciate success and good fortune, and cope with the sorrows of loss and failure. Adults do this by assisting children to develop an awareness of their own feelings, values, and attitudes. And finally, adults must help children to achieve a comfortable, realistic, and stable acceptance of themselves (Weinstein, 1995a).

## What Are the Principles of Surrogate Parenting?

From a practical perspective, children need parental adults to help them develop strategies and tactics, and provide resources for coping with life's challenges. From an emotional perspective, children wish for these adults to be in attendance when life's battles are joined, and to remain steadfast as helpers regardless of quality of performance or success of outcome.

A teacher can address these needs and wishes in reasonable ways. In practical terms, a teacher can reliably provide good instruction, coaching, and other assistance to help children solve academic problems and achieve success in school. From an interpersonal perspective, a teacher can behave as a stable, consistent, and benevolent figure regardless of performance or outcome. Teachers do this by continuing to embrace the child and his or her interests regardless of the child's ability and level of commitment. And, from an emotional perspective, teachers can cheer students on by means of positive expectations and hopes, acknowledgment and celebration of success, and continued optimism and enthusiasm in the face of difficulty. Of course, all these forms of support must be tempered by honesty and a realistic appraisal of potential and outcome.

There are several principles for teachers to use as guides for responses to these important emotional needs and wishes of children. The fostering of trust is the unifying theme through which each principle contributes to effective surrogate parenting. Each, to some degree, requires the teacher to subordinate his or her own personal needs to those of the children he or she serves.

In many ways, these principles are a test of a teacher's perspective on teaching. The teacher must ask, "Is my perspective primarily focused on my own needs and ambitions or on the needs and ambitions of my students?"

Because troubled children have little tolerance for adults' narcissistic self-gratification, teachers must focus on the needs and ambitions of students in order to accept the role of surrogate parent. Consequently, teachers can be neither self-indulgent nor cavalier about meeting students' needs for safety, instructional support, and adult supervision in class.

As a foundation for trust, children must view a teacher as using and sharing the power of his or her position in an organized, systematic, and positive way. Adult carelessness, disorganization, impulsiveness, poor preparation, lateness, insensitivity, and broken promises are dangerous experiences for children, especially troubled children.

## Principle 1: Stability

Teachers foster trust by responding to a child's need for stability. As stable parental figures, teachers must instill constancy into ways of relating, ways of doing things, and limits and boundaries of behavior. Rules, routines, and important expectations are not changed on impulse or whim. Teachers should keep ambiguity and painful surprises to a minimum to the degree that such control is possible. Thus, if the teacher announces that activities are to be held at certain times at specific locations, then the schedule and advance preparations must become the rule with only the most rare exceptions.

## Principle 2: Consistency

Teachers promote trust by responding to a child's need for consistency. Consistency refers to the regularity with which established expectations are met. Is a rule or routine followed one day and ignored the next? Is Johnny punished or rewarded for certain behavior while nothing happens to Billy for the same acts? To feel safe and trusting, children need to observe consistency between behavior and consequence regardless of who displays the behavior or when it occurs.

Similarly, children need to witness consistency between word and deed. Teachers and other adults foster trust when they display the basic honesty to share truth with children. A child needs to know that the adults in his or her life say what they mean and mean what they say (S. Weiss, personal communication, May 25, 1997).

## Principle 3: Benevolence

Teachers foster trust by displaying benevolence because children feel safe when they recognize that the teacher has their well being at heart. Children must observe a teacher to bestow rewards enthusiastically and withhold gratifications reluctantly. Children must also recognize that, as a benevolent adult, a teacher is willing to risk their anger to make unpopular decisions if such decisions are in their best interest.

## Principle 4: Flexibility

Teachers must be responsive to a child's need to see adults respond adaptively to novel occurrences and unexpected events. Children become suspicious when adults are rigid and arbitrary in adherence to established but no longer effective ways of doing things. This applies not only to environmental contingencies, but also to the idiosyncratic and developing inclinations of the child.

## Principle 5: A Healthy Perspective

Children need teachers to develop and maintain a realistic and appropriate perspective about the purpose and importance of activities in which they engage with children. In some instances where health and safety are at risk, neither children nor teachers can afford to be lax about order and discipline. In other instances, there is more freedom to make mistakes, to fail, or to laugh and play even when such behavior creates some problems.

Adults damage trust when they overreact or attribute exaggerated meaning to relatively minor events, or, on the other hand, when they minimize that which is serious to a child. Taking seriously a child's self-recrimination about a minor mistake, and keeping the meaning of activity and participation in proper perspective are both important to trust. The overly demanding and destructive antics of "stage mothers," some performing arts directors, and athletic coaches are negative consequences of an adult's loss of perspective (Weinstein, 1991). In the end, adults reinforce trust by stepping back from the heat of the moment to laugh about absurd events that seemed so important only a moment before.

### Principle 6: Crisis Management

Children need teachers to remain objective and calm during crises. At such times, when things seem to be getting out of control, children depend on the maturity expected of adults. Crises are not times for teachers to have temper tantrums or become hysterical. Nor, at the opposite extreme, are they times for teachers to become passive or indifferent and withdraw.

Children will become frightened and disappointed if they discover that the maturity they count on so much is only an illusion. A calm and deliberate search for solutions to the problem at hand and appropriate actions to make the best of difficult circumstances reinforces trust during any crisis.

## HOW CAN TEACHERS EVALUATE THEIR PERFORMANCE AS SURROGATE PARENTS?

Teachers need not extend themselves in unreasonable ways to adopt these principles as guidelines for the emotional care of children. As the principles imply, "being there" in a manner that all children can count on and that is appropriate to and highlights one's primary identity as "teacher" is basic to "good enough" surrogate parenting.

In this way, teachers can contribute emotional resources to help children rescue and heal themselves. The true heros are the adults who serve the child in a responsible, competent, and caring manner, and the children who use these adult contributions to transcend the adversity of their life circumstances. The process of rescue and healing is the same whether it occurs in the classroom, the school concert band, a local chess club, a bible study group, the ball field, or any of the numerous settings in which children and adults come together in schools and the community.

Because the best of care in the adult administration of this process offers no guarantees of success, the adult's primary concern should be about the process rather than the outcome. In essence, the teacher's role is to provide yet another lifeline for children to seize in their struggle to reach healthy maturity.

In so doing, teachers and other adults provide social raw materials that enable children to construct a manageable internal image of themselves and their world as trustworthy entities. When successful, children begin to take control over important aspects of their lives and to join peers and the larger community. Such success also promotes optimism and flexibility that enable children to derive meaning from experience, and to trust one's own feelings as a gauge of the impact of life's events. And most important of all, children begin to regard themselves as precious and worthy.

## SUMMARY OF KEY POINTS

From time to time, all teachers face the challenge of managing repeatedly disruptive students. These students, as well as other quiet and withdrawn children can be so frustrating and provocative that adults begin to see them as incorrigible and hopeless. As a result, many despairing teachers are tempted to reject such children at risk rather than face further annoyance and irritation that may come of trying to manage the problems they present in class.

Teachers become particularly pessimistic when they have information about a student's seemingly intractable emotional problems or disrupted family. However, observations of children who thrive despite such difficulties are encouraging. These observations consistently indicate that if children can form good relationships with adults outside of the family, the chances of a positive resolution to their problems increase dramatically. Consequently, the elevated health, social, and legal risks these children face can be attenuated by relationships with adults who serve, to some degree, as surrogate parents.

Teachers are in a very good position to offer just such an opportunity. In fact, the consequences of not doing so can be so severe that teachers should regard helping as an imperative in teaching.

This imperative does not require teachers to extend themselves in unreasonable ways. The important tasks are to create safe, predictable learning environments and develop trusting relationships with students. Under conditions of trust and safety, many needy students can form healthy attachments with competent, responsible, and caring teachers. In this way, teachers provide the social and emotional resources to help these students better cope with the adversity of their lives.

To appropriately fill the role of surrogate parent, teachers must behave in ways that are stable, consistent, benevolent, flexible, and reflect a healthy perspective on the purpose and meaning of their work. They must also be prepared to manage crises calmly, and with purpose. Children at risk will have rescued themselves when, as a result, they rekindle their capacity to trust, begin to take control of their destiny, and become optimistic about themselves and the meaning of events that punctuate their lives.

# 3

# School Violence and Substance Abuse Prevention

The goals of this chapter are to help teachers:

1. Understand the relation between drug control, drug use, and the upsurge in violence in the schools.
2. Grasp the impact of violence on the teacher's role as monitor of student behavior in the school.
3. Understand the relation between youth culture and violence.
4. Cope with security measures that now intrude on school life for both adults and children.
5. Recognize the events and processes through which violence erupts in the classroom and other school settings.
6. Develop and use strategies for preventing and managing violent conflict.

Since the 1970s, increases in youth violence have led some observers to describe schools as "combat zones" (Bynum & Thompson, 1996). Such words promote frightening and cynical stereotypes about adolescents, particularly about teens who are members of racial minority groups.

Reports of rare but dramatic occurrences perpetuate these stereotypes. Such reports cause alarmed parents and other community members to think deadly violence in the schools is more common than it is (Holloway, 1998; Lewin, 1997). President Clinton's glib comment that "High school seniors are more likely to take weapons to school than to take calculus in school" did not help matters ("Clinton Orders," 1997).

The large majority of young people are not violent, although more students behave violently, more often, and more dangerously than in the past (Wilson-Brewer, 1995). According to the U.S. Department of Education, 52 million students attend public schools, and although nearly 200 have been killed in school since 1992, children are safer at school than elsewhere (Lewin, 1997). Therefore, deadly violence remains an aberration of youthful behavior.

Furthermore, increases in youth violence are not limited to urban schools, despite stereotypes about them. Although increases are greater for tough inner-city schools, suburban and rural school districts also have suffered. This is evident in recent multiple murders in schools in small communities in Kentucky, Mississippi, and Alaska (Bragg, 1997; Lewin, 1997), and more recently in Arkansas, Oregon, and Colorado.

## HOW IS DRUG POLICY IMPLICATED
## IN SCHOOL VIOLENCE?

As school violence has grown, policymakers have associated it increasingly with drug use. This association is in part an outgrowth of recent studies of fatal and nonfatal community violence. These studies provide evidence that drugs or alcohol were present in the majority of violent incidents such as sexual assaults, marital aggression, and assaults among strangers (Fagan, 1993).

Some policymakers have rushed to conclude that violence occurs in thefts for money to buy drugs, and as a result of drug effects on user judgment, perception, and impulse control. Other policymakers argue that violence is an outgrowth of conflict between persons involved in the illegal drug trade (Goldstein, 1985).

Accordingly, the U.S. Department of Education renamed its Drug Free Schools and Communities Demonstration Program as the "Safe" and Drug Free Schools and Communities Demonstration Program. The New York City Public Schools include drug possession as a reportable violent incident for its school safety officers, and the security activities of many school districts include searches for drugs along with searches for weapons.

However, this association may have more to do with the politics of the war on drugs than on investigators' establishment of a cause-and-effect relationship between student drug use and school violence. It is true that some drugs, especially alcohol, have effects that weaken personal controls on aggressive behavior, and others, such as cocaine, can stimulate users toward wildly impulsive acting out, but other drugs, such as marijuana and heroin, are soothing and calming even to the point of immobilizing users.

As with many of the problems policymakers and the media attribute to drug use, the violence associated with drugs may be more a product of drug policy than drug use. Despite incidents of thefts for drug money and turf struggles between drug dealers, there is no clear evidence that alcohol and drugs directly cause much violence, and the evidence does indicate that most drug and alcohol users are not violent people (Fagan, 1993). As a covariate to violence, drug and alcohol use are more likely to provide a provocative context for violence than to cause it (Fagan, 1993).

This lends plausibility to Canada's (1995) claim that increases in school violence are a product of harsh drug laws first enacted in the 1970s. According to Canada, these laws amplified youthful violence by tempting adult drug dealers to recruit children into street-level drug trade. No doubt, some poor children with austere lives, few job opportunities, and whose tender age provides legal immunity, find the temptation of quick and plentiful drug money to be irresistible. In this way, dealers hoped to avoid arrest and long prison sentences that now face adults caught selling drugs.

The drug trade's school-age recruits formed vicious street gangs, and acquired deadly weapons including handguns(Canada, 1995). They did so to protect themselves in the dangerous world of drug dealing. However, these sources of violence began to infiltrate the porous boundaries of neighborhood schools, particularly in impoverished inner-city areas (Devine, 1996).

Such developments greatly increased risks associated with school discipline, normal interpersonal tension, and occasional minor social friction in the peer group. Teachers, students, and innocent bystanders are now in danger of disfigurement, maiming, and death as a result of occurrences that once were tame and even laughable.

In the past, teachers would intervene or peers could restrain violent behavior. However, the proliferation of weapons has changed the system of checks on school violence. Teachers can no longer safely control violent conflict, nor can peers stop a fight and declare a winner before serious injury occurs (Canada, 1995). Mischief that once led to blackened eyes, bruised egos, and a teacher's rebuke now puts blood on the walls, dead bodies on the floor, and generates strong pressures for a police presence in the schools.

Consequently, just a few truly aggressive and violent young people cause damage that is grossly disproportionate to their numbers. They can assault many victims, frighten numerous others, and seriously harm the social and physical environment (Canada, 1995; Devine, 1996; Fagan, 1993; Singer, Anglin, Song, & Lunghofer, 1995).

In fact, some schools are held hostage by the violent few (Canada, 1995). Frightened teachers turn a blind eye to dangerous students, and have abdicated responsibility for controlling destructive behavior (Devine, 1996). According to Devine (1996), in affected schools, stairways, bathrooms, and hallways are so perilous that even adult school guards avoid them and security personnel have begun to resemble paramilitary forces. In this atmosphere of fear, teachers' unions and the police direct teachers to avoid risk inherent to intervention into fights. Thus, teachers' loss of control has become a norm.

Perhaps the worst casualty of such schools is the voice of decency among the majority of students. This voice is silenced by a tyrannical peer culture of intimidation and violence (Devine, 1996).

Decent students struggle to remain decent while warding off their peers who are not. Canada (1995) reported that to do so, decent, usually nonviolent students who think adults cannot protect them devise ways to protect themselves. These students may carry weapons for protection, and use posturing, threat displays, and other behavior to appear dangerous and unmanageable.

Their hope is that intimidation will ward off predators over whom adults have relinquished control (Canada, 1995). Students use toughness and bravado as self-protective behavior, and these have become dominant indicators for social evaluation in the peer group. According to Devine (1996), this is the process through which decent students become transformed into proactive instruments of violence.

Consequently, dangerous crises can erupt with frightening suddenness, and the orderliness of the school becomes uncertain. Such was the case in a New York middle school in which two eighth-grade girls stole small needles from the school infirmary and then attacked 11 other students with them. This aroused fears of hepatitis B and HIV infection among the students who were stuck, their parents, and school officials, although the likelihood of infection is low (Roane, 1998). This bizarre example is one of many that demonstrates how a destructive few can change a whole school, reduce its environment to chaos, and lead innocent others to assume an aggressively self-protective stance.

## HOW DOES SCHOOL VIOLENCE CONTRIBUTE TO DRUG USE?

Earlier chapters of this book characterized the life circumstances of children at risk as disorganized and stressful. Violence in the schools is just one more powerfully disorganizing and stress-inducing influence for decent young people at risk of substance abuse.

According to one survey by Ferriera (1997), 64% of high school students have been victims of bullying by predatory classmates by senior year. The most common forms of bullying were name calling and psychological abuse and threats, although physical abuse and threats with weapons were less common. Nevertheless, some 30% of bullied students were so affected that they wanted to transfer to another school and 15% said they had considered suicide.

More directly, Singer, Anglin, Song, and Lunghofer (1995) found that adolescents' exposure to violence was associated with serious trauma symptoms. These included depression, dissociation, anger, anxiety, and posttraumatic stress.

For some such students, the uncertainty of living in dangerous and unpredictable homes and neighborhoods is worsened when the schools acquire the same aura of uncertainty and stress. Considering that more than 33% of students in a 1989 national survey reported being threatened and another 13% reported being attacked in school, the potential for such an unhappy occurrence is real (American School Health Association, 1989). Worse yet, the destructiveness of these experiences is amplified by students' sense that teachers have abandoned them to the predators in their midst.

Therefore, despite claims by drug control advocates that drugs have caused increases in school violence, it is also likely that drug policies and the violence they have precipitated contribute to drug use. These claims are perhaps another instance of drugs and drug users being made scapegoats.

Such claims have contributed to polarization among those concerned about educational reform. On one side, blaming drugs helps policymakers, educators, and whole communities to justify a school system that has never truly addressed populations of young people in greatest need. These are young people for whom racism, ethnic prejudice, poverty, and other life circumstances create the greatest risks. The risks include crime and delinquency, school failure, school drop out, teen pregnancy and parenthood, and substance abuse.

Those who are invested in the status quo of education often argue from a position of liberal denial. They deny the growth of violence or claim that reports of increasing violence are part of the rhetoric of racism. Now, even some who may grudgingly acknowledge rises in violence argue that dangerous problems that confront the schools are not the fault of the system, and that we must win the war on drugs rather than change the schools.

On the other side, there are those who argue from a position of conservative denial. They claim that the system does not work at all and should be completely dismantled. They argue for a new system that would provide access to private schools through vouchers; school choice in which parents may send children to preferred public schools; public schools operated by private, for-profit business interests; or parochial schools.

Despite this polarization that amplifies the inertia of school systems, the huge liabilities associated with violence have forced many districts to seek means to reduce the danger. One approach relies on technological, regulatory, and environmental security measures (Wilson-Brewer, 1995). These measures include the following:

*Security Technology*
1. Metal detectors and x-ray machines.
2. Closed-circuit televison in schools and on school buses.
3. Phones in classrooms.
4. Magnetic door locks.
5. Gun- and drug-sniffing dogs.

*Normative and Regulatory Measures*
1. Imposition of gun-free school zones.
2. Closed campuses.
3. Student identification cards.
4. Bookbag bans.
5. Dress codes.

*Environmental Security Measures*
1. Removal of lockers from school buildings.
2. Improved lighting and blackouts.
3. Landscaping.

*Personnel Actions and Security Activities*
1. Employment of nonteaching security personnel.
2. Police patrols.
3. Safe corridor and safe haven programs.
4. Locker searches

Canada (1995) and Devine (1996) challenged technological–regulatory–environmental violence prevention as an imposition of the police state and a prison atmosphere on the schools. Students not only must struggle with danger, chaos, and stress, but they now must suffer indignities and abuse at the hands of the system. Critics argue that if school is preparation for adult life in the community, then some schools are preparation for criminals who will spend adult life in jail.

Another approach is preventative and educational, and relies heavily on conflict resolution and mediation strategies. Other pieces to this approach include after-school activities, social skills development, advocacy of positive social values, recognition and avoidance of weapons and dangerous situations, stress management, and reducing race and ethnic prejudice. However, conflict resolution and mediation strategies are dominant in the middle and high schools (Wilson-Brewer, 1995).

Nevertheless, critics are cynical about educational solutions to the problem of violence, too. They challenge the theory behind educational school violence prevention programs, and doubt their effectiveness (Hawkins, 1993; Webster, 1993).

## HOW DOES VIOLENCE OCCUR IN SCHOOLS?

Many teachers view school violence as sporadic, random, isolated events induced by sudden conflict, irritation, frustration, and impulse among strangers. In this way, seemingly chance meetings produce predation and self-protection, or cause irritable people to fight.

Although random encounters such as these do happen, much school violence occurs between young people who know each other. Because antagonists often are bound together in classes or other school activities, circumstance and interpersonal friction can create a history of hostile interaction between them.

This history promotes violence because it evokes a state of defensive alert, taxes self-control, and fosters slights, insults, and other provocative behavior. Adolescent narcissism, immature social skills and values, peer pressure, aspirations for status and power in the peer group, fear of personal humiliation, and the possibility of becoming a scapegoat add to this risk.

According to Canada (1995), Devine (1996), and Milburn and Conrad (1996), many students are trapped in long-standing rituals of youth culture that support violent acting out. These authors agreed that violent and negative traditions of youth culture dictate that no one may back away from a fight and are powerfully reinforced by the peer group. Because of this, even minor accidental encounters between absolute strangers may escalate to tragic proportions as antagonists have more to fear from friends than from each other. If anyone backs away from a fight, these so-called friends may be relentless and merciless in persecuting that peer who they label as a "chicken" or "wimp."

Therefore, violence is a culminating event in a progressive and bankrupt social process. This process promotes increasingly hostile interactions, is open-ended, and is repetitive rather than closed and singular. It is bankrupt because antagonists abandon positive or conciliatory forms of relating. The process forces adversaries to discard alternatives to violence, whether they want to or not. Then, violence occurs as one or both antagonists, under the harsh scrutiny of peers, make an unrestrained attempt to seriously harm the other.

The process begins with acts of omission or commission. Acts of omission include slights, negligence, and other passive–aggressive forms. Acts of commission include predation, self-protective reactions, or impulsive expressions of irritation and frustration (Coccaro, 1995). Some antagonists initiate hostility to serve narcissistic (self-esteem), economic (money, property), social (image, status), or territorial (turf) needs. In other cases, adversaries join gangs or cliques who use violence to enforce group norms, and as a standard for self- and social evaluation.

Initial provocations may be mild, but subsequent behavior is increasingly intense, harmful, and hostile as the process unfolds (Coccaro, 1995). Assaultive acts become more numerous and damaging, and adversaries commit more and more energy to them. Attacks may be physical (assault), verbal (insults, harassment), social (embarrassment, ostracism), or material (vandalism, theft).

Initial provocation, whatever its form, generates a second stage defined by reactive hostility in which offended parties seek to avoid humiliation, exact revenge, and protect self. The process then moves to a third stage marked by reciprocal and escalating reprisals and antagonism. At the fourth or end stage, adversaries lose internal control, abandon hope, and cease efforts for conciliatory disengagement.

*Fist Stick Knife Gun*, the title of Canada's (1995) "personal history of violence in America" captures the essence of this process. An initial provocation, intended or not, leads to angry words, angry words to pushing, pushing to shoving, shoving to punching, fists to knives, razors, and box cutters, and more recently, to guns. Each antagonist struggles mightily to dominate, punish, and do harm to the other with little if any regard for bystanders or the environment. The process continues until one of the adversaries retreats, a truce is called, others intervene, or tragedy occurs.

In the aftermath, there may be social, legal, and health consequences for combatants, victims, bystanders, and witnesses. And, there may be damaged or destroyed equipment, facilities, and personal property.

If the process reaches the fifth and chronic stage, each adversary views the other as a sworn enemy, and a feud begins. Violent exchanges recur, and everyone tries harder to "win," over and over again.

Furthermore, adversaries may recruit siblings and friends, and the struggle will then expand from a fight between individuals to a war between groups. Violence becomes more cold-blooded as passion yields to cold blooded premeditation, more vindictive as provocations and retaliations intensify, and more destructive as energies of individuals are multiplied by resources of allies. In some bizarre instances, misguided parents become embroiled in violent acts against their children's antagonists, too ("Students Stepfather," 1997).

## What Do Young People Fight About?

Teachers should understand that young people struggle against each other over the same things people have struggled about since human beings emerged on this planet. Conflict is neither bizarre nor unhealthy and is consistent with many positive social values.

We teach assertiveness, competition, and self-efficacy and recognize each to be important to health, happiness, and success. Therefore, the problem is not conflict, per se, but rather how it is resolved. From this perspective, arguments, disagreement, bickering, and conflict are neither synonymous with nor inevitably resulting in hostility, enmity, or violence.

Although the specific concerns over which young people can get into squabbles are too numerous to list, these concerns fall into two broad categories, the first of which is *rational issues*. These issues emerge in connection with material or practical needs and desires. Some are obvious, as in the case of competition for limited resources such as space, supplies, and equipment. An issue that is ancillary to this is that of ownership.

Less obvious are practical issues that surround group participation in activities. These issues include struggles over the goals of activity, the methods to be used in pursuing the goals of activity, and the needs and values to be pursued in the process of participation.

A group of kids who want to ride bicycles together cannot just hop on bikes and ride off. Bikes must be available and participants must decide who gets to ride which bike. This last issue is usually, but not always, resolved on the basis of ownership.

Furthermore, they must decide on a destination (a goal) and a route (a method or means to get there). Trickiest of all, they must decide whether the ride is to be leisurely and chatty (emphasizes social interaction); whether it will have stops at scenic points on the route for viewing and picture taking (emphasizes environmental appreciation and aesthetic values); whether it will be high speed (emphasizes competition and fitness); or will be consistent with any other values held dear by one or more participants. The process of reaching agreements about these concerns is rife with opportunity for conflict.

Students address analogous concerns in school when they plan and implement class projects and other group learning activities, or when they play together. Inevitably, in the course of such activities, students will have to work out problems about sharing and taking turns with supplies, materials, and equipment. They also will address issues about end products, how to create them, and what benefit each student seeks to derive from participation.

The second category of concerns is that of *emotional issues*. These issues address self-perception and interpersonal relationships. Such issues emerge out of needs for social power and personal control, acceptance and belonging, freedom and choice versus conformity to norms and expectations, personal enjoyment, pride in self, and authenticity and truthfulness, particularly about self. These issues are far more abstract, but nevertheless are loaded with potential for fiery encounters.

Teachers also must recognize that struggles between peers are not the only dangerous moments for students. Other such moments include conflict between students and teachers, and between students and cultural mandates of school, such as rules and regulations. Conflicts between adults such as teachers or administrators or between adults and cultural mandates such as between teachers and personnel policies can energize students in negative ways.

Nevertheless, despite the variations in context described in the preceding paragraph, the struggles address rational needs for resources or emotional needs for narcissistic gratification and some kind of reciprocity in interpersonal relationship. In summary, conflict arises when people seek material resources or emotional gratifications, and feel that they will be deprived of or must defend these important supplies.

Students beliefs and attitudes about conflict influence the manner in which it is resolved. Some attitudes and beliefs contribute to violent resolutions. One such belief is that disagreement is equivalent to hostility or, in extreme cases, enmity. Another is that resolutions to conflict must inevitably produce a winner and a loser. A third is that students can use conflict to extract bribes and favors from adults seeking "peace at any price."

Furthermore, some students believe that agreements are binding only to the degree they offer personal advantage. These students may violate public agreements or disclose private agreements to others for personal advantage. And finally, some of the most difficult problems emanate from personal beliefs and grass-roots ideologies that generate race hatred and conflict (Pinderhughes, 1997).

## What Provocations Should Teachers Watch For?

Fagan (1993) emphasized the importance of a focus on events and behavioral interactions rather than on persons as a framework for prevention of and intervention into violence. In the schools, inflammatory behavior and hostile exchanges are no longer merely unpleasant. They now are very dangerous. Therefore, the notion of provocative events and hostile interaction among students is important to teachers.

In this interaction, real or imagined acts provoke or are pretexts for hostility. As described previously, a social process aided and abetted by peers escalates this hostility, and peer pressure often forces antagonists to abandon conciliatory nonviolent strategies. Following is a list of provocative acts to which teachers should be responsive in preventing violence in the classroom.

Verbal provocations include:

1. Hostile or antagonistic tones, language, or gestures (mean and nasty talk).
2. Mean-spirited, insulting, or provocative comments.
3. Menacing gestures or verbal threats.
4. Veiled threats in word or tone.
5. Students screaming and yelling angrily at one another.

Prejudicial actions include:

1. Hostile expressions about a peer's race, ethnicity, or gender.
2. Insults about sexual orientation.
3. Derogatory comments about a peer's parents or other family members.
4. Taunting or harassment about physical characteristics or anomalies (i.e., height, weight, skin conditions, glasses, orthodontic braces, etc.).
5. Taunting or harassment about behavioral traits or anomalies (i.e., speech impediments, shyness, dress, etc.).
6. Inappropriate sexual advances, teasing, or harassment (including comments, grabbing, ogling, fondling, etc.).

Passive–Aggressive behavior includes:

1. Hurtful or embarrassing pranks.
2. Physically hurtful actions such as poking, pinching, "nuggies," done playfully or in a hostile manner.
3. Hostile humor or practical jokes.
4. Subtle expressions of contempt or disdain (sly or sneaky put-downs).

Social provocations include:

1. Students plotting and scheming against another student.
2. Students forming groups against individuals or other groups of students.
3. Students pressuring or goading other individuals to put on a dangerous or violent show when there is a dispute (egging them on).
4. Leftover disputes and arguments emanating from participation in sports and games (who really won, who caused a loss, who cheated, who committed what foul, etc.).
5. Courtship spats (lovers' quarrels).

**6.** Courtship competitions (lovers' triangles).
**7.** Impolite behavior and rudeness.

Betrayal, abandonment, and violations of trust include:

**1.** Students violating confidences or disclosing private information about another student.
**2.** Students refusing to help or support another student.
**3.** Students denying acceptance into or rejecting another student from group activity.
**4.** Students lying to or cheating a peer.
**5.** Recruiting adults for hostile purposes (i.e., tattling, lying to a teacher to get another student in trouble, etc.).

Assault, vandalism, and theft include:

**1.** Violent assaults or retaliations (punching, hitting, kicking, biting, wrestling, throwing a peer to the floor, etc.).
**2.** Assault with weapons or objects used as weapons.
**3.** A student purposely damaging or destroying another's personal property.
**4.** Muggings, thefts, and holdups.
**5.** Forcible rape.

The 32 items in the preceding lists are grouped somewhat arbitrarily. Although one can easily recognize overlap between categories, the items express the multitude of ways that young people can generate social tension.

Furthermore, some of the items represent far more provocative behavior than others. No doubt, various forms of assault, vandalism, and theft are violent expressions of hostility. However, in many instances, violent actions emerge out of other, more mild, provocations. Therefore, teachers must be prepared to intervene in a timely fashion when they observe seemingly mild provocation, and they must try to prevent or minimize the frequency of such occurrences. The guiding principle is that the more often students have hostile interactions, the greater their exposure to and risk of violent crises.

## How Can Teachers Prevent Hostile Interaction in the Classroom?

Teachers can implement a strategy of primary prevention against hostile interaction in the classroom. When teachers employ this strategy effectively, they lower the frequency of hostile behavior. They also reduce the harm-reduction burden of addressing, secondarily, each instance after the fact of its occurrence.

Secondary prevention, or preventing hostility from escalating, can be a distracting and exhausting ordeal for teachers. This is especially so in classes in which the same students are at the center of recurrent conflicts, students polarize into warring factions, or antagonists are intransigent and unyielding. To students and teachers, hostility in the classroom is a problem for which an ounce of primary prevention is worth many pounds of secondary-prevention cure.

The strategy that follows addresses these problems, and also risk factors in drug use and negative peer influences on academic achievement (Weinstein, 1996, 1997a, 1997b). The strategy requires educators to perform three important quasiparental tasks. These tasks are as helper, protector, and supervisor in creating safe classrooms and preventing student violence (Weinstein, 1995b).

Teachers perform these tasks by providing a stable and consistent learning environment, fair and benevolent treatment, assistance to resolve conflict, social skills instruction, and advocacy for positive social values. Furthermore, teachers must recognize latent hostility, set limits on its expression, and seek constructive resolution. The goals and methods of these tasks for teachers are outlined in the following lists.

Because ambiguity is the enemy of violence prevention, it is important to create a well-defined classroom culture by:

1. Establishing clear and stable behavioral norms. These norms are a product of policies, rules, and procedures, plus students' expectations that adherence to them and their application will be consistent.

2. Providing a clear rationale for policies, rules, and procedures. Emphasize the best interests of students and learning as a focus of explanation. Avoid sounding arbitrary or self-serving.

3. Providing explanations, demonstrations, and rehearsal for special skills and routines that are part of classroom behavioral norms. Even the most well-intended students will have difficulty with behavioral norms for which they lack necessary skills and understanding.

4. Establishing effective routines for managing transitions between classroom activities or into and out of class. Transitions generate activating emotions such as anxiety, frustration, or anger, and are the most volatile moments in peer social interaction.

5. Demonstrating flexibility and adapt to change as needed. Students see a rigid teacher as arbitrary, and become resistant, untrusting, and reactive. If the teacher is too formidable, then angry students may act out against peers.

6. Establishing effective mechanisms for resolving conflict in the classroom. Clear, stable policies, rules, and procedures for resolving conflict, and consistency in applying them, are most important.

Because unfair treatment is an enemy of violence prevention, it is important to model equity, justice, and benevolence as positive social values:

1. Provide students with equal access to resources and opportunity in the classroom. Materials, supplies, privileges, chores, and responsibilities should be divided equitably among all students.

2. Provide assistance, protection, and supervision evenhandedly. The teacher's "self" is a special and important resource. Students will resent and act out against teachers who do not offer them a fair share, and against those other students who seem to be favorites.

3. Balance issues of "need," "merit," "entitlement," and "privilege" fairly when offering resources, opportunity, and service to students. Classroom wealth has finite limits and its distribution is a zero-sum game. That which teachers give to one student must be taken from others.

4. Define benevolence as "in the best interest of students and learning" and repeatedly demonstrate that this is the guiding principle in setting limits on behavior in the classroom.

5. Be just and fair in distributing rewards and imposing penalties. Over-reactions and dismissive responses to success or negative behavior foster problems of trust, later.

6. Advocate equity, justice, and benevolence as principles for resolving or mediating conflict.

Because secondary violence prevention is a fall-back position when primary prevention falters, it is important to be vigilant and skillful in monitoring social functioning and hostility in the classroom:

1. Assess students as a group for their level of social functioning. High-functioning groups need less adult help than lower functioning groups in managing conflict and other issues.

2. Assess each student's needs for adult support and supervision in peer relations. Be prepared to assist those individuals who need help.

3. Assess latent hostility and antagonism between students. Often students send signals that trouble is imminent. Some of these signals will be pleas for adult assistance.

4. Create buffers between volatile students. Use space, distance, helpful peers, and activity as creative forms of insulation between potential antagonists.

5. Monitor the classroom group for scapegoats. The peer group can be merciless when it turns its resentment or frustration inward at the expense of its most vulnerable members. Be prepared to protect the goat and help the rest of the group to address its problems directly and constructively.

6. Monitor the classroom group for moblike reactivity. The peer group can sweep its members along like a wolfpack in a rampage of destructiveness. Try to defuse the energy that drives this outward expression of anger and frustration before it gains momentum.

7. Monitor the peer group for dangerous trends and fads. Many such gradual changes in norms are harmless or even positive. Others such as drug fads, carrying weapons, and sexual acting out are dangerous and destructive.

8. Monitor the peer group for coercive social pressure. Students often push peers to behave in ways they ordinarily would not. These peers comply to fend off hostility and threats. Violence is a classic example as students are forced to fight by a violent youth culture.

9. Be prepared to intervene preemptively. Once control is lost, it often cannot be regained until destructive energies are dissipated.

Because social ineptitude and poor communication skills leave students trapped in helplessness and violence, it is important to prepare students for independent violence prevention:

1. Teach language as a basic tool of conflict resolution and violence prevention.

2. Teach communication skills as violence prevention. Speaking is one half of the equation. Listening is the other half.

3. Teach negotiation strategies. Compromise, trading, sharing, and taking turns are the long standing methods through which humans have managed to avoid extermination. As con-

cepts, they are easy to understand but require skill for their execution.

4. Teach mediation skills so that peers may help each other resolve conflict peacefully. The assistance that students can provide each other strengthens their relationships and makes life easier for everyone, including teachers.

5. Advocate equity, justice, and benevolence as important social values in peer relations.

## SUMMARY OF KEY POINTS

Since the 1970s, school violence has been a growing problem for teachers, parents, and children. Policymakers claim that this frightening trend is a product of drug use. However, other observers argue that it is an outgrowth of drug control in that harsh laws have led adult drug dealers to recruit children, who are immune to adult penalties, into the drug trade. This has produced vicious street gangs who bring their weapons, antisocial attitudes, and violent behavior into the schools.

In the schools, these changes have had serious impact on the traditional checks and balances of youth culture. Teachers and peers can no longer safely intervene to stop violent exchanges. Consequently, decent students have begun to use weapons, hostility, and violence to protect themselves because they can no longer depend on adults for protection.

The schools have responded with a myriad of security measures that have changed the learning environment in ways that raise serious questions. At issue is the potential of such measures to impose a prison atmosphere on school life, and criticism of the theory and effectiveness of educational programs for conflict resolution and mediation.

A new approach to preventing violence relies on intervention into the process through which violence occurs. The strategy requires that teachers develop learning environments in which the potential for hostile interactions is minimized. Teachers may do this by creating a well-defined classroom culture in which fair treatment is a dominant social guideline. Also, the teacher must monitor and promptly intervene in provocative student behavior. And, in the process of intervention, the teacher helps students to acquire social and verbal skills for resolving and mediating dangerous encounters on their own.

# II

## Theory and Practice
## in Drug Education and
## Substance Abuse Prevention

# 4

# Moral Admonition and Secular Propaganda: Failed Strategies in Substance Abuse Prevention

The goals for this chapter are to help teachers understand the following:

1. Drug use and drug control are long-standing universals in the history of human societies.
2. Moral admonition and secular propaganda are neither new nor unique to modern efforts to prevent substance abuse.
3. Substance abuse prevention in the United States has become a political issue because it is entangled with efforts to legislate morality.
4. The intrusion of drug control into education exposes teachers to social risks and hazards that threaten job security.
5. Moralistic appeal and propaganda have little, if any, effect on drug use.
6. Informational strategies to prevent drug abuse have produced disappointing results.

People have been using psychoactive drugs for more than 10,000 years (Goode, 1993). Not only is this history lengthy, but evidence from it suggests that nearly every human community extracted mind-altering substances from plant life in its habitat. Each community integrated these substances into its culture to serve religious, medicinal, and social purposes.

The evidence indicates that prehistoric humans, tribal societies, and ancient civilizations each used alcohol, marijuana, cocaine, opium, tobacco, or hallucinogenic plant products. In fact, drug use

**55**

would be universal among human communities but for the Inuits (Eskimos), who may not have used psychoactive drugs at all. This probably is attributable to their inhabitation of an environment that is inhospitable to plant life from which drugs can be derived.

Nevertheless, the extraction and use of drugs is among the oldest of technologies for those people whose habitat contains drug-producing plants (Rudgley, 1993). Furthermore, pharmacology, the study of medicines and drugs, has origins in ancient Egypt and India that are several thousand years old. In fact, pharmacology is one the earliest forms of scientific inquiry.

Therefore, efforts to prevent drug abuse, particularly alcohol abuse, date back to antiquity. Historical evidence about ancient civilizations, including those of the Hebrews, Egyptians, Greeks, and Romans reveals that all addressed the problem of alcohol abuse.

Furthermore, the prevention strategies of ancient civilizations were similar to those used by present-day societies. Strategies to control supplies of drugs included prohibition and taxation. Attempts to control demand for drugs relied on moral education and admonition by religious leaders and teachers. Such efforts to curtail or limit availability, drive up costs, instill or appeal to moral standards, and to teach and persuade continue to this very day in the United States and other modern countries.

## WHAT FORCES DRIVE SUBSTANCE ABUSE PREVENTION IN AMERICA?

The U.S. impulse to turn morality into law (Garvey, 1986) has led the United States to push traditional substance abuse prevention strategies to remarkable extremes. In the early 1970s, as the drug explosion of the 1960s peaked, and again in the late 1980s during the most recent drug panic, national leaders reinvigorated the war on drugs by officially declaring war. To be sure, this meant more than catchy sloganeering.

The explosion of cocaine use among yuppies and other fashionable, well-to-do people, and crack cocaine use among the poor, ignited the sparks of panic during the 1980s (Goode, 1993). Then, the drug-related deaths of several prominent athletes and entertainers, a conservative political climate, broad belief in a mythical epidemic of cocaine-impaired crack babies, and sensational reports by the media fanned these sparks.

Consequently, the problem of drug use was recast from a "drug users' health risk" to "an act of treason." In this context, drug use became an easy target for politicians seeking to convert morality into law. And, at no time is the raw exercise of power more transparent then when it is joined with moral purpose (Noble, 1990).

This occurs because morality permits its proponents to derive absolutes from even innocuous behavior. Reformers may then easily convert morality into drug law because, according to moralists, all recreational drug use is absolutely bad, and bad is equivalent to illegal.

Consequently, drug users, who policymakers had ambivalently tolerated in the past and defined as victims, became targets for punishment along with drug dealers. Users were attacked as a "moral scourge," "a threat to our way of life," "co-conspirators with criminals," and as "murderers" of small children and loved ones (Hepburn, 1995). With amplification from the media and an update in style, the prohibitionist forces behind this rhetoric were at least as powerful, if not more so, than they ever were.

Thus, the archaic and seemingly dead moralistic zeal of alcohol prohibition had reawakened in word and deed. Politicians jumped on a "Get tough on drugs!" (Sandor, 1995, p. 515) and "Get tough on crime!" (Porter, 1995, p. 44) bandwagon to please an anxious public and reap political advantage from the panic. And, the media sold newspapers and hiked television ratings with sensationalized and biased reporting (Goode, 1993).

Also, as first lady, Nancy Reagan, chose drug use as a theme to escape her public image as a cold, uncaring, insensitive, petty, and self-involved person (Jensen, Gerber, & Babcock, 1991). In 1981, by speaking out against drugs, she found a safe venue from which to illuminate herself as a socially concerned citizen and first lady. What could have been safer than her simplistic mantra of "Just say no!" to drugs?

Oddly, she may not have deserved her coldly negative image in the first place, according to Miles Davis. Davis was an award-winning and internationally known Black jazz musician who had used drugs much of his adult life. He was addicted to heroin for 4 years, used heroin from time to time after kicking his habit without relapse into addiction, used cocaine, and was a heavy drinker.

Davis' opinion is important because his sensitivity about racism and racist stereotypes about Blacks, especially among Whites who have wealth and power, bordered on paranoia. He was notorious for his hostile reactivity and outspokenness to even the most subtle affronts about or exploitation of his race or history of drug abuse.

After meeting Nancy Reagan at a White House dinner honoring Ray Charles in 1987, Davis revealed in his autobiography that her abundant warmth and charm had outshone that of her husband (Davis, 1989). And, if anything, Ronald Reagan's charm was his most powerful political asset (Wills, 1996). These personal qualities were contrary to

Nancy Reagan's public image, and although she may not have realized it, Davis' response was a genuine victory for her.

No doubt, Davis would have expressed his displeasure had he thought she behaved badly toward him. Davis reported in his autobiography that he did respond negatively toward Barbara Bush, the wife of then Vice-President George Bush, when he met her at the same dinner.

Despite her needless and brief foray into substance abuse prevention, and the seeming innocuousness of her words, Nancy Reagan's "Just say no!" had a deeper and more cynical meaning. Implicit within this directive was the idea that people use drugs because they lack the strength of character and moral will to control their own sinful impulses, and resist peer and other social pressures.

Her words fed the panic and empowered the "punitive parent" of conservatism to elbow aside the "caring parent" of moderation in the policy debate surrounding drug control. The stage was set for conversion of morality about drug use into national law, and a harsh, vengeful, and punitive law, it is.

Consequently, the previously described events and Nancy Reagan's effort to bolster her image contributed to passage of the Federal Anti-Drug Abuse Act of 1988. Drug users now can be evicted from their homes, denied government entitlements, subjected to involuntary drug testing, heavily fined, and even denied driver's licenses.

Also, users may have their personal property confiscated and lose their jobs. Although the legislators who framed this law claim that these last two provisions are aimed at profits derived from drug sales, one cannot help but wonder if such penalties specifically targeted well-to-do drug users. Affluent people were using cocaine in the bathrooms at fashionable parties and expensive night spots such as Studio 54 in New York (Hackett, 1989; Kirkland & Lawrence, 1992). Wealthy party givers, yuppies who traveled to them in their expensive cars, and nightclub owners had much to lose if police caught them with drugs in their homes, automobiles, and business establishments.

So extreme and intense was the panic and government reaction that foreign countries were invaded or their governments destabilized, and foreign policy was skewed to wage the war on drugs (Zeese, 1989). Although the Reagan and Bush administrations have come and gone, and the panic has subsided, the war continues.

As with all wars, the costs of the war on drugs in resources, social displacement, and public confidence have been enormous relative the true magnitude of the problem it seeks to crush. One may liken the meager gains achieved by its many heavy-handed efforts to shooting with an elephant gun at a mouse, only hitting the tip of its tail, and killing half the neighbors with the ricochet. Illegal drugs are still available, people still buy them, although costs of some drugs may be higher, and the country awaits the next drug fad.

In the next 5 to 10 years, the growing wave of methamphetamine and heroin use (Johnson, 1996; Sandor, 1995) and recent reversals in downward trends in drug use among adolescents are likely to precipitate yet another panic. Consequently, the reactions of the late 1980s are only the latest of many such events in 200 years of evolution of drug policy. More panic is sure to come.

## WHAT DO MORAL ADMONITION AND SECULAR PROPAGANDA ABOUT DRUGS MEAN TO TEACHERS?

The teacher's role as an agent of substance abuse prevention has followed dutifully along the same evolutionary path that produced our current status quo. From the late 1800s to 1930, school systems demanded that teachers provide moral inspiration. From the early 1930s, after repeal of alcohol prohibition, to the early 1960s, communities recruited teachers to disseminate "hard sell" antidrug propaganda. Throughout the remainder of the 1960s into the early 1970s, teachers provided "soft sell," though more objective, negative information about drugs and the dangers of drug use.

Throughout the remainder of the 1970s into the mid-1980s, prevention strategists asked teachers to be mental health workers. From the late 1980s through the end of the 20th century, communities demand that teachers act as authoritarian agents of drug control.

Although most observers agree that education is the best hope for drug abuse prevention, the results of teachers' efforts have been uniformly disappointing. This may have happened because communities have always pressed teachers to serve in ways that resemble education in form but not in substance.

Clearly, substance abuse prevention in the schools has fallen short of educational ideals such as truth, meaning, choice, and personal responsibility. Educators and policymakers have always championed these ideals as necessary for constructive participation in democratic community life.

However, in response to moral issues such as drug use, many communities have been overtly hostile to these cherished values. Recently, resistant elements in some communities have argued that such ideals are part of a dangerous ideology called *secular humanism*. Although secular humanism is a social theory, members of these communities view it to be a "godless religion." They argue that it rejects any notion of devine guidance or purpose, absolute or objective moral standards, and embraces "an anything goes" morality based on personal needs and desires (Noble, 1990).

Secular humanism has become the latest enemy in an effort to impose a universal morality on a heterogenous and multicultural society. Those who have identified it as the enemy struggle mightily against any existential resolution that meaning, purpose, and morality emerge from within the individual human being and are independent of the "hand of God."

In this way, substance abuse prevention has become entangled in an ideological struggle. It is embroiled along with issues such as separation of church and state, school prayer, book banning, pornography, abortion, and moral relativism. Freedoms associated with all of these issues are periodically attacked by political conservatives across the country.

Consequently, history reveals that substance abuse prevention has long ignored teachers' most valuable assets. These assets are teachers' commitment to education, enthusiasm, training, rationality, humanitarianism, and teaching skill. No doubt, many teachers are caring, charismatic, and persuasive, but they are not preachers, propagandists, psychotherapists, or policemen.

## HOW DOES THE HISTORY OF SUBSTANCE ABUSE PREVENTION RELATE TO TEACHING IN THE SCHOOLS OF TODAY?

Although reflection about the past is revealing, the material that follows is not a comprehensive history of U.S. social and educational policy about drugs. Rather, the narrative provides some history in order to expand on five specific issues important to teaching. These issues were presented in chapter 1 because they are important to teachers' decisions about doing substance abuse prevention work.

However, these same issues also provide teachers with a legitimate link between substance abuse prevention and the academic curriculum. The issues are as follows:

1. Teachers' efforts in drug education and substance abuse prevention have an historical context that has meaning in the classroom.
2. The role of teachers as agents of prevention is defined within the contexts of culture and social policies regarding drugs and drug use.
3. Teachers who serve as agents of prevention risk identification with abhorrent motives and events associated with U.S. drug policy.
4. Drug policy clashes violently with many dearly held social and educational values.

**5.** Teachers' exposure and vulnerability to pressures to violate these values is a problem in drug education and substance abuse prevention.

The material that follows expands on each issue, and provides perspectives that have curricular relevance to many school subjects. These subjects include history, social studies, literature, art, drama, music, economics, religion, humanities, and philosophy.

For example, history reveals that substance abuse became a social policy issue just after the United States achieved independence from colonial rule. Benjamin Rush, a signatory of the Declaration of Independence and America's first surgeon general, became alcohol abuse prevention's first prominent advocate in the new world.

Rush was also the nation's first professor of medicine. In 1785, he published a pamphlet (Conner & Burns, 1995) that became the first scientific (Levin, 1995) paper to criticize the intemperate use of distilled spirits. In attempting to educate the citizenry with this pamphlet, Rush achieved yet another first with his proposal that addiction to alcohol is a disease and a medical problem (Levin, 1995).

Twenty years later, Thomas Trotter, a British naval physician, expanded on Rush's ideas and proposed that heredity and adverse childhood experience produce alcohol addiction (Levin & Weiss, 1994). Considering that the proposals by Rush and Trotter are 200 years old, they are remarkably consistent with modern thinking.

In 1825, the American Society for the Promotion of Temperance emerged in Boston. By 1830, the society had circulated more than 200,000 copies of Rush's pamphlet.

The temperance movement subverted Rush's effort to teach and educate, and to bring rationality to the problem of alcohol abuse. Rush's statements became the first sparks of a fiery struggle about alcohol and other drugs that still continues. So began what Connor and Burns (1995) described as "America's 200 Year War on Drunks."

This war began in 1825 Boston. By the 1820s, Boston was the busiest center of commerce and trade in Massachusetts, and was rapidly becoming one of the busiest in a then-young United States. The Puritan world of Massachusetts, of which Boston was the center, had a rigid code of morality in which decency was measured by religious scruples (Noble, 1990).

Anything religious leaders thought would corrupt, debauch, unleash lustful desires, and cause lewd, wicked, and scandalous behavior was a target for suppression through excoriation and, if necessary, prosecution. These targets included any potentially corruptive influence that might enter the minds or bodies of the citizenry, and especially children. Consequently, books and booze became easily identified objects of condemnation in this tight-minded (Noble, 1990) Puritan stronghold.

In 1873, at the same time as the temperance agenda shifted toward prohibition, Anthony Comstock, an ardent crusader against alcohol, founded the New York Society for the Prevention of Vice. Then, in 1878, Comstock met with a group of ministers in Boston, and soon they formed the New England Watch and Ward Society. Literary censorship and book banning was the principle activity of these self-appointed moral watchdogs, but their existence was born at the same time and of the same righteous indignation as the prohibition movement. This war against alcohol, begun in Boston, and its logical extension to other drugs is one in which teachers long have been valued as recruits. However, teachers have had an ambiguous and confusing role. The troublesome questions have always been: Do teachers accede to moralistic demands and political mandates to serve the cause of abstinence and prohibition? Or, do teachers challenge these demands and mandates by adhering to cherished educational and democratic values? These values advocate personal freedom and choice, moderation, reason, and temperance.

Clearly, these are but two of many questions that challenge academic freedom. The tenure system was created because of the threat inherent to such questions. Although the system is not absolute in its protection, its purpose is to protect teachers from assaults on their freedom to pursue truth, as they see it.

Because tenure is not ironclad, teachers feel vulnerable around issues related to politics, sex, religion, and drugs. Therefore, as described in chapter 1, many teachers refuse to participate in substance abuse prevention and drug education. They behave as draft resistors to the war on drugs which, to them, may be the perplexing and dangerous equivalent of a domestic Vietnam War.

These teachers' assessments may be reasonable because many battles have been won for and against drug prohibition, but the war lingers on with little, if any, hope of a satisfactory conclusion. To teachers, substance abuse prevention may seem like a minefield in which there is little to gain and much to lose.

The past may offer some understanding of this problem to teachers of today. History suggests that teachers' ambiguous and confusing position emerged out of prohibitionists' subversion of Rush's well-intended and rational ideas.

People's all too human capacity to subvert great ideas with self-serving distortions of reality (Beyerstein & Hadaway, 1990) presents an interesting question to teachers. Teachers may challenge their students with this question: "Can one bring reconciliation between emotionally based arguments, as are the prohibitionists', and a reasoned position such as Rush's?" U.S. education idealizes rationality, and the forces of suppression cling tenaciously to their powerful emotional investment in morality.

Prohibitionists raised this question by selectively attending to Rush's words. They had to do so because Rush was not a prohibitionist, and the religious leaders of prohibition did not share Rush's or Trotter's view that addiction is a disease.

These leaders viewed addiction as sin or moral weakness, just as many individuals continue to do to this day. According to prohibitionists, alcohol corrupted good people, weakened their character, and turned them into sinners. In so doing, alcohol was a moral scourge that destroyed individuals, families, and communities. The irony is that Rush, long after his death, remained a powerful influence, and his writing a rallying doctrine of the prohibition movement in America. This happened despite the fact that his thinking was antithetical to prohibition.

As the goal of the temperance movement shifted to prohibition, the battleground for this struggle became the national marketplace for demon rum. The prohibitionists' view was that to save society from rampant alcohol abuse, the marketplace must be restricted or shut down.

This is important to teachers because prohibition is a statement about human nature. It is an early rendition of the "Theory X versus Theory Y" argument about whether people are inherently good when they have opportunity to show their true nature, or inherently evil. Many teachers organize their classes and relate to their students in accordance with one or the other of these polar opposite beliefs about children. And, many teachers are not conscious of the feelings that have driven such choices.

The prohibitionist position is that all common people are evil and corruptible, and few, if any, are capable of temperate drinking. Therefore, the prohibitionist claim is that members of society who possess the purpose, pride, and honor, have a duty to deny that which corrupts (contrary ideas, free expression, sensuous experience, alcohol and other drugs) to the rest.

According to some observers (Noble, 1990), such individuals acquire the power to do so when they convert their arrogance to social and political influence. They express their arrogance in claims that by breeding, education, and experience, they are superior to the commoners among the masses they seek to protect.

Despite fundamental disagreements with Rush's ideas as previously discussed, and an unenthusiastic response by the general public, the prohibitionist movement acquired enough power and momentum to gain passage of the Volstead Act of 1917. In 1920, prohibition of the sale of alcohol in the United States became law as the Eighteenth Amendment of the Constitution. It remained so until the amendment was repealed in 1933.

However, prohibition is not merely a failed social experiment or an historical relic of antiquated ideas (Roman & Blum, 1995). Prohibitionist strategies flourished anew in America's continuing and recently reinvigorated "One-Hundred-Year War on Drugs" (Connor & Burns, 1995; Roman & Blum, 1995; Sandor, 1995).

The alcohol prohibition movement started to gather strength during the Civil War, and gained further momentum through the Industrial Revolution. Then, the arrival of large numbers of immigrants attracted attention to opiates, cocaine, and marijuana and each, in turn, became a target of prohibition (Musto, 1987; Rumbarger, 1989).

By the end of the 19th century, derivatives of cocaine and opium had become common additives for patent medicines. These medicines were intended to treat pain and diarrhea, and continued to be available over the counter until the eve of World War I.

However, as the nation entered the 20th century, various states and localities began to pass laws prohibiting their use. Then, their representatives in the Federal government pressed for national legislation. Consequently, the Pure Food and Drug Act of 1905, the Harrison Narcotics Control Act of 1914, and creation of the Federal Narcotics Board in 1922 imposed powerful national restrictions on narcotic production and distribution.

This process recurred in connection with marijuana. Although local laws prohibiting marijuana use started in El Paso, Texas, in 1914, marijuana became a regional issue in the southwest following the Mexican Revolution of 1923 (Musto, 1987). Large numbers of Mexican immigrants came into the United States seeking jobs and competing with U.S. workers for unskilled employment. In 1937, Congress passed the Marijuana Tax Act, imposing prohibition on that drug. Since the 1940s, similar scenarios have continued to take place as scientists synthesize or discover new drugs and government agencies respond to them.

Thus, for teachers of language arts, Sandor's (1995) use of metaphor is of interest because he drew a poignant analogy between the history of U.S. drug policy and its similarity to "a long-running musical" theater production. Sandor painted a word picture of this history as one in which the songs and the story have remained the same despite the passage of many generations of performers.

New agencies are formed and become new theaters for the same production. New drugs are added to lists of restricted substances, thus becoming new sets and props. New people are appointed to lead the struggle as producers and directors come and go. One might find it all to be great comedy except that, tragically, new victims of drugs and drug policies continually appear in the headlines and obituaries.

For teachers, this history reveals that the task of addressing the issue of drug use in the classroom is not clear cut. The teacher's intention may be to help children find insight, enlightenment, and wisdom about drugs and other issues of living. Certainly, health, safety, and security for individuals, families, and communities are very acceptable goals. However, in pursuing such seemingly beneficial ends, teachers will enter a battleground of competing agendas, fanaticism, values conflicts, and distortion. This battlefield is one on which combatants have been at each others' throats for a long time.

The drug issue contains many smaller, but nevertheless, complicated problems. The health and social problems caused by drugs are but one concern. Another is problems caused by efforts to prohibit drug use. And, another is the troubling messages the preceding problems convey about U.S. culture, the national character, and Americans' struggle to balance money, morals, and personal freedom.

These problems provide rich but dangerous opportunities in the classroom for great teaching and learning. Because of the danger, teachers should be alert to the likelihood that the following may occur:

1. Any reasoned middle ground about these drug-related issues may be besieged by reactive elements of the community. Their emotionally based positions on a variety of issues are not so reasoned.

2. These reactive community members may view teachers as either "for drugs" or "against drugs." They base their view on vague understandings of any teachers' actions in the classroom or elsewhere.

3. Beneath community members' emotionally based reactions is a belief that they and their children are fundamentally corruptible. Words and ideas contrary to their own values and morals are, therefore, dangerous.

4. Most of the people who react in these ways are not crazies or extremists. They are anxious and concerned about the well-being and future of their own children and the children of others. They are acting to protect children from what they see as evil.

5. These fears about drugs often have been fanned by misinformation, selective attention to truth, and media attention to rare but sensational drug-related events.

6. Fear is a driving force behind intransigence and reactive, moralistic, and aggressive behavior regarding many social issues,

including drug use. Such fear is largely unassailable by facts, reasoning, and other elements of rational problem solving.

**7.** Any school district may have some administrators who resist educational activity that disturbs their all-too-comfortable complacency or "rocks their boat."

**8.** Other teachers may be embarrassed or threatened by the prospect of negative reaction within the community.

**9.** Among the reactive, some colleagues, parents, and other community members will be tenacious and extreme in attacking teachers they identify as the "enemy" on issues about drug use.

## WHY DOES PROPAGANDA FAIL AS A STRATEGY FOR SUBSTANCE ABUSE PREVENTION?

Consistent with its prohibitionist origins of the late 1800s, early educational efforts to prevent substance abuse pursued inspirational strategies. Relying on impassioned dissemination of negative information about alcohol abuse, the earliest education efforts resembled religious missionary work.

These efforts were, for all intents and purposes, sermons laden with scare tactics, preaching, and emotional fervor (Mathews, 1975). Moral admonition became a central theme. The puritan ethic was reaching its high point as a force shaping U.S. culture and social policy regarding alcohol use.

This is not surprising because religious leaders were at the forefront of the prohibition movement. However, prohibition was never very popular in the community, and the economic boom of the Roaring 20s marked the beginning of the demise of the movement. Alcohol prohibition came to an ignominious end with the repeal of the Volstead Act in 1933.

Although alcohol prohibition ended, Congress created the Federal Bureau of Narcotics to enforce prohibition of other banned drugs in 1930. Under the leadership of Harry Anslinger, the bureau mounted massive propaganda campaigns against marijuana, the "evil weed," and then against opiates and cocaine.

Prevention education, finally unburdened of the strategy of religious admonition and moral appeal, followed this lead. Initially, educators adopted Anslinger's hard sell propaganda tactics. Scare tactics and horror stories attributable to substance abuse comprised significant portions of the curriculum for more than 20 years.

These antidrug programs of 1940 to 1960 failed to differentiate between the dangers and effects of different drugs. Also, just as Bohemians and beatniks had before them, in the 1960s, increasing numbers of young people began experimenting with marijuana and discovered, firsthand, that antidrug information was not to be believed.

In response, drug education shifted to a soft sell strategy in the 1960s and 1970s. Educators began using methods that provided factual information about specific drugs and the dangers inherent to each of them.

Implementors of these methods promoted them as offering a dispassionate focus on scientific facts, but these methods, too, were blatantly biased toward "no use" goals. The information was often invalid, exaggerated, or overgeneralized and recognized as such by groups at whom it was directed (Avis, 1990; Carroll, 1985; Fields, 1992).

Then, in the early 1970s, reviews of evidence about information dissemination to prevent drug abuse stimulated a major change (Carroll, 1985). The reviewers found that information did not reduce drug use (Hanson, 1982; National Institute on Drug abuse, 1984;). In fact, some evidence raised suspicions that broad and indiscriminate dissemination of drug information may stimulate drug use rather than reduce it (Avis, 1990).

Perhaps it is no wonder that the mass of this evidence indicates that informational strategies for substance abuse prevention have been ineffective or counterproductive (Botvin, 1995; Hanson, 1982). Although 20/20 hindsight requires no prescience, many plausible hypotheses might explain the disappointing results of information strategies.

One explanation is that people are not rational and will not use information appropriately in making decisions about their own behavior (Steuart, 1969). A second is that teachers do not have the knowledge, skills, or the enthusiasm to effectively communicate drug abuse information to their pupils (Botvin, 1995). A third explanation is that the forces that promote drug abuse in the peer group, the home, and the community are far more powerful than teachers could ever hope to be in opposing drug use (Goode, 1993). Therefore, children use drugs as they wish because they ignore the facts about danger, teachers are unconvincing in presenting the facts, and teachers occupy too small a place in children's lives to exert meaningful influence.

Another way of stating this theory is that children, especially those at greatest risk, view teachers to be trifling irritants, irrelevant, and untrustworthy. Rather than seeing teachers as good helpers, children may view teachers to be incapable of meaningful assistance, uncaring and unresponsive, or reactive and punitive (Weinstein, 1995c).

Particularly with regard to drugs, children may see middle-class, traditionally trained teachers as ignorant, insensitive, and rigid in promoting an abstinence agenda (Wepner, 1984). Furthermore, many children expect teachers to be socially and emotionally remote to youth and popular culture, and to a child's life at home and in the community. The "generation gap" becomes a great and uncrossable abyss in such instances.

Consequently, children expect teachers to be unsympathetic to that with which they identify most closely. This includes norms and values through which children pursue self-esteem and social status among their peers, in their family, and in their neighborhood. Probably, to some degree, for some teachers, with some children, and under some circumstances, each of these pessimistic expectations is valid.

Thus, as with all stereotypes, some children's stereotypes of teachers may contain a kernel of truth (Harding, 1964). Such a kernel of truth, no matter how improbable, gains status as a well-earned reputation that a child can attribute to all teachers. Those children at greatest risk of drug use are most likely to accept these powerful negative stereotypes about teachers.

Some school systems examined the previously mentioned ideas in what Wepner (1984) referred to as the "ex-addict epoch" of drug education. During the early 1970s, school districts recruited graduates of drug-free therapeutic communities. They thought that streetwise ex-addicts might be better able than professionally licensed teachers to form attachments with drug-using children.

Initially, parents, teachers, and school administrators resisted the employment of ex-addicts in the schools. But, ex-addicts soon were accepted members of pupil personnel teams. They received drug education training along with counselors and teachers, and became socialized into the substance abuse prevention strategies of the time. However, appraisal in 1973 and subsequent disillusionment with many of these strategies led to their discontinuance, as well as cessation of employment of ex-addicts.

We all may be seduced by our desire to appear brilliant in trying to understand the failures of substance abuse prevention. As a result, our attempts to construct insightful understandings about such complicated problems often overlook or disregard the obvious. The obvious about prevention may be that information strategies presented information that was patently untrue, distorted, or selective and biased. Therefore, information strategies did not present information. They presented propaganda.

In accordance with 1800s folk wisdom, one can fool some of the people some of the time, but not all of the people all of the time. Thus, as Abraham Lincoln warned, the truth will be and was found out about drugs. In the 1960s, personal experience and the peer group repudiated the lies of drug propaganda, and discredited the liars.

Furthermore, negative findings about informational strategies introduces a refreshing possibility that people, once they have believable facts, are reasonable, rational, and realistic in indulging their propensities for pleasure and risk-taking. The facts about the consequences of casual drug use, in the very large majority of cases, do not approximate the horrors of antidrug messages. This is true even though some people experience horrors and terrible misery in connection with abuse of some drugs.

If the actual incidence and prevalence of these horrors and miseries confirmed the claims of antidrug messages, most of the millions of people who engage in casual drug use would not do so. Thus, information strategies did not deter drug use because reasonable people reject and resent lies, and then respond to truth with suspicion and distrust. This distrust is truly unfortunate because some drugs and some circumstances in which people use them are truly dangerous for everyone.

Nevertheless, for many adventurous souls, claims by drug-using peers, their own individual experience, and the lack of convincing opposing authoritative evidence settle the issue. For them, casual drug use is in the same ball-park as other more socially endorsed but equally risky activities. Many people do not indulge in risky but socially accepted activities, and fewer people are accepting the risks of drinking, drugging, and smoking.

Although all of the previously mentioned hypotheses about the failure of information strategies are speculative, the failures themselves brought propagandistic drug education in the schools to a screeching halt. In 1973, the federal government imposed a moratorium on funding for curricular innovation. Too late, perhaps, because prevention efforts by teachers had damaged the credibility of drug education in the schools. Teachers' efforts continue to arouse suspicion, especially among children who are in greatest jeopardy.

## HOW HAVE INFORMATION STRATEGIES CHANGED SINCE 1973?

Although information about drugs remains important to educational strategy, an evolving consensus of experts recommends that careful selectivity be exercised. This consensus has produced guidelines that urge moderation and caution about the kind of information to be disseminated, the settings in which it is to be provided, and the personal qualities of persons providing it. Thus, prevention experts now advocate educational temperance for teachers.

These experts began to recognize that trustworthiness and credibility of teachers are indispensable elements of drug education. Also, guidelines now direct teachers to provide information in small doses rather than in overwhelming exposures. Preferably, teachers should provide this information in response to their pupils' need to know rather than to impose it outside the context of such need.

Furthermore, guidelines urge teachers to teach about substance abuse in an emotionally low-key manner, and to avoid histrionics and emotional fervor. Alternatives to the standard educational approaches of lecture, reading, and writing also are important. This last recommendation is particularly meaningful to teachers in special education and in the arts.

Content should emphasize the immediate effects and adverse consequences of drugs rather than their long-term dangers. Realistic appraisals of drug use rates among peers are particularly important because children tend to overestimate drug use in the peer group. Furthermore, messages should acknowledge the following:

1. Drug use is a complex rather than simple problem.
2. Stereotypes do not apply because drug users form a heterogeneous population.
3. Social policies governing drug use are inconsistent.
4. Society contains great variations in behavior and lifestyle.
5. Drug effects are produced by the interaction of many factors.

Alternatively, prevention messages should refrain from scare tactics, and avoid providing inadvertent training about how to take drugs. Also, messages should avoid emphasizing illegal drugs to the exclusion of legal drugs that are abused at times.

Thus, the reappraisal of 1973 produced recommendations that drug education curricula should be designed on a foundation of trust, credibility, moderation, truth, and the needs of children. These recommendations urged that drug education be more consistent with traditional educational values, but unfortunately, eventually placed it at odds with drug policy.

Consequently, policymakers have created a dilemma for teachers. In the most simple terms, current policy is that "If our abstinence position is too weakly supported by truth to be convincing, and if we cannot use deception to achieve adherence to our position, we will use coercion!"

Therefore, teachers find themselves in the midst of the ongoing struggle between individual rights to truth, freedom, and the pursuit of happiness and the restrictive power of the community. The struggle is not between the forces of good and evil, but between the youthful spirit of freedom and adventure, and the elders' wisdom of restraint and security. However, evil emerges when proponents and advocates of either of these two forces violate our most cherished democratic values to impose their will.

## SUMMARY OF KEY POINTS

Nearly all human communities have integrated mind-altering drugs into their cultures, and all have had to address the problem of drug abuse. Regardless of time, place, and level of technological development, the problems and methods of prevention have been similar for tribal societies, ancient civilizations, and modern nations.

However, Americans have raised the issue of drug use to unusual prominence and have been extreme in their attempts to eradicate it. Prevention is now entangled with efforts by policymakers' to legislate morality and a contentious political issue. Political leaders have recast the problem of addiction from an illness to an act of treason. In this way, leaders have urged the nation to return to times when it viewed drug use as a moral scourge. Consequently, we are now waging an unending and unsuccessful war on drugs.

Moral admonition and propaganda have been overused but ineffective weapons in this war and they have damaged the position of teachers in the prevention effort. In addition, drug control has intruded on drug education and substance abuse prevention. Truth has become a casualty in the war on drugs, and teachers who examine truth about drugs jeopardize their reputation and their jobs. Furthermore, informational strategies no longer have a prominent place in prevention efforts.

# 5

# Current Thought About
# Substance Abuse Prevention

The goals for this chapter are to prepare teachers to:

1. Understand the troubled relations between drug control, drug education, and substance abuse prevention in the schools.
2. Manage the schism between drug education and substance abuse prevention.
3. Translate theories about drug use into action in the classroom.
4. Understand substance abuse prevention's shift away from a focus on drugs to a focus on the drug user.
5. Establish realistic goals and objectives for substance abuse prevention in the classroom.
6. Understand drug use as a behavioral pattern that emerges from a normal developmental process.
7. Help children effectively resolve drug-related developmental issues so that they may safely integrate legal medicines and drugs into adult life.
8. Understand the distinctions between substance use, misuse, and abuse.

Educational prevention strategies now withhold information rather than distort or misrepresent it. They do so to preserve teachers' credibility, avoid stimulating children's curiosity about drugs, and maintain some children's fearful attitudes toward drugs. Therefore, drug education curricula and prevention programs contain less propaganda, and modern instructional guidelines urge teachers to act with restraint when presenting accurate scientific knowledge to students.

This change reflects expert consensus that neither knowledge nor propaganda are effective independent deterrents to drug use. Prevention experts especially doubt the deterrent effect of drug information that teachers provide in purely didactic fashion (Botvin, 1995), outside the context of trusting student–teacher relationships, and without meaningful student discussion in the classroom (Ellickson, 1995; Ennett, Tobler, Ringwalt, & Flewelling, 1994).

Nevertheless, knowledge and its derivatives such as insight, wisdom, and enlightenment are cherished and legitimate goals of education (Kilpatrick, 1963). Such goals represent education's role in preparing thoughtful citizens who can use the past experience of our culture to infuse rationality into society's present actions (Dewey, 1916).

Thoughtfulness and rationality are the enemy to many Americans whose emotionally based arguments dominate the political struggle about drugs. According to current policies, the narrow raison d'etre of substance abuse prevention is to suppress indiscriminately any and all illicit drug-taking behavior. This is policymakers' definition of prevention's intent even though such controversy rages about drugs that issues of meaning and purpose have never been more relevant to the formulation of U.S. drug policy (Goldberg, 1996).

Consequently, the search for the purpose and meaning of drugs in our society has become a marginal concern of education. Knowledge and attitude are no longer the bread and butter of substance abuse prevention in the schools, and objectives that define the educational end products of the search for meaning have become irrelevant. These educational traditions are vital to education's capacity to contribute thoughtful and humane solutions to social problems related to drugs and crime.

To policymakers, the many possible meanings with which drug availability challenges society now are relevant only if these meanings influence drug use. Therefore, if prevention experts were to suspect that wearing red neckties deters drug use among children, policymakers would direct the energies of teachers accordingly. This is evident in the current debate about school uniforms in public schools.

Furthermore, substance abuse prevention presses for the abandonment of other cherished social and educational values of drug education. Current policy sacrifices enlightenment that comes with the discovery of meaning in a naked attempt to control actions by controlling minds. What is more, educators who seek to inform drug-taking behavior are at odds with policy and those who enforce it. As a result, drug education is now, for all intents and purposes, an educational relic, despite the legitimacy of its place in the school curriculum.

Such losses occurred because truth became a casualty of the war on drugs. The real truth about drugs is not horrible enough to deter drug use, and the experiences of millions of casual users and their friends during the 1960s and 1970s discredited the horrible images presented in propaganda. However, the 1980s cocaine drug panic reversed this liberalizing trend as public sentiment became increasingly conservative and liberal educational thinking fell from favor. Consequently, under pressure to act, politicians of the 1980s would no longer tolerate the complexity and ambiguity of educators' theories about the connection between meaning, behavior, and drug use.

In turning away from educational thought, policymakers rejected hard-earned wisdom that, for better or worse, human behavior is complex and often inscrutable. Policymakers and others under pressure to take corrective action were sorely tempted to sidestep the complexity of some social problems and impose simple solutions on them.

As has been the case for drug policy, such solutions usually are ineffective and create many new and more complicated problems. Furthermore, such disappointments with drug policy cannot be separated from other disappointments that have eroded Americans' faith in national leaders and institutions. Public confidence in government, the press, major companies, universities, and the professions has slipped dramatically since the 1960s (Samuelson, 1995). All have participated in the continuing national debate about drugs and have been implicated in problems surrounding drug policy and drug use.

## CAN TEACHERS TRANSLATE EDUCATIONAL THEORY INTO SUBSTANCE ABUSE PREVENTION PRACTICE IN THE CLASSROOM?

Teachers who attempt to translate theory into substance abuse prevention practice have difficulty because the complexity of even small segments of the behavioral world is overwhelming. Because we cannot address simultaneously all significant elements of complicated environments, we cope by narrowing our view to a more manageable size. In so doing, we hope we have included that which is most relevant and have not excluded too much that is important.

As an illustration of the complexity of educational thought, theorists describe the relations between behavior, knowledge, and attitude to be reciprocal. Knowledge and attitude precede but then are altered by behavior and then again predispose behavior's future intention and direction. Bloom (1956) and his associates described *knowing* to be complex and to occur at many levels of thought and action ranging from simple recall to higher levels of understanding, analysis, creative synthesis, and evaluative judgment. Similarly, Ajzen and Fishbein (1980) described *attitude* to be not merely a positive or negative predisposition toward some behavior or object, but to include dimensions such as beliefs, feelings, and intentions.

Broader, holistic explanations, such as Lewin's (1951) field theory, Bandura's (1977) social learning theory, Becker's (1974) health belief model, and Jessor's (1992) theory of adolescent risk behavior are even more complex. These theories characterize behavior to be the result of many interacting psychological, social, and biological factors.

In his general theory of behavior, Lewin described human actions to occur in response to the objects and events of one's "life space" or "social space," and to be the product of the many forces that promote behavior and oppose it. Bandura described how social influences, such as role models, imitation, and social reinforcement effect the learning of behavior.

Narrowing his field of view to health, Becker proposed health behavior to be the product of one's concerns about susceptibility to a given health threat, its seriousness, barriers and cues to preventive action, and many other moderating factors. With greater specificity to drug use, Jessor described the health- and life-compromising outcomes of using drugs to be produced by complex interaction between many risk and protection factors, and behavior and lifestyle.

Although such complex theories are elegant and make good sense, they challenge teachers at two levels. At the descriptive level, the theories propose an overwhelming assortment of factors to be influences on behavior. At the dynamic level, they identify the processes and outcomes of an almost geometrically increasing multitude of interactions between these factors.

Despite their complexity, these theories are useful guides to planning. However, they are almost impossible for teachers to think about when teaching because there is just too much to remember and control. The teacher's responsibilities in an action-oriented and fluid environment such as a classroom leave little time for abstract thought, outside of the curriculum. Consequently, trying to translate into practice more than isolated components of complicated theories often places a teacher in the position of a juggler who must keep too many balls in the air. For teachers, these theories are too complex for practical application in the real world of teaching, except in limited ways.

The aforementioned difficulties do not mean that elegant theories should be disregarded, or that teachers should throw up their hands in surrender to the overwhelming complexity they portend. Rather, these difficulties mean that teachers must carefully and selectively incorporate limited and manageable elements of each theory into teaching practice as they apply. This is exactly the path of new educational strategies and tactics in substance abuse prevention.

## THE HYPOTHETICAL CASE OF BOBBY

The hypothetical case of Bobby, that follows, was contrived for illustrative purposes only. It is an instance of just one child who has begun to experiment with drugs. The case becomes increasingly intricate as the narrative unfolds, and interpretive comments inserted among the events of Bobby's life reflect the theoretical perspectives discussed previously. Though Bobby is a male high school student, the descriptions apply also to female students.

## Bobby's Life

Bobby is a teenager who loves (attitude is positive toward) ice cream. During early childhood and elementary years, Bobby's parents used ice cream to reward good behavior (equated ice cream with love). As a result, Bobby not only enjoys the sensuous gratifications (likes the sweet flavor and creamy texture) of ice cream, but also finds that eating it is reassuring, and calming (conditioned response that provides secondary rewards).

There is more to Bobby's life than ice cream. Bobby is a fairly good student with above-average grades (successful in school) and has begun thinking about going to college. Bobby believes that college acceptance is achievable, but acceptance to one of the schools he prefers may be more unsure. As a result, Bobby is nervous about forthcoming SAT examinations.

Also, Bobby has studied clarinet since grade school and is assistant leader of the clarinet section in the school band and orchestra. Bobby is proud of this accomplishment but experiences some uncomfortable performance anxiety about solo parts he must play during school concerts.

Recently, Bobby began participating in weekly rehearsals and occasionally performing with an adult community band. This band has some members who are professional jazz musicians. When Bobby mentioned his performance anxiety, one of these players advised him to take a beta blocker (proprolanol, a blood pressure medication) before a scary gig (jargon among musicians meaning "playing engagement") to stay calm. Bobby admires this adult's playing and worldliness (status as an insider among really cool musicians), and is flattered by the interest he has shown (the jazz musician is an attractive role model).

Bobby goes to the library to look up "beta blocker" in a medical reference book. Bobby suspects that if his parents knew that the jazz musician had suggested a drug, they would forbid him to continue his participation in the community band, and possibly create a fuss with the band's director. Because the music teacher at school had referred Bobby to the community band, this would have been too embarrassing. Therefore, Bobby never discloses the older musician's advice or what the reference book said about beta blockers.

Also, Bobby enjoys recreational athletics. Bobby at one time had dreams of making a school team, but his parents forced a choice between music and varsity sport. To this day, Bobby thinks he could have handled both and is irked about having to give up one.

Bobby thinks that had his parents known of what was said in the community band, they would have pushed him toward sports. Bobby giggles about the irony of this. He has heard of some of the school's star athletes using steroids during training, other drugs during games and matches, and boozing it up at parties.

Also, Bobby has seen both his dad and mom relax with their martinis from time to time, although they are not heavy drinkers (parents model moderate drug use and instrumental drinking—using alcohol for its effects). Bobby's dad smokes a pack of cigarettes a day and coughs and wheezes a bit with strenuous exertion (accepts certain health risks to maintain his nicotine addiction).

Bobby learned in elementary school that smoking was hazardous to health. Some of the things Bobby learned about lung cancer and heart disease were scary and made him anxious about losing his father to such terrible diseases. Bobby talked to his dad about quitting smoking, and his Dad agreed that he should stop, but never did.

Although angry, Bobby now ignores the smoking and drinking (denies his fear about losing or being rejected by his dad, and his guilt about anger toward both parents). Also, Bobby' mother and one sibling are overweight, but Bobby looks the other way about that concern, too (body weight has acquired symbolic meaning in the separation process).

Currently, these issues are more prominent because Bobby is separating (is developmentally adolescent) from his family. Bobby thinks the family is meddlesome and intrusive (has problems with interpersonal boundaries). Therefore, Bobby is reluctant to seek help from family members about many of his concerns for fear of showing weakness and never hearing the end of it (dependency conflict).

Furthermore, Bobby is in the process of forming a romantic attachment (involved in courtship) with a partner to whom he is strongly attracted (life is becoming more complicated). Several of Bobby's friends have romantically paired with other members of the peer group over the past year (introduced a new peer group norm in response to emerging biological, psychological, and social needs).

Bobby wants very much to keep pace with the crowd (maintain membership and status in the peer group). To cover the costs of dating, and other personal interests, he occasionally takes odd jobs, babysits, and earns a few dollars. Bobby likes the feeling of independence that comes with some cash in hand, but his budget is always tight.

Bobby suspects (is anxious and insecure) that his partner is ambivalent about continuing the relationship. As a result, Bobby is dieting continually in order to calm fears (problems with self-esteem) about being physically unattractive to the romantic partner, and to make a "separation" statement (I'm independent, different, and not fat!) to the family.

Consequently, Bobby is struggling mightily to avoid eating ice cream (self-denying an important gratification) and resents it (feels unfairly deprived). Bobby is tormented by intense hunger (craving) whenever he thinks about ice cream. This happens often when Bobby is under time pressure or other stress (conditioned reaction to circumstances that elicit unconscious wishes for parental love and support).

So, Bobby seeks relief through what friends said were diet pills (illegally obtained drugs of uncertain identity but probably amphetamines). The pills were offered to Bobby by these friends (drug-using peers) at no cost.

Bobby accepts and tries the pills despite "school-taught" understanding (knowledge) that drugs can be dangerous, and "church-taught" beliefs (negative attitudes) that using them is a crutch for the weak (holds a moralistic view). These same friends ease Bobby's internal conflict about using the diet pills by offering many comforting reassurances (provide social support and rationalizations).

The diet pills work (provide reinforcement for continued use) to reduce the hunger pangs, but cause Bobby to feel edgy and irritable (side effects). They seem to amplify the nervousness he feels (subjective experience of stress) about so many aspects of the transition to adulthood (school grades, future plans for college, dating, musical participation, family issues, money, etc.). Bobby thinks about the beta blocker and another friend offers Bobby some marijuana to "mellow out" ...

## An Analysis of Bobby

Bobby's needs, developmental struggles, personal issues and fears, and social circumstances are common challenges in growing up, and are not the problems of a freak or crazy person. In fact, Bobby probably is typical of many children teachers see daily in the junior and senior high school classroom.

Clearly, the psychological, social, and biological elements of Bobby's circumstances are neither extreme nor unusual. The drug users' stereotypes of alienation, poverty, estrangement from parents, social deprivation, abuse, neglect, and school failure are not factors in Bobby's case.

Although this case is fictitious, it has many possible variations and permutations that are true to life for most adolescents. For example, Bobby demonstrates how information strategies may strengthen students' knowledge and negative attitudes about drugs, but also that the relations between knowledge, attitude, and behavior is not direct. As Lewin, Bandura, Becker, and Jessor claimed, knowledge and attitude are buried in interplay between a variety of powerful forces that are internal and external to the individual. The notations within the parentheses in the narrative demonstrate that this interplay occurs at many levels. Right or wrong, friends, family members, and admired role models, by word and deed, are supportive of self-medication and recreational drug use to cope with self-doubt, stresses, and pressures of an active life.

At the narrative's end, Bobby is not in any immediate danger attributable to his drug use. Furthermore, Bobby has some strong protective factors such as parental support, protection, and supervision, school and church attachments, involvement in a variety of activities, commitment to positive future-oriented ambitions and aspirations, and adherence to many prosocial values. Therefore, if Bobby were real, the odds of his emerging unscathed from this episode seem very good, although there are no guarantees.

Realization by prevention experts that most children who experiment with drugs do not fit any stereotype as social misfits, and delinquents, and that students such as Bobby are not unusual has produced a major reorientation in substance abuse prevention. This reorientation, as described in the following section, has stimulated new optimism and created new problems.

## WHAT NEW AND USEFUL THEORIES ARE AVAILABLE TO TEACHERS?

Disaffection with traditional substance abuse prevention, the shift to a more pragmatic approach to deterrence, and the complexity of drug use have produced an important change. This change in strategy for substance abuse prevention emphasizes the drug user rather than the troublesome attributes of drugs, as was the focus of the past. The attributes that make drugs tempting but dangerous now are in the background rather than the foreground of substance abuse prevention.

Consequently, newer strategies focus on people and their social environment, and seek to intervene into aspects of each that play a role in reducing or promoting drug use. These strategies apply theory and research from public health, social psychology, and observation of smoking prevention programs.

The public health concepts around which modern substance abuse prevention strategies revolve are health promotion and wellness; and risk, protective, and resistance factors. Realizing that much illness and mortality are products of social influences and behavior, public health advocacy began to move beyond disease prevention (Butler, 1994; Gerbner, 1990). Because preventing disease by attacking the agents that cause it is but one limited possibility, health advocates now promote more expansive, aggressive, and proactive strategies.

Health care workers now attack agents of disease, but also seek to reduce personal risk factors that make people susceptible to illness, and strengthen attributes that provide protection. Thus, the strategy is to help people avoid agents of disease, increase their resistance to disease, and mobilize resources that protect them from harm.

For example, if the three little pigs had decided to live where wolves would not go, had taken karate lessons, and all built their houses of brick, the big bad wolf would have been less of a danger. But, not entirely! If on a sunny afternoon, a deviant wolf with a black belt in martial arts passed by as a little pig snoozed in his yard, chances are the pig would have been lunch for the wolf. Thus, avoidance, preparedness, active self-protection, and vigilance help to preserve and strengthen wellness even though they do not guarantee it.

Consequently, the world of disease prevention, health promotion, and wellness is one of odds rather than absolutes, and probabilities rather than certainties. In this world, one must acknowledge that life is a crapshoot, but by identifying and controlling forces that are acting on the dice, we can improve our chances.

In simple terms, the public health message is to stay away from noxious environments; to eat, sleep, and exercise well; to manage stress effectively; to avoid dangerous objects, substances and materials; and to keep one's immune system in good tune. The substance abuse prevention mission is to promote abstinence, and failing that, postpone use, reduce dosages, frequencies of use, and the potency of drugs of choice. Accordingly, teachers may contribute to this mission by creating drug-free environments, helping students recognize and resist pressures to use drugs, and providing opportunities for successful participation in social relations and activities that have protective value.

## WHAT PROBLEMS DOES THE NEW FOCUS PRESENT TO TEACHERS?

Although the shift in focus from drugs to the drug user is promising, it has created new problems. For example, abstinence is now an even more strident message of substance abuse prevention and reflects a redoubling of America's long-standing emphasis on primary prevention (preventing exposure). Despite the continuing ebb and flow of drug use by millions of people, secondary prevention (illness prevention and responsible use) is increasingly the neglected stepchild of substance abuse prevention.

Primary prevention is the prohibitionist agenda of U.S. drug policy, and prohibitionists are willing to sacrifice drug users to preserve that agenda. They argue that secondary prevention transmits the wrong message to young people. Accordingly, they resist needle exchange programs, the placement of methadone treatment facilities in their communities, and press for even more draconian drug laws.

Also, some problems emanate from a troublesome group of theories about the causes of drug use. These theories, in one way or another, claim that drug use is a symptom of personal deficiency that makes drugs attractive or impairs resistance to them. Deficiency theories propose that drug users suffer from preexisting disorders, inadequacies, or deficits that make them vulnerable to drug use. They claim that these deficiencies exist within them, their families, or their communities prior to any exposure to drugs. According to deficiency theories, drug use is an attempt to treat these problems through self-medication.

Such proposals would be easily disregarded if they were not so seductive and dangerous. They are seductive because the consequences of substance abuse are easily confused with the causes (Fishbein & Pease, 1996). Also, difficult living conditions imposed by poverty and other life circumstance are easily confused with conditions produced by self-destructive behavior such as addiction. And finally, a middle-class perspective may lead many observers to conclude that difficult living conditions are profoundly and invariably destructive to all who are subject to them, and are a cause of addiction.

Deficiency theories are dangerous because they are untrue and potentially misleading to substance abuse prevention, especially primary prevention. Although personal deficiencies probably play some part in drug use, this part is small relative to the larger picture. Many people who suffer from personal and social inadequacies and live under difficult circumstances do not abuse drugs. Conversely, most casual or recreational drug users are reasonably intact and functional people, and most of the small minority who develop drug problems were fairly healthy and robust when they began using drugs.

In simple terms, too large a portion of the general population has used or use drugs to consider all users to suffer from severe personal, social, or environmental problems. And, too many drug users emerge unscathed from their drug experiences to suspect that they ever had unusual problems.

Consequently, experimentation with drugs and casual drug use are not meaningfully related to preexisting capacities for self-care, social responsibility, and life enjoyment. Thus, for the vast majority of casual or recreational users of legal drugs, the cold beer on a hot day, the glass of wine with dinner, and the cigarette and coffee before work are the representative models of use. For casual or recreational users of illegal drugs, occasional use of marijuana, cocaine, or other substances in search of transcendent experience, to have fun with friends, or to reduce tension are parallel models.

To some extent, deficiency theories are a remnant of the alcohol prohibition era, in which readiness to "blame the victims" of substance abuse, and to "save them from themselves" were prominent explanations of drug use and its prevention. Reformers preached that drug use is a sign of flawed character, moral depravity, and a lack of personal strength and willpower.

This readiness to believe that something is fundamentally wrong with drug users contributed to misrepresentation and distortion of later, more scientific ideas. Many scientific ideas reflect a bias toward deficiency theory because much of the thinking about drug use emanated from the addiction treatment community. Mental health professionals involved with recovery and rehabilitation saw only the casualties and the aftermath of substance abuse.

These casualties were damaged and deficient, obviously, and they generated claims that preexisting psychological damage causes addiction. However, addiction can cause damage seen in treatment, and damage can exist separately as neither a cause nor consequence of addiction. The best evidence indicates that addiction can be extremely damaging to addicted people, but damaged people are not much more likely to become addicts than are other people. Those with preexisting mental health conditions are overrepresented, but they comprise a small minority of the population of addicts. Consequently, we are not able to use mental health indicators to predict, with any confidence, who will or will not become an addict.

Many people use drugs in ways that do not cause harm, but some integrate drug use into their life in ways that are dangerous. Therefore, a reasonable counterproposal to deficiency theory is that all people are vulnerable and no one is immune to addiction. Some people may be more or less vulnerable, but many risk and protective factors have nothing to do with traits or qualities representing personal deficiency. Rather, people get into trouble when the dosages, frequency of use, and the reinforcing properties of their drugs of choice are excessive to the point of producing compulsive use.

These excesses are worsened by compulsion, and then precipitate progressively worsening social, health, economic, and emotional crises for the user. Eventually, these crises become extreme and the user can no longer recover the losses attributable to them. Although troubled people have a greater likelihood of developing dangerous patterns of drug use, many such individuals do not. Conversely, many seemingly robust individuals do develop dangerous patterns and fall victim to addiction.

Despite these observations, the hypothesis that preexisting damage and deficiency cause addiction remains a tempting explanation, especially for zealots. The medical profession's disease model and later findings of genetic links to alcoholism are easily reinterpreted to support this position.

Concepts such as the *addictive personality* and *social deviance model* also give plausibility to such interpretations. The former describes drug users as having personality traits that liken them to accidents looking for a time and a place to happen. The latter proposes that people retreat into drug use because they cannot adequately adjust to the social demands of community life. Despite a long history of extensive examination, little, if any, supportive evidence exists for either concept (Fishbein & Pease, 1996; Lindesmith, 1947; Vaillant, 1983; Winick, 1986).

Consequently, just as the alcohol prohibition movement subverted Rush's advocacy of temperance and moderation (see chapter 4), those committed to drug prohibition continue to claim that drug use is a symptom of preexisting disease. With a little polish, they argue that drug use is an attempt to self-medicate against a wide range of personal and social inadequacies. Those who argue this position join the rhetoric of moralism with the rhetoric of science and medicine.

These troublesome notions continue to hamper substance abuse prevention efforts. Although mental and social health problems do contribute to some individuals' use of drugs, prevention efforts based on correcting personal deficiency have been ineffective. Also, such theories may be disruptive to community life because they contribute to stereotyping and bias about the poor, and members of racial, ethnic, and cultural minorities.

Deficiency theories are particularly problematic for the special education student. These students and their families often are stigmatized in subtle and not so subtle ways. First, stigma is associated with special education placement, and placement diminishes a child's social status. Second, schools make a disproportionate number of special education placements for members of ethnic and racial minorities. This aggravates sensitivities about stereotyping and bias.

Therefore, applying deficiency theories to special education students is particularly problematic because the schools have publicly labeled such students to be deficient. Teachers committed to substance abuse prevention for special education students must avoid stimulating further risk attributable to labeling and discrimination.

## WHAT ARE REALISTIC GOALS FOR SUBSTANCE ABUSE PREVENTION?

The preceding material and previous chapters describe a complex and ambiguous arena into which teachers step when they incorporate substance abuse prevention into classroom teaching. In all instances, teachers who choose to do this work find themselves to be but one player amid a dizzying array of pro-drug and antidrug-use influences. When confronting these influences, teachers face the challenge of becoming a central figure in children's lives rather than remaining on the periphery, as teachers often do.

Children who are reared in our culture observe, are targets, and are immersed in a seemingly unending struggle between economics and morality. Furthermore, social policies that staunchly and ardently demand drug abstinence and prohibition as the true resolution to this struggle create an illusion for young children. This illusion is that morality is the winner.

However, this illusion dissipates and the money-versus-morals dilemma becomes increasingly perplexing as children mature. With the onrush of adolescence, young people begin to recognize inconsistencies in drug policies, and are disillusioned by the hypocrisy, deceit, opportunism, and duplicity of figures prominently associated with these policies. They observe loved ones, friends, and other role models exhibiting drug-using behavior that seems far more truthful about the realities of drug use than do messages from those who are agents of drug policies. The moralism that underlies these messages becomes increasingly untenable as the rich and famous, politicians, educators, clergy, police, entertainers, artists, writers, musicians, athletes, and other prominent figures are rocked by scandal about sex, drugs, graft, and corruption.

The media not only sensationalizes these disappointing events, but directly and indirectly glamorizes the behavior that leads to such falls from grace. Advertising campaigns for alcohol, patent medicines, and tobacco often target youth. Television, film, the recording industry, and publishing seek ratings and profits, by favorably presenting drinking, smoking, and drug using in dramatic portrayals, novels, and song lyrics (Greenberg, 1984; Greenberg, Fernandez-Colado, Graef, Korzenny, & Atkin, 1984).

Furthermore, popular culture makes its own statements about drug use as each succeeding generation attempts to separate from the generation of its parents. Young people conform to new expectations in order to be included among peers in the dream of a freer, brighter future. Not infrequently, drug use is woven into the fabric of trends and fads through which popular culture bestows acceptance and status on its young members.

In facing all these challenges, teachers may find themselves in a delicate position of balancing social values such as honesty and democracy against personal needs such as professional survival and credibility. Therefore, teachers should have a clear understanding of the possibilities and limits of such work before they accept the opportunities, responsibilities, and dangers inherent to this simultaneously rewarding and frustrating endeavor. The narrative that follows identifies and defines these limits and possibilities and their meaning relative to drug policy and broader social issues.

## HOW SHOULD TEACHERS PURSUE GOALS OF ABSTINENCE AND POSTPONEMENT OF DRUG USE?

Abstinence from illicit drug use and postponement of experimentation with alcohol and tobacco until legal age are the prevention goals of the schools. Although these goals are attractive at first glance, their moralistic underpinnings present serious problems to those who are realistic about children, U.S. culture, and teaching.

In part, these problems plague teachers because of the narrow and severely limiting definition of illicit drug use that is an outgrowth of drug control. Furthermore, *illicit drug use* and *substance abuse* have become interchangeable terms. To use any illegal drug, any legal drug that one obtains illegally, or to use any legally obtained drug in ways that are contrary to its prescribed purpose is the current definition of illicit drug use. Therefore, all illicit use is substance abuse. According to drug control advocates, this is so regardless of the harmlessness of the drug, the limitations of use imposed by the user, the circumstances under which the user takes an illicit drug, or the purposes of use.

This definition places goals such as responsible drug use and harm reduction out of reach for teachers. *Harm reduction*, which is assisting recovery and rehabilitation from problems attributable to substance abuse, is not realistically within teachers' professional domain.

Furthermore, a teacher cannot suggest safe or responsible ways to try drugs for those children he or she knows are determined to experiment. In the current social and political environment, teachers who do so risk attack by angry parents, anxious colleagues, and reactive administrators, and risk losing their jobs. Therefore, teachers inevitably must confront the problem of how to address drug use in realistic terms in an atmosphere circumscribed by both realistic and unrealistic proscriptions.

This obstacle is surmountable if one views substance abuse prevention from the broader perspectives of the place of education in human development, and U.S. cultural reality. From these perspectives, people grow up, finish or leave school, and emerge from family and school as autonomous, independent members of a drug-using society. Most people exploit, from time to time, the benefits of various drugs, licitly and illicitly. And, as discussed repeatedly in this book, most emerge unharmed from their experiences. In basic terms, the mission of all teachers is to prepare children to cope effectively and constructively with drugs in their challenging transition into adulthood.

## HOW DO PEOPLE INTEGRATE DRUGS INTO THEIR LIVES?

Clearly, excessive or compulsive drug use is not a problem that emerges suddenly and as a surprise, although some people have trouble immediately. Rather, it usually is the product of a process through which people integrate drug use into their lives (Fields, 1995). Almost all members of U.S. society begin this process during adolescence when drug availability forces young people to make decisions and choices about drugs.

This is an important developmental task (Jessor, 1992), the completion of which has serious meaning and consequences throughout life. The question each of us must ask and answer, eventually, is how we will fit alcohol, tobacco, and other drugs into the routines and patterns that define our lifestyles.

Some people complete the resolution of these issues in a purposeful and deliberate manner. Others do so with limited awareness of the acts of omission or commission that eventually produce an identifiable pattern of drug use. And, some never come to terms with these issues. However, even the most stable patterns of drug use can be altered by stress and troubling life events.

In many cases, individuals take drugs without even realizing they are doing so. Often, this happens because foods, beverages, and over-the-counter medicines contain drugs about which the consumer is unaware. Coffee, tea, soft drinks, chocolate, cheeses, cold products, cough suppressants, and mouthwashes are a few examples.

Nevertheless, each individual establishes a pattern of drug use that fits within the surrounding culture, and is usual and customary for him or her (Avis, 1990). This pattern is defined by the dosages, frequencies, duration of episodes of use, rates at which episodes occur, potency of drugs of choice, circumstances, and purposes for use.

Patterns usually fit into four broad categories: non-use, experimental use, regular use, and heavy use (Polich, Ellickson, Peuter, & Kahan, 1984). However, each of these broad categories contains subcategories that may be of value to teachers in establishing substance abuse prevention goals. Accordingly, teachers can place drug use on a continuum as follows:

1. Abstinence: never or rare use.
2. Occasional and irregular: very infrequent use and as random singular episodes, dosages light relative to potency of the drug of choice, drug effects only important to user to the degree that the episode is for purposes of experimentation. Control is strong and not an issue.
3. Irregular but periodic: repeated use for brief periods interspersed with periods of nonuse, dosages light relative to the drug of choice, some interest in experiencing drug effects. Control is an occasional thought but not yet a concern.
4. Regular: steady rate of use for extended period of time, dosages light relative to the potency of the drug of choice, moderate interest in drug effects. Control is an emerging but relatively minor concern.
5. Regular and moderate: same as regular but with heavier dosages, drug effects important as is control.
6. Regular and heavy: same as regular but dosages bordering on excessive, drug effects important and concern about control eroding.
7. Excessive use: frequencies, dosages, and durations of episodes sufficient to produce tolerance, and, eventually, compulsive use. Drug effects very important and control receding to status as an irritating but minor afterthought.
8. Compulsive use: user cannot stop despite progressively worsening costs and consequences. Control reemerging as an important concern, but seems out of reach and impossible to regain.

As can be observed, each pattern of use represents increases in dosages, frequencies, duration of episodes, and rates at which episodes occur. However, the continuum should not be viewed as sequential or as a hierarchy. That is, each pattern is not necessarily dependent on the adoption or completion of preceding patterns for its establishment.

Nevertheless, in realistic terms, Patterns 1 through 5 seem to be reasonable goals toward which teachers may aim educational efforts. These are patterns of temperance that most people establish with or without drug education in school. However, for better or worse, abstinence is the preeminent goal, the simplest to pursue, and the easiest to which to apply public health strategy.

Public health thinking advocates that all organs of society present a united front so that mixed messages and equivocal policies of temperance may be avoided. Temperance, by its very nature, is equivocal.

## WHAT ARE TEACHERS TRYING TO PREVENT?

Clearly, the problems associated with substance abuse manifest themselves most often in Patterns 6 through 8, even though some individuals suffer terrible consequences, illness, and death in connection with initial or early exposures to some dangerous drugs. Overdoses, mental illness, accidents, violence, and communicable diseases are among these dramatic negative outcomes.

Therefore, reducing the incidence of higher risk patterns of use, and cavalier or nihilistic behavior when taking drugs should be the targets of prevention. Success here can lower the odds of disaster, even though the possibility of tragic consequences may never be totally eliminated.

However, definition of the phrase *tragic consequences* is central to prevention and represents the final point of appraisal for prevention efforts. Although there are other dramatic negative outcomes, the major tragic consequence against which prevention efforts are aimed has always been and continues to be addiction.

In the past, experts defined addiction in the purely physiological terms of *drug effects*. An addict was a person who had used an addictive drug enough to incur metabolic changes, develop a tolerance for the drug, and experience withdrawal symptoms on cessation of use. Modern definitions of addiction go well beyond the narrow confines of this early thinking.

Now, addicts are identified in accordance with psychological, medical, behavioral, and social criteria, too. From a *psychological* perspective, addicts are individuals who can be described as follows:

1. Their drugging or drinking behavior displays obsessive–compulsive qualities.
2. They are unable to stop drinking or taking drugs despite repeated attempts and great effort.
3. They continue to drink or take drugs despite accumulating and progressively worsening consequences.

From a *social* perspective, addicts are individuals who can be described as follows:

1. Their drug use and drinking behavior have caused legal, financial, occupational, and family problems.

**2.** Their peers, friends, business associates, health care providers, and family members have labeled them as addicts.

From a *behavioral* perspective, addicts are people with the following characteristics:

**1.** Their lives and waking hours are dominated by activities necessary to obtaining and using drugs.
**2.** They have lost interest in social networks of which they were a part prior to becoming addicted.
**3.** They have abandoned activities and interests in which they participated prior to addiction.

From a *medical* perspective, addicts are individuals who demonstrate the following:

**1.** They display physical signs and symptoms of illness attributable to taking and using drugs.

These are the tragic consequences for drug users who fall victim to addiction. However, these do not represent the costs to other, nonaddicted or nondrug-using individuals who may suffer from addicts' behavior. These include the following:

**1.** People who are injured or killed as innocent victims of accidents, violence, and assault.
**2.** People who become infected with sexually transmitted diseases as a result of sexual contact with addicts, or addicts' contributions to the spread of such disease.
**3.** Children and spouses who are abused or neglected in families that are disrupted by addiction.
**4.** Community members who pay the financial costs of health care and legal systems burdened by addicts.
**5.** Community members who have become impoverished and homeless in economically deteriorating neighborhoods.
**6.** Other victims of addicts' self-neglect and risk-taking behavior.

## SUMMARY OF KEY POINTS

Disappointments about the effectiveness of information dissemination as an independent strategy have produced a search for new theories and methods for substance abuse prevention. The search for ideas has been burdened with intrusions into the processes of drug education and substance abuse prevention by the demands of drug control.

This encumbrance presents teachers with many problems related to credibility, academic freedom, and job security. These problems just serve to complicate the difficulties teachers face when attempting to integrate behavioral theory into traditional teaching–learning processes related to substance abuse prevention.

Nevertheless, disaffection with traditional approaches produced a shift in focus away from drugs *per se* to the drug user. This shift opened new opportunities, but at the same time, has been plagued by drug control biases. These biases continue to influence prevention theory and practice. Principle among these biases is the acceptance of deficiency theories to explain drug use. These unsupportable theories claim that people use drugs to self-medicate against deficits in personality and social adjustment.

Teachers should avoid approaches predicated on the notion of personal deficiency and pursue prevention goals that are more consistent with the realities of drug use. Although abstinence and postponement of drug use are valid goals of primary prevention, teachers will recognize that all people integrate some drugs into their lives in various ways as part of adolescent development.

These patterns can range from a glass of wine with dinner or a cold beer on a hot day, a cigarette and coffee before work, to the regular use of over-the-counter and prescription medications, or even the purchase and use of illicit drugs such as marijuana, heroin, and cocaine. Problems of illegality are certainly complicating factors, but all citizens must come to terms with the opportunities and problems associated with drug availability.

Because both legal and illegal drugs serve needs, all users face the risk of developing risky patterns of use. The level of risk associated with any pattern of use is the defining characteristic through which one may distinguish between drug use, drug misuse, and substance abuse. In the last analysis, the challenge of substance abuse prevention is to help students avoid patterns that will later lead to compulsive use and its severe physiological, behavioral, psychological, social, and health consequences.

# Social Influences and Drug Use

The goals of this chapter are to help teachers accomplish the following:

1. Understand social influences on drug use.
2. Grasp the importance of the family as a risk factor for drug use among children.
3. Recognize various self-evaluative dimensions that are risk and protective factors in drug use.
4. Strengthen children's resiliency and optimism as protective factors in substance abuse prevention.
5. Recognize the interplay between adolescent development and drug availability in personal decisions about drug use.
6. Understand that all people are vulnerable to the dangers of substance abuse, not just those with emotional or adjustment problems.
7. Use strategies in the classroom that reduce risk and strengthen resistance to drug use pressures.

Researchers generally agree now that substance abuse is a social disease, and that social relationships are major sources of risk and protection (Ellickson, 1995). This potential to generate risk or protection is inherent to family life, and the friendships and cliques of the peer group.

Researchers have also identified factors that promote or inhibit the spread of drug abuse in the community. They generally agree that interpersonal communication and the community's transmission of its norms and standards effects the spread of drug use and abuse.

Close friends and members of cliques communicate directly with one another. However, people who may not know each other communicate, too, although in more subtle ways (Steinberg, 1996). These cohorts or crowds develop norms and standards that members share and internalize into their sense of self. Their common identity becomes visible to them as they co-participate in fads, trends, and social movements. The messages in their norms and standards can exacerbate or inhibit the spread of drug use and abuse.

Although these socially mediated risk and protective factors increase or decrease the likelihood of drug use, they guarantee nothing in either direction. Goode (1993) captured this uncertainty in his statement that "Almost everything in the world of drug use is a matter of odds," and "a matter of degree" (p. 13). Goode's observation pertains to both the precursors and the consequences of drug use.

## WHAT ARE INDIRECT AND DIRECT SOCIAL INFLUENCES ON DRUG USE?

Social influence (Bandura, 1977), resistance to social influence (McGuire, 1964), and coping, adaptation, and social deviance (Jessor, 1992) are relevant to drug use. Research into the relation between drug use and measures of these concepts consistently indicates that social pressure is an important risk factor. Conversely, resistance to social pressure has protective value.

This is especially true for teenagers because peer pressure is most powerful during adolescence. They are insecure about their identity and judgment and are therefore more subject to the influence of others (Steinberg, 1996).

Also, adolescents are at the stage of life where the availability of drugs first becomes an issue for them. This confronts teenagers with the problem of whether and how to integrate alcohol, tobacco, and other drugs into their emerging adulthood. Therefore, risk is intimately connected with important challenges of adolescent development.

Furthermore, aversive life circumstances frustrate normal developmental needs. These frustrations exert indirect pressures to use drugs, which are amplified as adults and peers offer social incentives, and advocate or model drug use.

Children feel indirect social pressure when parents force them to independently satisfy needs that adults should manage. For example, some parents do not adequately support their child's participation in growth-promoting activities. Parents may withhold resources and assistance, or fail to teach their children how to behave in various community settings. These children must define the limits and boundaries of acceptable behavior for themselves, although they are poorly equipped to do so. This is particularly important to activities in well-supervised, drug-free environments, such as school, church, recreation centers, and other community facilities.

Consequently, neglected children miss opportunities for growth because of ignorance, poor social skills, immature judgment, and bad choices. These children may not recognize available options, or they may be too fearful to independently seek access to them. Sometimes adults in charge deny them access to activities because these children behave inappropriately or are disruptive.

Furthermore, some parents provide inadequate protection and leave children to fend for themselves in perilous circumstances. These parents may too often expose children to risks of injury, tension, and stress. Common examples are parents who repeatedly allow children to use dangerous household appliances with lax adult oversight, or fail to intervene when their children are victimized by neighborhood bullies or predatory classmates.

Conversely, very protective or strict parents may impose rigid rules or endless demands on children. Overly stringent curfews, too much time caring for younger siblings, or ceaseless household chores can obstruct important activity. No doubt, parental acts of omission and commission make the family a source of indirect social pressure and a risk factor in drug use. As the preceding examples reveal, these acts can deprive children of opportunities that are necessary to growth and development, and expose them to inordinate and unnecessary dangers. Clearly, drug use and abuse is a family problem (Fields, 1995; Heinicke & Vollmer, 1995).

Disrupted family circumstances can lead to poor adult care of children at home, but this can also happen in the school and the community (Hawkins, Lishnen, Jenson, & Catalano, 1987; Kumpfer, 1987). Children can exacerbate problems that begin in the family through their own self-defeating behavior, outside. When clumsy or provocative pleas for help fall on the seemingly deaf ears of teachers and other adults outside the family, the child in trouble is truly alone. This is the core of risk for substance abuse.

Children with immature skills, in difficult circumstances, who are too alone in the struggle to achieve healthy maturity are at greater risk of developing dangerous patterns of drug use. This core of risk grows malignantly as children's difficult circumstances expose them to major negative life events and worsen levels of daily irritation. These, in turn, elevate stress and lead these children to spend more time with drug-using peers (Kumpfer, 1987).

Risk is further increased when children cannot find any responsible adults from whom to obtain assistance. Parents and other adults who might serve as parental surrogates may not be available or have taught children not to bother them. In the latter case, some adults respond in ways that are too chaotic and disorganized to be effective. Other adults are reactive, intolerant and punitive, or so rigid and unyielding as to convey indifference to their children (Weinstein, 1995b).

And finally, poor coping skills complete this tragic portrait. The core of risk becomes particularly noxious when children begin to act out ineffectually against the adversity of their circumstances. Destructive expression of anger, acquiescence, and helplessness, and withdrawal into fantasy add to the pain and to the risk of drug use (Wills, 1991).

## HOW DO SOCIAL INFLUENCES MAKE
## SELF-ESTEEM A FACTOR IN DRUG USE?

Neglect and frustration are corrosive to self-esteem. Theorists propose that people derive self-esteem from two sources. The initial and primary source is an parent' love during infancy and early childhood (Kohut, 1977). The other source is an individual's successful use of his or her own abilities to achieve valued goals (Digorry, 1966). In the circumstances described previously, parental love is suspect and a child's failure to achieve goals, especially in school, is too common.

Most observers define *self-esteem* as self-liking or self-acceptance. However, if self-liking is tied to abilities, social status, and other personal attributes necessary to goal achievement (Digorry, 1966), then social skills enter the self-evaluative process, too. Social skills influence self-esteem to the degree that they help children obtain social acknowledgments for personal success. Thus, a varsity athlete's touchdown or home run is gratifying, but the cheers in the stands also are important.

These skills are relevant to drug use. They enable a child to gain acceptance and affection from significant individuals and groups, and they permit the child to exercise some control over the obligations and rewards of these social relationships. Also, they enable a child to be flexible and assertive in coping with challenges and adversity that sometimes emerge as a by-product of such relationships.

These abilities each play a part in self-evaluation (Weinstein, 1995b), and protect against drug use. Conversely, their lack is an indicator of susceptibility (Hawkins et al., 1987; Kumpfer, 1987). Such skills are particularly relevant to teachers because success in each is the product of learning that students can achieve in the classroom.

## HOW DO ADULTS CONTRIBUTE
## TO A CHILD'S EXPERIENCE OF FAILURE?

Clearly, inadequate adult care, poor social acceptance, little fun, and abundant self-doubt are socially mediated frustrations. And, they generate indirect pressures that promote dangerous drug use. For children and adults, frustrating, unpredictable, and stressful life circumstances create much disappointment, trauma, and unhappiness.

As a result, a child's search for love, self-acceptance, control, and freedom can lead to dead ends, blind alleys, and slippery slopes. No doubt, if life circumstances are miserable enough, one may resort to extreme measures to find relief from disappointment and to find inner peace.

Because most children are not deaf, blind, or stupid, many attribute their difficult life circumstances to the actions of adults. Consequently, when children's protests do not secure a positive response from grown-ups, despair and withdrawal will follow. Some of these despairing children withdraw from adults by assuming a posture of pseudo or pretend self-sufficiency, and by becoming overly dependent on the peer group for support and protection. This places them at greatest risk of drug use and abuse.

The disappointment and trauma described in the preceding paragraphs are important to teachers for many reasons. First, negative histories with parents can exaggerate children's sensitivity and reactivity to other grown-ups. For these children, defensive attitudes and hypervigilance distort immediate experience in the classroom. Interested teachers often find themselves handling such children with "kid gloves" and "walking on eggs" when relating to them. This work can be draining and thankless as these children react against what they need and want most: a caring and available adult!

Clearly, a child may protest and then withdraw in many ways, including drug use. However, the likelihood that a child will choose to use drugs increases when direct pressures to do so are exerted by peers, siblings, parents, and admired role models. Friends, family members, and others do this when they advocate drug use, use drugs themselves, or approve of doing so.

This is particularly true in environments that are rife with drug-using role models, offer easy access to drugs, and have social norms that support drug use. Such environments make drugs an attractive option and lower barriers to use.

## HOW CAN TEACHERS BE A PROTECTIVE
## SOCIAL INFLUENCE?

The circumstances described in the previous section are implicated in a range of self-destructive behavior, including dangerous drug use. However, they do not guarantee disaster. Many children emerge reasonably intact and do thrive despite horrendous living conditions. Yet, some people emerge in terrible straits from seemingly ideal situations.

Children who thrive in the face of adversity share at least one common attribute: All are able to form attachments with positive adults outside of the immediate family. Teachers and other adults in the schools often become surrogate parents and perform marvelous rescues without even realizing it (Weinstein, 1995a). Other protective factors appear to help some of these children, too. An important factor is resiliency—the ability to bounce back from traumatic events and frustrating experiences (Anthony, 1987; Garmezy & Masten, 1986; Kobasa, Maddi, & Kahn, 1982). According to Wills (1991) and Savage-Supernaw (1991), resiliency itself is strengthened by a number of tools for adaptation and coping. Fortunately, teachers can teach these tools to children.

One such tool, *spirituality*, is not limited to religious participation, and therefore, has a place in the schools. It extends to children's personal interests in the meaning and purpose of life, the place of humanity in the grand scheme of existence, and an interest in the metaphysical.

Another tool for resiliency is *positiveness and optimism*. This refers to a child's readiness to interpret adversity as challenge rather than threat, and to see painful experiences as transient setbacks rather than chronic conditions. Implicit to positiveness and optimism is an expectation that one will overcome adversity, and gain strength from the experience.

A third tool is *flexibility*, which is the capacity to change strategies and tactics in response to outcomes of efforts and actions. The ability to retain that which serves one's purposes, relinquish that which impedes them, and experiment with new approaches supports resiliency.

The fourth tool for resiliency is *direct problem-solving action*. One's own intervention into troublesome conditions negates inclinations to be acquiescent, passive, and fatalistic. Actively making things right rather than hoping or surrendering strengthens adaptation, and, thus, resiliency.

And, finally, *physical activity* is almost synonymous with participation and is important to resilience. Sports, games, and action heighten mood, physiological immunity, and endurance. Adversity frequently tests just these capacities in the struggle to adapt.

## WHAT THEORY OF DRUG USE IS APPROPRIATE TO TEACHERS?

Teachers are not psychotherapists, pharmacologists, or police officers. Furthermore, the theories and knowledge base that guides substance abuse prevention practice in these fields are remote to teachers. Clearly, teachers are lay persons in regard to mental health issues, drug effects and chemistry, and law enforcement. Therefore, teachers must have a frame of reference for teaching if they are to understand their role as agents of substance abuse prevention.

Because teachers know about teaching, any theory that will be of use to them must be appropriate to what teachers know and do. The *functional theory of drug use* that follows satisfies this requirement. This theory argues that people use drugs because drugs are available, serve functions or purposes for users, and that the decision to use drugs is the product of a socially mediated process. This theory acknowledges that all people are vulnerable to the dangers of drug use and no one is immune to these dangers; some people have tragic experiences with drugs and alcohol, but many more others, leading reasonably normal lives, use drugs and suffer few, if any, negative consequences (Avis, 1990); and most health, legal, and other problems associated with drug use are consequences rather than causes of drug use.

The following tenets outline the functional theory of drug use:

1. Drugs are available and the United States is a drug-using society. Therefore, resolving personal issues about using drugs is an important developmental task of adolescence in U.S. culture. Drug experimentation and use are normal to this developmental stage rather than a sign of mental illness or social deviance.

2. Of the population of casual drug users and addicts, few began using drugs to solve mental health problems, or to compensate for personal deficits. Therefore, primary prevention by teachers is not mental health treatment, even though some children may derive mental health value from it.

3. Life circumstances and social pressures raise and lower likelihood of drug use, and these are external to the user. They do not guarantee immunity or dangerous exposure to drugs, but teachers can increase resistance by helping children adapt to and cope with difficult circumstances and social pressures. Teachers do this by teaching skills and providing social support.

4. People use drugs because of the function or purposes these substances serve for them. In general terms, people use drugs to have transcendent emotional experiences, to have fun with friends, to achieve tension release, and to obtain social rewards that are at times associated with using drugs.

5. Drugs satisfy needs that are neither bizarre nor unusual, and other safer and more socially endorsed behaviors can satisfy these needs, too. However, some socially endorsed alternatives are just as dangerous as some drugs, if not more so. Teachers can promote positive, drug-free alternatives and equip children to pursue them.

6. Drugs serve the needs of the user needs in two ways: Through the drugs' pharmacological effects and through the social meanings that individuals, families, other primary groups, and communities have linked to usage. Teachers can explore these meanings in the curriculum.

7. For teachers, a realistic goal for substance abuse prevention and drug education is postponement of experimentation by children. Postponement should be aimed toward a time when greater maturity provides better judgment about drug use, and acquired skills provide alternative means that may serve the needs served by drugs.

8. A second goal for teachers is the teaching and learning of skills, insights, and alternatives so that children, as they mature, do not integrate drugs into their lives in potentially dangerous patterns of use.

In simple terms, the theoretical proposal offered here is that all people reach a point in life (usually during adolescence) at which they must come to terms with the availability and meaning of drugs, and that people use drugs because drugs feel good. In most cases, drugs are positively reinforcing because they enable people who feel fine to feel even better. In a minority of cases, drugs are reinforcing because they provide relief to people who feel bad.

Among the many possible soothing, good feelings drugs induce are tension reduction, social acceptance and status, pleasure, altered perceptions of self and environment, stimulus control, various imagined or placebo effects, and enhanced engagement with spiritual beliefs (Avis, 1990; Levin, 1987). It should be noted that these functions address needs that are neither bizarre nor uncommon.

People find drugs attractive because they work and they work quickly (Ray, 1972). Furthermore, users can be passive after taking a drug because drugs generate desired effects without effort by the user (Fields, 1995). Those drugs that are most dangerous work most quickly, have the most powerful effects, and require the most frequent readministration to sustain their effects.

Clearly, many people willingly accept risks associated with drug use, even when informed about the dangers (Blachly, 1970). This is important because Americans value and reward risk-taking. Thus, drug effects and social reactions offer rewards that are powerfully reinforcing to drug use.

Teachers should not infer from the preceding theory that an individual's integration of drug use into his or her life is a simple process. Individual decisions and actions that produce patterns of drug use emerge out of a complex interaction between social forces, biological traits, and psychological characteristics. The principle actors who exert social influences are the family, the peer group, and the culture of the community.

Teachers also should recognize that alternate paths exist for children's use in meeting needs served by drugs and alcohol. However, teachers must be aware that some of these alternative paths (e.g., overeating, bad relationships, gambling) are potentially destructive, too (Blachly, 1970). Still others are healthier, but may require long delays in gratification and much effort (e.g., pursuit of career, psychotherapy, acquisition of expensive items, good relationships).

Nevertheless, drug availability creates additional choices about how to satisfy needs. Availability also forces people to confront pro- and anti-use pressures while they make choices about whether and which drugs to use. Consequently, decisions about drug use become personal and social issues for all to whom drugs are available.

Fortunately, the resolution of these issues is a window of opportunity for teachers. Although postponement seems to be all that is possible for some individuals regarding some drugs, resolution toward abstinence from illicit drug use is socially endorsed at the time of this writing. For better or worse, this is consistent with the wishes of parents and others who support substance abuse prevention efforts.

## HOW CAN TEACHERS TRANSLATE
## THEORY INTO STRATEGIES FOR ACTION?

The functional theory of drug use offers a variety of strategies to relieve internal pressures to use drugs. Certainly, frustration can generate many such pressures in children. Therefore, teachers should help children develop social and personal skills to better meet their own needs, and to bolster self-esteem. Also, this theory suggests strategies aimed at heightening alertness to external pressures to use drugs, and helping children resist these pressures (Ellickson, 1995).

Therefore, school-based substance abuse prevention can be based on understandings of social influences on drug use as follows:

1. Teachers can teach social and personal skills to help children reduce susceptibility to drug use. Frustrated personal and social needs, and low self-esteem that comes of disappointment and failure increase susceptibility.

2. Teachers can increase resistance to drug use by alerting children to subtle and obvious social pressures exerted by friends,

family, and media. Vigilance about such pressures has protective value.

3. Teachers can reduce susceptibility to drug use by exposing children to drug-free activities and environments, and helping children avoid those where drug use is a contagious presence. Providing alternatives enhances avoidance and reduces risk.

4. Teachers can strengthen protection against drug use pressures by teaching children skills they can use to resist peer pressure. Peer pressure is a major vector in the spread of drug use, misuse, and abuse.

5. Teachers inoculate against pro-drug use messages by exposing children to these messages in advance and in a safe setting. Preemptive prior exposure protects against undue influence by such messages.

6. Teachers can strengthen protection by modeling equity, justice, and benevolence in their working relationship with children, thereby increasing bonding and attachment to school. These prosocial values and strengthened attachments have protective value.

## SUMMARY OF KEY POINTS

Observers generally agree that drug use is a product of interaction between many social influences and the personal characteristics of the user. These social influences exert both direct and indirect pressures that effect patterns of use. Social influences also effect the consequences such patterns impose on individuals, families, and communities.

Indirect pressures for children emerge from disappointments and trauma that frustrate developmental needs. Significant individuals and groups exert direct pressure to use drugs through role modeling, advocating drug use, and providing social and cultural incentives.

However, teachers can mobilize important resources to help children cope with difficult circumstances and resist negative social pressure. These resources include a workable philosophy of living, spiritual understanding, positiveness and optimism, adaptability, active problem solving, and engagement in constructive physical activity.

Teachers can help children develop and use these tools to resolve the issue of how to integrate alcohol, tobacco, and other drugs into their emerging adult lifestyles. To do so, teachers must acknowledge the purposes that these substances serve for users, that drugs are but one approach of many that may serve these same purposes, that most people are unharmed by their drug experiences, and that no one is immune to the dangers associated with drug use.

Consequently, the teacher's role is one of helping young people sort through the conflicting messages and potential choices that challenge them on route to healthy maturity. Teachers may do this by helping students develop the skills and insights they will need to cope with the social influences and pressures, and the adversities they will inevitably face as they near adulthood.

# IIII

# Drug Education and Substance Abuse Prevention in Curricular Contexts: Social Policy and Government

# 7

# Substance Abuse Prevention in the Context of Social Policy

The goal of this chapter is to describe U.S. social policy so that the following can occur:

1. Teachers can use the study of social problems, issues, and policies as a vehicle for substance abuse prevention.
2. Teachers can help their students examine issues of individual freedom as they relate to drug use.
3. Teachers understand how social problems of poverty, crime, family disruption, and health care influence their role as agents of prevention.
4. Teachers who work in communities that are disorganized, provide poor social support, and are poverty stricken will be prepared to help students examine these social problems as they relate to drug use.
5. Teachers will be knowledgeable about the broader social policy issues related to drug use and may address them in a manner that is consistent with important democratic and educational values.

Disillusionment with social policies that govern community life contributes to alienation and other risk factors in drug use. Therefore, this chapter provides a brief primer about social policy because students' disillusionment with community life often challenges teachers' substance abuse prevention efforts. Although this chapter offers suggestions for using classroom activities to address disillusionment, it is largely preparatory to later chapters.

## WHAT IS SOCIAL POLICY?

Communities work best when their members create stable and consistent expectations to guide exchanges of goods and services and participation in community activity. These expectations must be flexible and responsive to crisis and change. Also, they must reflect the purpose and meaning of community life and promote fair and benevolent relationships between community members.

Therefore, any examination of social policy must include the notion of "community" and the understanding that people create communities to meet their own economic and social needs. Community members sustain life for themselves and their families when they cooperate to produce food, shelter, clothing, health care, and protection. Because life ends quickly in the absence of these supplies, survival is the basic need out of which people live in communities.

U.S. communities meet the material requirements of survival by organizing around capitalism and the market system. In this system, community members create formal and informal arrangements for voluntary exchanges of goods and services. In free systems, markets expand and contract as a result of these voluntary exchanges. In this way, people give and receive what they and others need and want.

Political economists theorize that community members participate in these arrangements out of self-interest rather than altruistic motivations. Most people enter the market as both buyers and sellers and receive benefits that are proportionate to the value of what they give. However, the system generates an illusion of altruism because participants do well for themselves by doing well for others.

In addressing disillusionment with students, teachers may examine these ideas about the interplay between human nature and the economics of community life. A "yes" answer to the first three and a "no" to the last three of the following questions reflects disillusionment with community life. A "no" to the first three and a "yes" to the final three questions conveys optimism and enthusiasm about community life.

1. Are people just lazy, willing to accept a free ride, and unwilling to work unless threatened with deprivation or punishment?
2. Do people want to get as much as they can while giving as little as possible in return?
3. Are people fundamentally "me-oriented" and unwilling to participate in "we-oriented" community activity without some personal gain beyond that shared by everyone?
4. Are people balanced in their orientation to giving and receiving?

5. Do people's needs to be independent, useful, deserving of rights and privileges of community membership, and providers for their families foster work and productivity?
6. Are people inherently creative and industrious? If given the chance, will they be productive for personal satisfaction, altruism, or the sheer joy of creative activity?

These questions imply that the market system is not perfect. Clearly, the freedom to create agreements and contracts, the power to enforce agreements, and the right to hold property are necessary to the market system. However, the system does not work well in the absence of enforceable laws that define the rules.

Therefore, policing against problems such as fraud, theft, and vandalism are important. But despite such protections, the free market incurs many problems that threaten its stability and are painful to community members. Some general examples are frequent occurrence of unemployment of willing and able workers, the over- or under-valuing of some market offerings, the inability of some community members to contribute because of age, infirmity, or disability, and the exploitation of the system by some young and able "free riders," who give nothing in return. Many community members view drug use to be a serious contributor to these problems of the market.

Some other specific problems are as follows:

1. Unwanted side effects of production and distribution such as pollution, crowding, traffic congestion, accidents, illness, and property damage.
2. Securing payment for "public" goods and services such as roads, bridges, trash removal, fire fighting, and police.
3. Unequal and unfair competition among producers that may raise costs for consumers or reduce the quality of goods and services.
4. Uninformed consumers who are cheated by unscrupulous producers and sellers.
5. "Boom-or-bust" fluctuations in market activity that effect employment, inflation, and income.
6. Inequitable distribution of goods, services, and wealth.
7. Production and marketing of goods and services that the community sees as a threat to its economic, social, or moral integrity (drugs, weapons, gambling, pornography, prostitution).
8. The costs of doing business such as advertising, payment of intermediaries, and record keeping.

These problems can be so costly or damaging that communities have turned to the political process to guide private economic activity. Consequently, government has imposed programs, laws, and regulations, and created agencies to control the "unseemly, raucous, and self-interested competition of the marketplace" (Mitchell & Simmons, 1994). The phrase *social policy* refers to the politically derived definitions, strategies, and practices that guide these government efforts.

Through its social policies, a community assigns role and status, rewards and penalties, and rights and entitlements to community members. These assignments define members' behaviors and positions in its social and economic structure. Social policy also provides mechanisms through which individuals acquire wealth, and those in positions to do so redistribute wealth among community members.

Each community implements its policies in territories controlled by it. Social policy reveals itself there in customs, laws, and standards by which community members interact in the exchange of goods and services. More specifically, community members observe the exercise of policy in the following:

1. Public ownership and operation of facilities, services, and resources.
2. Criminal laws to protect life, liberty, and property, and to enforce rules of the market place.
3. Civil laws to settle disputes between community members.
4. Taxation.
5. Spending to support activities and people.
6. Monitoring, investigation, and inspection of the marketplace and actions of community members.
7. Licenses and franchises to regulate various market and community activities.
8. Information dissemination, information suppression, propaganda, and publicity about goods and services, and community events and activities.

Because these policy exercises have such serious meaning, community members often band together in subgroups and coalitions to protect their interests. Each interest group presses for policies that serve and resists those that threaten its members' special needs.

Furthermore, social policy defines the degree to which the community may impose its will on individual members in the interest of the common good. And conversely, social policy protects the rights of the individual to pursue private interests unencumbered by others. Policy in the letter and spirit of its laws must effectively balance the needs and security of the community against those of the individual. The political struggle over drug policy revolves around this key issue.

To exert effective control, policies must provide consistent responses to opportunities and crises, and must be fair and benevolent for community members to abide by them. Clearly, these core values strengthen support for the politics of community life, although tension and conflict surround most policy issues. Teachers can remind students that the French Revolution and the American Revolution were both community protests against policymakers' failure to adhere to these values.

In the United States, equity, justice, and benevolence are organizing principles of the constitution and the democratic system. Unfortunately, there is much in U.S. policy history to indicate that raw economic and political power often distorts the marketplace and subverts these core values. Disillusionment is a major consequence of these problems.

Consequently, core values are foundational to the democratic ground rules of policy debate and trust in the system. Under the ground rules, policy advocates can lobby, propagandize, and electioneer, but, they cannot offer bribes, suppress ideas, or use violence to get their way.

The gray area between what is permissible and what is not is where many individuals and interest groups seek to unfairly influence policy debate (Mitchell & Simmons, 1994) Politicians and their staffs often become covert lobbies for the industries from which they were drawn and to which they expect to return after public service. And, many politicians count heavily on the money, social connections, and endorsement of various interest groups in order to win elections.

Thus, interest groups exert influence through campaign contributions, personal favors, and promises to open or threats to close plants and facilities in officeholders' districts. These potentials are broadly recognized and are the stimulus for proposals to limit time in office for elected officials and to impose controls on campaign contributions.

In view of the problems just described, trust and effective ground rules are especially important. This is so because policy emerges as the end product of conflict between interest groups in all communities (Peltason, 1967). However, students of government ponder the degree to which policy resolutions reflect the influence of small groups of wealthy, better educated individuals, the will of the common person, or the decisions of bureaucratic managers (Mitchell & Simmons, 1994).

Because of these fears about democratic processes, trust is a major element of peaceful coexistence and conflict resolution between interest groups. It is often the deciding factor in whether policy emerges through force, suppression, and armed warfare, or through dialogue and negotiation.

This is particularly true for what professional political operators of the 1980s referred to as *wedge issues* (Patterson & Kim, 1994). These divisive issues press people to view policy conflict as a struggle between "villains and heros," "good guys and bad guys," or "the government and the people" (Peltason, 1967, p. 1). Such seems to be the case in the "pro-life" versus "pro-choice" abortion debate, the National Rifle Association (NRA) versus gun control advocates, liberals versus conservatives, industry versus the environmentalists, drug prohibition versus drug legalization, labor versus management, and so on *ad infinitum*.

In the classroom, students may debate the following issues about government's role in managing tensions among the aggregate of community members, various interest groups, and individuals. A "yes" answer to the first three questions and a "no" to the last four indicate disillusionment, and a "no" to the first three and a "yes" to the last four indicate optimism and enthusiasm about policymakers.

1. Is government separate from the masses and do its officers represent a superior, more knowing, and elite social class?
2. Is government's role to create and impose policy on the people?
3. Do officers use their position to promote their own special interests and those of their supporters?

And, conversely:

1. Is the purpose of government to protect the people from tyranny by special interests?
2. Is government an instrument through which its officeholders promote the best interests of the people?
3. Is the government joined with the people so that the self-interest of officeholders is consonant with the needs of their constituencies?
4. Is government's role to mediate debate and to supervise the actions of people and interest groups when events and crises raise policy issues?

In the United States and other democracies, the government generally serves as a mediator, and because of the electoral system of government appointment, the majority rules, usually. When politicians do not deliver the goods or displease more voters than they please, they will be voted out of office.

However, many people of voting age in the United States have withdrawn from the electoral process (Moore, 1996). For example, more than 60% of U.S. voters did not vote in the 1994 elections.

The general perception of voters is that party politics and the enormous expense of election campaigns has subverted the electoral process. The average citizen cannot afford to mount a meaningful campaign for office without support from a major political party. And, parties nominate candidates who are supported by powerful, wealthy, and contributing interest groups. Consequently, interest groups may control elections and policy by controlling nominations.

As public disclosures of campaign contributions reveal, interest groups often contribute simultaneously to both the Democratic and Republican political parties. In this way, these groups attempt to maneuver into a "no-lose" position regardless of the outcome of an election.

Consequently, one complaint among reluctant voters is that nominated candidates are more alike than different on major policy issues. For powerful interest groups, interchangeable political candidates are just fine as long as the needs of these interest groups are protected. In this way the unseemly, raucous, and self-interested competition of politics has been added to the unseemly, raucous, and self-interested competition of the marketplace (Mitchell & Simmons, 1994).

The following questions may be addressed in classroom discussion. Do voters stay away from the polls because:

**1.** They are indifferent, ignorant, or careless?
**2.** They feel that candidates differ in unimportant ways?
**3.** They believe that voting will not improve their lives?

## WHAT IS THE SOURCE OF U.S. SOCIAL POLICY?

The purpose and meaning of a community's social policies emerge from members' collective consciousness of values, mores, and identity. Consequently, social policy is the product of interaction between government and culture.

By the beginning of the 20th century, millions of immigrants came to America because they shared a collective consciousness that portrayed the nation to offer unlimited prosperity. In fact, the U.S. standard of living doubled every 21 years for the nation's first 150 years (Council of Economic Advisors, 1991; Thurow, 1992). The image of the United States as a melting pot became vivid following World War II, and was captured with great clarity by John F. Kennedy (1986) in his book *A Nation of Immigrants*.

Therefore, teachers must examine the collective U.S. consciousness if they are to help students grasp the purpose and meaning of U.S. social policies in relation to the problem of drug use. In this context, both the process through which communities create policy and the content of policies are important to study in the classroom.

One important element of the U.S. consciousness is a pioneering spirit of adventure and discovery. Within this consciousness is a sense of sharing a special mission and a unique destiny in which all will thrive (Patterson & Kim, 1994).

The pioneering spirit drove Americans' ancestors to uproot themselves and travel enormous distances to begin a new life in the new world. For many, arrival in America was achieved at great risk (Moore, 1996). Clearly, early American immigrants bestowed a consciousness suffused with powerful wishes for unbridled expansiveness, new horizons, and a future that is better than the present.

Inherent to the U.S. pioneering spirit is a drive toward individual autonomy and the rags-to-riches "American dream". All is made possible by sacrifice, the virtue and salvation of hard work, and rugged individualism that may be eccentric, even to the point of criminality (Ellwood, 1988). In the pioneering spirit, husband and wife support each other to make the family an economic and social force from which children may be launched into a better life than that of their parents.

It is this pioneering spirit that led to human discovery of the new world. It drove early Asians to walk across the Bering Land Bridge between Siberia and Alaska 20,000 to 40,000 years ago. And, by 12,000 years ago, they were dispersed throughout North America and through to the southern tip of South America. The descendants of the early Asians were the "Indians," as Columbus inaccurately named them, who later greeted European explorers.

Not only did these earliest of Americans spread to the furthest reaches of the new world, they carried evolving cultures with them. Many gradually transformed their economies from hunting and gathering to farming by about 9,000 years ago. Plants were domesticated to provide food, fibers and other raw materials, and drugs.

These people used drugs as medicines, poisons, hallucinogens, and stimulants. The most widely cultivated was tobacco, but mescaline, peyote, cocaine, and numerous other plants containing intoxicating substances were grown and used, too. Beers and wines were produced from corn, persimmons, and a variety of fruits, vegetables, and grains.

The same spirit drove the Vikings, the first Europeans to find the new world, in 1000 AD. Later came English and Portuguese fishermen in the 1400s, and then Christopher Columbus in 1492. Subsequently, the spirit of exploration and discovery drove Meriweather Lewis and William Clark's 1804–1806 expedition. This opened the far west to European newcomers of the American people. Europeans brought with them distilled alcohol, diseases, and racist social policies that eventually caused the death of 80 million Native Americans.

Nevertheless, the same spirit drove Neil Armstrong, who, on July 20, 1969, became the first person to walk on the moon. Clearly, the pioneering spirit has led Americans to the deepest recesses of the sea, the highest mountain peaks, and even to leave the planet.

Furthermore, it has led many Americans to explore the spirit itself, the innermost recesses of the mind, and new frontiers of altered consciousness. Usually, exploration of the physical world is supported by science and technology and exploration of the metaphysical has been supported by the arts, philosophy, religion, and the mystical.

However, science and technology crossed long ago into the realm of the impalpable with discovery and production of drugs. Native Americans made major early contributions to this crossover. And, to some degree, the spirit of adventure and discovery continues to support illicit individual drug experimentation, especially with LSD and other hallucinogens.

Nevertheless, aspirations propagated by the metaphysical and chemical would be only dreams without policies that encourage individual freedom and tolerance of the new and the different. U.S. social policy promotes individuality, exploration, and discovery. However, it discourages the use of drugs to pursue individual freedom and novelty even though U.S. culture presents messages to the contrary.

A second aspect of the U.S. consciousness is that of the nation as "haven to oppressed peoples" (Darman, 1996a). The U.S. desire for community is strong, and the social relatedness and empathy it creates evokes compassion and concern for others (Ellwood, 1988). These are displayed in the charity, acceptance, and inclusion Americans extend to those who find their way into the melting pot.

Although some people think of the melting pot as a process through which immigrants assimilate into a new and uniquely U.S. identity, that has never been the case. Instead, the freedoms guaranteed by U.S. social policies support a rapprochement between immigrants' ethnic identity and the demands of the mainstream of U.S. community life.

As a result, some immigrants assimilate unreservedly into U.S. community life and others maintain strong ties to their ethnic identity. Therefore, assimilated and nonassimilated immigrants enjoy religious freedom, cultural expression, native language use, and freedom to live amid their ethnic brethren.

However, U.S. social policies demand that they do business in English, offer equal opportunity to other Americans regardless of ethnic origin or other characteristics, practice monogamy, provide for their children, register for the military draft, and obey drug laws. Also, increasing numbers of immigrants are seeking dual status by gaining U.S. citizenship, while also retaining their nationality of birth (Sengupta, 1996). The question of dual citizenship raises complicated problems about taxes, allegiances, military duty, and extradition in criminal cases.

Despite the U.S. spirit of charity and acceptance, the pendulum of inclusion has swung back and forth between greater and lesser tolerance. Throughout the 200-year history of the United States, advocates of every stripe have joined the push and pull for limiting immigration, imposing American nativism, and recently, demanding multi-cultural separatism (Schlesinger, 1992). At the close of the 20th century, 8.7% of Americans are foreign-born as compared to 22.7% for Australia, 18.5% for Switzerland, and 16.1% for Canada (Moore, 1996).

It is here that American wishes for expansiveness, exploration, and opportunity collide with the spirit of charity, acceptance, and inclusion. When Americans become pessimistic about future opportunity, their ideals of charity and inclusion become dim. As this occurs, optimism about the future is replaced with anger and fear (Patterson & Kim, 1994). During bad economic times, the pendulum of social policy swings toward intolerance, and during good times it swings toward acceptance.

Currently, Americans are not willing to do much for the poor or the half million homeless people who sleep on the streets of U.S. cities every night. Few Americans are willing to pay more taxes, sacrifice their own government benefits, or take the time and effort to do volunteer work. At this time of a widening income gap between rich and poor and government financial exigency, most people just want the poor and the homeless to disappear (Patterson & Kim, 1994; Sanger, 1997).

Accordingly, U.S. communities have passed repressive social policies and used them as weapons most often during bad economic times. Recently, New York City evicted homeless people from Tompkins Square Park, Chicago shut O'Hare Airport to the homeless, Santa Barbara banned sleeping on public streets, and other communities have outlawed "aggressive begging." The state of Arkansas began 1997 by executing three criminals in 1 day. And, 1996 welfare reform imposed harsh time limits on welfare eligibility and all but eliminated transitional services to those for whom benefits will expire.

During difficult times, policymakers have instituted drug laws against real and imagined threats to "born-in-America" hegemony about jobs, sexual mores, and social influence. Consequently, for immigrants, Blacks, Chicanos, Chinese, and other minority groups, drugs have powerful associations with the dark side of the U.S. spirit (Musto, 1987).

## HOW DOES SOCIAL POLICY RELATE
## TO SUBSTANCE ABUSE PREVENTION?

Social policy is important to substance abuse prevention because drug use is associated with many social issues. Among these issues, poverty, family disruption, crime, violence, and health care are prominent. But, policy failures and disappointments, and arrogance and dishonesty among policymakers raise serious drug-related concerns. Therefore, drug policy is but one of many social policies that impact drug use.

As history reveals, U.S. communities and those of nations around the world have struggled most intensely with drug problems when social policy is ineffective and unfair. Currently, the United States is struggling with crises caused by just such policy failings. These crises are as follows (Patterson & Kim, 1994):

**1.** A lack of confidence in government leaders.
**2.** Community polarization around morally divisive issues.
**3.** High government deficits and indebtedness.
**4.** Crime and violence.
**5.** A troubled education system.

What is more, U.S. communities frequently worsen these crises because they fail to provide adequate material and social support to the poor. Consequently, the poor's basic needs often go unmet, and, too often, they become scapegoats for the broader ills of society.

Clearly, the consequences of poverty are neither abstract nor dismissible. For every 1% increase in unemployment there are increases of 6.7% in homicides, 3.4% in violent crime, 2.4% in property crimes, 5.6% in fatal heart disease, and 3.1% in death by strokes (Moore, 1996). Also, there are $75 billion in lost productivity, $25 billion in lost taxes, and $5 billion in unemployment compensation. And, poverty is clearly intertwined with racial, ethnic, and class struggles. As a result, life for the U.S. poor often is chaotic and stressful. These conditions are risk factors in substance abuse.

As these figures suggest, to survive, some of the poor meet their needs via antisocial and illegal activities. Drug dealing on the street is a tempting form of such activity. Still others, who are not poor but are contemptuous of the system, violate its rules with impunity (Sales, 1996).

In committing drug-related crime, poor and wealthy alike drain community resources. They also risk imprisonment, injury or death, and disruption of their own families. Furthermore, their behavior promulgates trauma and malignant cynicism among other members of the community. No doubt, poverty, family disruption, crime, and health care are interrelated problems that impact drug use and with which U.S. policymakers have struggled for 200 years.

As this suggests, a community's social policies can summon the best and the worst of the human condition. For example, policies that prevent abuse and neglect of vulnerable people such as children and the aged demonstrate admirable ideals. So do policies that resolve community tensions through cooperation rather than armed confrontation. The same may be said of policies that lend aid to those in need.

Therefore, in the United States, improving education, reducing crime, eliminating drug addiction, strengthening the family, and enhancing the economic security of the citizenry are universal wishes. To these ends, many policy initiatives have come and gone since the 1930s. So have several wars on poverty, crime, and drugs. The catchy terminology and sloganeering used to promote each are as follows:

1. Franklin Delano Roosevelt's "New Deal."
2. Lyndon Johnson's "Great Society."
3. Richard Nixon's "New American Revolution."
4. Ronald Reagan's "Reagan Revolution."
5. George Bush's "kinder, gentler America."
6. Bill Clinton's "Health Plan."
7. Newt Gingrich's "Contract with America."

## WHAT SOCIAL POLICIES ADDRESS ISSUES RELATED TO DRUG USE?

To stop discrimination and abuse, and to redress injustices of the past, the following policies were enacted since the 1960s. All have direct and indirect bearing on poverty, crime, and the family, and impact the U.S. drug problem.

### The 1964 Civil Rights Act

The 1964 Civil Rights Act was one of many dating back to 1866 and including those passed in 1870, 1871, and 1875. The 1964 act addressed "equal opportunity" and offered solutions to problems of discrimination in employment and education.

The provisions of Title VII of the 1964 act prohibit discrimination in employment on the basis of race, sex, national origin, and religion, and established the Equal Employment Opportunities Commission (EEOC). Two central concepts of the act define discrimination as unequal treatment, or unequal results in hiring and employment practices, especially for protected groups. The first refers to fair competition for jobs and the second to retention, salaries, and promotions. Consequently, the law guarantees all individuals a fair opportunity to get a job and enjoy a work environment that is free of discriminatory intimidation, ridicule, and insult.

Because direct evidence is difficult to obtain, the law permits investigators to infer discrimination from indirect evidence. Indirect evidence includes incongruity between proportions of a protected group's numbers in the work force and the numbers employed by any particular employer.

One derivation of this was the Equal Employment Opportunity Act of 1972. This act mandated affirmative action for federal, state, and local government employment in public agencies and by government contractors and subcontractors. Affirmative Action is a formal effort to use "proportionality" to assure employment of protected groups and to make up for past injustices.

At the time of their enactment, such laws appeared to be real victories for civil rights advocates, but the enthusiasm that drove their passage has waned over the years. Despite civil rights victories following the Civil War, the 1896 U.S. Supreme Court upheld the principle of "separate but equal," thus disconfirming early civil rights gains and confirming racial segregation of Blacks and Whites. Not until 1954 did the Supreme Court overturn this regressive 1896 ruling.

Similarly, the policy momentum behind the 1960s civil rights legislation appears to have faded, too. The Reagan and Bush administrations resisted school desegregation efforts and affirmative action. Both administrations stacked the courts in opposition to these laws, and the movement faltered. And, voters have passed anti-Affirmative Action referendums in several states.

As the Oakland, California, School Board's 1996 decision to list "Ebonics" (Black vernacular) as a distinct language suggests, even members of groups who suffered most because of previous injustices seem to be retreating into a more isolated position. Not only are they losing enthusiasm, their children have begun to fall behind again after years of gains (Applebome, 1996; Education Trust, 1996). Some of the lost ground is attributable to the ills of inner-city life, but the major problem is a growing disparity in educational opportunity between minority and White students. As these observations indicate, the gains achieved by egalitarian social policies appear to be neither permanent nor self-perpetuating.

## The 1965 Voting Rights Act

Earlier voting rights acts in 1957 and 1960 sought to protect the voting rights of Black voters, and the Twenty-Fourth Amendment (1964) banned the imposition of poll taxes in federal elections. The 1965 act authorized the U.S. attorney general to register Black voters and suspend literacy tests in states with low voter registration rates. The act was effective enough in reducing Black disenfranchisement to be enacted again and strengthened in later years.

## The 1968 Fair Housing Act

The problem of racial discrimination and segregation in housing was attacked in this 1968 act. The Department of Housing and Urban Development (HUD) serves for housing as does the EEOC for employment. In 1988, amendments added addicted persons and the mentally ill to those who were protected under the 1968 law. However, the protections for addicted persons have eroded in recent years.

## The 1974 Child Abuse Prevention and Treatment Act

Despite many deeply rooted reservations about incursions into the fundamental right of family privacy, concern about child abuse and neglect rose dramatically in the 1960s. Before that, U.S. communities paid extremely limited attention to the needs of children (Mezey, 1996). This is two despite the fact that reports of child abuse date back to 1655, and the notorious case of Mary Ellen Wilson, which occurred in 1874.

From the late 1800s to the mid-1930s, policymakers instituted only true important policy initiatives. These were congressional regulation of child labor at the turn of the century and the inclusion of Aid for Dependent Children as part of the Social Security Act of 1935.

However, since the mid-1960s the federal government has created a variety of programs to help and protect children who are at risk because of poverty, disability, and family circumstances. These include food programs for Women, Infants, and Children (WIC), and Head Start.

Also, public interest groups such as the Children's Defense Fund, the American Civil Liberties Union, and the American Bar Association have instigated and assisted legal actions on behalf of children. As a result, the federal courts have become advocates for children in litigation concerning sufficiency of welfare assistance, interstate enforcement of child support decrees, performance of state child welfare agencies, and equality of children's rights under the Constitution.

The most prominent of these policy initiatives is the Child Abuse Prevention and Treatment Act (CAPTA). Walter Mondale of Minnesota sponsored CAPTA in the Senate and Patricia Shroeder of Colorado sponsored it in the House of Representatives. Congress passed the act in 1974 and has reauthorized it every 2 to 3 years since then. Policymakers also expanded CAPTA to address issues of adoption, child pornography, and child medical care. In 1988, they amended CAPTA to address the needs of children of drug and alcohol abusers.

CAPTA defined child abuse, established the National Center for Child Abuse and Neglect, funds research and disseminates information, and provides grant monies to the states. States' eligibility for these funds was conditional on their passage of laws defining and prohibiting child abuse, and creating procedures for reporting abuse.

The act provides resources and incentives to child protection agencies for investigating reports of child abuse, foster care placement and mental health treatment of young victims, and prosecution of perpetrators of child abuse. Most states now have laws that require teachers and health care providers to report suspicions of child abuse to a child protection agency in their community.

The child protection system has encountered many serious problems since passage of the 1974 act. It has been deluged with reports, of which too many are frivolous and some are opportunistic or vindictive sequella of divorces and child custody battles. These consume the resources of investigative agencies at a time when Congress has eroded funding for many provisions of CAPTA.

Observers now describe the federal government's fragmented role in child protection as inadequate, misdirected, and lacking coherence (Mezey, 1996, p. 97). State agencies struggle with the following:

1. Unreliable information.
2. Poorly trained staff.
3. Inadequate numbers of case workers relative to the size of the case load.
4. Ineffective and inefficient procedures.
5. Poor administrative oversight.

Sexual abuse cases considerably worsen these problems because the courts struggle with the reliability of child witnesses, and the investigative procedures of child protection workers (Ceci & Bruck, 1995; Ney, 1995). Consequently, prosecutors have wrongfully imprisoned people on the basis of questionable evidence, and may have freed guilty parties because evidence they needed for a conviction was tainted by investigators.

Legal experts have strongly criticized Attorney General Janet Reno for just such action when she was Florida's state attorney. Some observers accused her of heavy-handed zeal and exploitation of the child abuse issue to promote her career. Courts have overturned verdicts in several child abuse cases with which she was involved.

## The 1977 Community Reinvestment Act

Policymakers intended this act to restrain banks from accepting deposits from residents of impoverished neighborhoods and then loaning the money to people with stronger credit ratings in more affluent communities. In this way, "fair lending" prevents discrimination when members of protected groups seek loans from banks and other financial institutions.

This has created problems in the banking industry. The law requires banks to make riskier loans at lower interest rates and some members of protected groups organize to make extortionate demands. These organized community groups do so under provisions that permit them to negotiate unfairly with bankers in the context of community reinvestment (Bovard, 1995).

Since the 1980s, federally insured banks and the savings and loan industry have had problems of their own. These problems cost U.S. taxpayers more than $200 billion, but 98% of U.S. banks are in compliance with this 1977 act.

### The 1990 Americans With Disabilities Act

In the 1970s, the independent living movement started and gained momentum across the United States. The movement urged that disabled people have the same opportunity to live and work independently as do the able-bodied, and that they be freed of their dependency on family and institutional supports.

Legislators passed numerous federal, state, and local laws to remove barriers and enhance disabled persons' access to education, employment, transportation, and community facilities. A 1975 federal law guarantees disabled children the right to public education in the least restrictive setting possible, and the 1990 Americans with Disabilities Act extends comprehensive civil rights protections to the disabled.

One problem that the nation has faced since passage of this act is that of defining the term *disabled*. Many people have sought to extend protection in unexpected ways. Some argued that obesity, allergies, safety-sensitive health conditions, dangerous emotional problems, alcoholism, and drug addiction should be covered under the act. These arguments present employers and others with expensive issues and accommodations.

## WHAT HAVE BEEN THE OUTCOMES
## OF SOCIAL POLICY INITIATIVES?

Many of the problems at which these bold initiatives were aimed remain and some have worsened. This is so despite government expenditures of trillions of dollars and extensive voluntary and legally mandated accommodation in the private sector.

Urban decay, crime, poverty, substance abuse, growing health care costs, and a paralyzing national debt continue to plague the nation. The AIDS epidemic and a lagging education system only add to the litany of woes.

Deficits and government indebtedness reduced availability of public sector employment in good government jobs. Most government financial problems are attributable to middle-class entitlements and defense spending.

Furthermore, the U.S. tradition of benevolent and paternalistic employers who provide lifetime security to loyal workers has vanished. Large companies have been reducing their workforces and streamlining operations in quest of efficiency and profits. The private-sector transformation is toward small-scale employment of an elite, highly paid workforce comprised of employees who get lots of overtime (Rifkin, 1995).

Interestingly, this has strengthened the economy, created many more jobs than it has destroyed, and has lowered unemployment to levels far below that of many western European countries. However, employees who are casualties of "downsizing" are experiencing great difficulty finding equivalent positions in other companies and industries.

From 1989 to 1995, more than 25 million people were laid off, and among those who lost long-term positions since 1993, only about one third have secured jobs of similar or higher pay (Lohr, 1996). The remaining two thirds are still job hunting, working part time, self-employed, or have taken full-time jobs for salaries lower than before their layoff.

Consequently, the U.S. middle class is shrinking. In the United States, 54% of the population is middle class as compared to 90% in Japan, 73% in Norway, 79% in Sweden, and 70% in Germany (Wolff, 1992). Although more U.S. Blacks have joined the middle and upper classes since the civil rights initiatives of the 1960s, only 47% are middle class or better as of 1986. Nearly 20 million of those who lost jobs to downsizing are living below the poverty level (Moore, 1996).

This has been both distressing and disillusioning because layoffs continue despite huge profits by many companies and unprecedented salaries for corporate officers. These companies walked away from communities that extended assistance to them during difficult financial times, and fired many loyal long-term workers.

According to former Labor Secretary Robert Reich, corporate America has abandoned the "implicit social contract" it maintained with workers since the late 1940s (Sanger, 1997). This contract, according to Reich, is one in which U.S. industry tried to include almost everyone in its prosperity, and shared increasing profits by offering workers higher wages, better health and pension benefits, and greater job security.

This is no longer the case. Less skilled workers are now relegated to piecemeal work in temporary positions (Rifkin, 1995). Temporary workers receive less pay and get few fringe benefits. What is more, they have much difficulty seeking redress for unfair treatment or discrimination in hiring or firing.

Clearly, new technologies and U.S. corporations' use of inexpensive labor abroad have contributed to this reduction in workers' security and income. However, social policies intended to stimulate trade and protect specific groups of workers have permitted, and to some extent driven, workers' losses, too. In contrast, many European countries prevent layoffs for all workers by levying tax penalties and applying powerful social pressures to restrain employers.

In the United States, equality of opportunity guarantees may have strengthened the hand of employees to the point where hiring U.S. workers has become too risky and expensive for profit-oriented employers. Because there are no restraints, employers can hire small, elite workforces to reduce the scale of many burdens besides salaries.

These include fringe benefits such as health insurance, pension plans, and unemployment insurance. Employers also reduce problems and demands imposed by a morass of regulations. These include potential intrusions of the equal economic opportunity and disabilities mandates, the National Labor Relations Act, and Occupational Health and Safety Act. And, they reduce the likelihood of expensive struggles with disgruntled employees who are seeking redress under these mandates.

Glaring examples of such problems are Texaco Oil's $140 million settlement of a discrimination lawsuit by minority employees, and the National Labor Relations Board (NLRB) directive to Caterpillar, Inc., the largest U.S. manufacturer of earth-moving equipment. The NLRB charged Caterpillar with discrimination against its striking employees and ordered the company to compensate 9,500 strikers for special benefits provided to nonstrikers. These special benefits included free lunches, breakfasts, picnics, beverages, catered meals, tee-shirts, flu shots, and unlimited ice cream and popcorn. Despite this victory, unionized employees have been unable to secure a contract with Caterpillar for 5 years.

Originally, U.S. policies had evolved to establish some reasonable balance between capitalist greed and workers' safety and security. Social security, child labor laws, safety standards, and minimum wage standards are among the many efforts toward that balance. The system seems to have lost its equilibrium.

To many Americans who are struggling for jobs, unable to afford health insurance, and toiling under a troublesome tax burden, preferential treatment for protected groups, set-asides, and a variety of other expenditures are unfair. There was little evidence that many policies and the programs through which they were implemented would work, and after the fact, many Americans think that they did not (Darman, 1996b). Teachers should have no doubt that disillusioned parents pass on these disillusioning sentiments to their children.

## SUMMARY OF KEY POINTS

Social policy has enormous meaning for teachers committed to substance abuse prevention. Any understanding of social policy is intimately connected with understandings of the purpose and meaning of community life, and community members' consciousness of their shared values and destiny.

The U.S. consciousness has been shaped by its origins in a nation of immigrants. This consciousness is one of pioneering adventure and rugged individualism coupled with a spirit of charity and humanitarian acceptance. Americans have not been unwavering in living up to these romantic ideals. The actions of leaders and the people have at times displayed the best and the worst of the human condition.

Central to these understandings is the role of social policy in U.S. community life. Social policy has been a form of control and redress when the U.S. consciousness has become distorted or subverted in ways that are harmful to community members. Among the damaging consequences that policy must address are poverty, crime, family disruption, and unmet needs for health care. All of these have powerful associations with drug use.

Teachers can help students understand that the policymaking process is imperfect and is subject to many influences that shape it. At this time in history, there is increasing evidence that many of our social policies have produced mixed results and have created additional problems, too. Because the efforts of policymakers can be disappointing, teachers must also help students resist disillusionment. This is important to preventing many forms of antisocial and destructive behavior, including drug use.

Furthermore, teachers must help students understand the linkages between drug use and socially and morally divisive issues. These issues include racial discrimination, social class conflict, abortion, capital punishment, gun control, and sex discrimination, to name just a few. Examination of these issues will invariably force confrontation with many risk factors associated with substance abuse.

# Substance Abuse Prevention in the Context of Social Disillusionment

The goal of this chapter is to describe disillusionment about social policy so that the following can be accomplished:

1. Teachers can understand how disillusionment emerges from social conditions and policy failures at school and in the community.
2. Teachers can understand how disillusionment is a risk factor in substance abuse.
3. Teachers can help students understand how the U.S. political process addresses poverty, crime, family disruption, and health care.
4. Teachers can help students understand the challenges policymakers face in the political process.
5. Teachers can help students remain active in school and community life when frustrated or disappointed by school and community response to personal and social issues.
6. Teachers can help their students use activism as a deterrent to disillusionment and drug use.
7. Teachers who work in troubled communities may encourage students to become active in the process of change in the school and community.

Children become disillusioned when acts of omission or commission by parents, teachers, and the peer group produce painful disappointments. The "system" or the "establishment" of school and community policies and adult leaders also can produce painful disappointments. Consequently, disillusioned children believe that home, school, and community are unfair places in which to compete for life's rewards. Among the disillusioned, the world is inherently unjust and heartless, and distrust and cynicism are dominant attitudes. *Alienation, anomie, dropping out*, and *disengagement* are terms for disillusionment about community life.

For children from good homes, disillusionment may begin in school because it is where young people regularly experience community life outside of the family. On the other hand, school can be a blessing to children whose disrupted family life and nightmarish struggle on the streets has disillusioned them. Therefore, teachers are in a powerful position to make school a positive experience and offer respite to children who are struggling at home and in their neighborhoods.

Because disillusionment and its various manifestations can be so destructive to community life, social scientists have studied the problem for 100 years (Bynum & Thompson, 1996). In 1897, Emile Durkheim produced the first of a number of "social strain theories" when he observed the association between suicide and contradictory social expectations and outcomes. In 1938, Robert Merton examined the association of deviant behavior with discrepancies between culturally promoted aspirations and socially mediated means for their attainment.

In the United States, social strain is visible in frustrated aspirations to make money and accumulate material possessions. Financial success is a standard that drives people to achieve status based on wealth and occupation (Bynum & Thompson, 1996). Accordingly, U.S. communities deluge their members with many tempting aspirations and also define the route to attaining them.

The problems that arise when economic and social obstacles frustrate these aspirations are not unique to the United States. Europe, too, now struggles with these problems, particularly among its adolescents. Europe's post-welfare state, post-Cold War, postindustrial society, and post-baby boom transition has broken many promises of a more prosperous future (Cowell, 1998).

Consequently, diminishing optimism has generated an explosive mix of unemployment, alienation, and substance abuse in western European countries. Furthermore, powerful advertising and peer pressure to pursue expensive symbols of success drive this disillusionment, and have yielded increases in violent crime among Europe's teenagers (Cowell, 1998).

In contrast to theories about disillusionment, Hirschi (1969) presented social bond theory to describe how community members behave when they are optimistic and trusting about achieving a community's vision of success:

1. They develop social attachments with sensitive regard for and genuine caring about other people in the community.
2. They make personal commitments to socially acceptable goals and means for success.
3. They invest time and energy in activity that the community values and rewards.
4. They believe in the correctness, moral worth, and viability of the community's norms and values.

People derive many individual benefits from such actions. These benefits include optimism and a readiness for action, and when the social bond is formed, as Hirschi described it, self-evaluative benefits also come. As cited in Weinstein (1995b), these self-evaluative benefits are as follows:

1. A sense of social integration in which people celebrate each other's triumphs and mourn each other's losses. Also, they share resources, benefits, and costs of each other's actions in an atmosphere of trust and loyalty.
2. A sense of personal freedom to explore positive options and the belief that others will help if an experiment in living does not work out well.
3. A sense of personal control in which one sees the world to be responsive to one's own actions and efforts.
4. Self-acceptance and esteem that comes of one's own success in achieving valued goals and subsequent acknowledgment by others.
5. Clarity about values, goals, moral positions, and the meaning and purpose of community life.

According to the American dream, people enjoy health, wealth, and wisdom if they attend school, work hard, and are virtuous, thrifty, and patient. As described in chapter 7, U.S. communities have instituted numerous policies, regulations, and programs to remove obstacles that restrain vulnerable individuals and groups on this path to success.

Despite these efforts to help people, many community members find such aspirations and means for their attainment to be unrealistic. For these people, disillusionment strains social attachments, weakens personal commitments to the community's norms and values, and attenuates personal involvement in community activities. As a result, social integration changes to social isolation, a sense of personal freedom changes to feelings of entrapment, a sense of personal control becomes a feeling of helplessness, self-esteem turns to self-repudiation, and moral clarity becomes moral confusion. These changes produce painful reappraisal, a loss of faith in the meaning of community life, and powerful feelings of self-doubt.

When social policies institutionalize sources of disappointment or fail to protect community members from them, victims may become cynical and nihilistic (Weinstein, 1995a). Then, the process of disillusionment is fueled by frustration, bitterness, and fear. These are human responses to the betrayal, abuse, neglect, exploitation, and abandonment through which disillusionment is generated.

Generally, disillusionment is an end stage of extremely negative experience and is preceded by protest and then despair. It is associated with depression and withdrawal at one extreme and rage and rebellion at the other. Both of these responses can be destructive of self and others and are associated with drug use. In the community, they feed into and are amplified by poverty, crime, family disruption, and poor health care. In school, aggression and withdrawal feed into and are amplified by academic failure, punitive or indifferent teachers, victimization by the peer group, and inadequate support, protection, and supervision by adults.

Young people very clearly expressed rebellion at the reactive extreme and "dropping out" at the apathetic extreme during the 1960s. They did so in connection with racism, social injustice, the military draft, the Vietnam War, and cries for academic relevance in the schools. This period was swept by an unprecedented tide of drug use that Americans never fully extinguished and is threatening to surge anew.

## WHY IS FAITH IN THE SYSTEM IMPORTANT TO SUBSTANCE ABUSE PREVENTION?

To explain U.S. policy disappointments and protracted struggles with social issues, some cynical observers theorize that the following:

1. Efforts by leaders have been subverted by political ambition and patronage.
2. Government has been untracked by corruption and inefficiency.
3. Policymaking has been paralyzed by ideological conflict.
4. Policymaking has been defeated by ignorance.
5. Policymaking has been misled by persons of radical and disruptive purpose in conscious conspiracies.

In this view, all policymakers are painted into corners. The corrupt ones lie, cheat, and steal; incompetent others waste resources and opportunity; and still others subordinate the public good to personal and ideological ambition.

To those who subscribe to such disillusioning theories, and to significant portions of the electorate, U.S. social policy is the product of a "crapshoot" by uninformed leaders who are luckless opportunists. At best, to such individuals, U.S. policymakers look like riverboat gamblers with a penchant for making bad bets rather then wise and thoughtful decisions (Darman, 1996b).

Teachers who address the issues and problems associated with U.S. social policy must realize that faith in the system is an important element of substance abuse prevention. Teachers should present the truth that the unhappy theories and perceptions cited in the preceding paragraph explain some disappointments and failures of U.S. social policy, but not most. Therefore, teachers must help their students discover and internalize the good reasons for being tenacious about community issues and active in the political process.

Teachers should emphasize that self-aggrandizement, lack of understanding, back room intrigue, and just plain lying, stealing, and cheating occur at times, but the U.S. political system of checks and balances provides powerful counterforces to these dangerous possibilities. Furthermore, the system's purposeful efforts to avoid these problems have a long history, and these efforts have become increasingly aggressive (Anachiarico & Jacobs, 1996).

Following the Civil War, reformers made great efforts to undo the machine party politics in which politicians passed down the spoils of their election victories to supporters, family members, and hangers on. This movement claimed that good government was a product of virtuous and altruistic leadership as opposed to patronage, cronyism, and graft. To reformers, the ideal person for office was an exemplary citizen, placed the public interest before self-interest, and put the good of the community ahead of party politics. Furthermore, this person remained incorruptible, modest in financial ambition, and was to be rewarded through meritorious service (Truman, 1981). Reformers of that era argued that good people produced good government.

However, by the beginning of the 20th century, reformers' views shifted to a belief that good government came of the separation of public service from party politics. Early 20th-century reformers argued that elected politicians can appoint public administrators to government posts, but once appointed, administrators should continue in their posts beyond the term in office of those who appointed them. Such appointees could not be removed from office without just cause and therefore, in theory, would be independent of the politicians who hired them. In this way, good government would come of separating the duress and temptations of politics from public service.

Following the Great Depression of 1929–1933, reformers again changed their approach. The advocates argued for creating a government structure of formal rules, policies, and procedures that channeled public servants' activities in directions necessary to good government. Organizational science and the experience of industrial organizations was to inform this structure. They argued that efficient, effective, and economical government emerged out of sound organization and appropriate administrative oversight to monitor and evaluate the work of the bureaucracy.

Since 1970, those concerned about good government seem to have abandoned these earlier views that good people, isolated from politics, and provided with clearly defined expectations and supervision would serve good government. The new perspective is that government work offers irresistible opportunities and incentives for selfish opportunism.

Consequently, reformers have imposed new controls. These controls strongly imply that all officials will eventually be corrupted by the power of government. This is disillusionment in its most extreme form in that government itself has become angry and disillusioned about its own workings.

Subsequently, 1,000 public officials were indicted or convicted of criminal offenses between 1970 and 1977. These officials had positions ranging from county sheriff to a U.S. vice president (Spiro Agnew). During the Reagan era, more than 100 federal officials were indicted or convicted, and so too have been several members of the Clinton administration (Anechiarico & Jacobs, 1996).

Therefore, modern reformers argue stridently that the only route to good government is constant vigilance. They claim that hidden surveillance and covert investigation, backed by sanctions such as jail, fines, and loss of jobs and pensions are requisite to controlling mismanagement, corruption, and other problems of government.

Since Watergate, Congress passed the Ethics in Government Act of 1978. The act established the Office of Government Ethics, and contains independent counsel provisions. This law requires that the U.S. attorney general petition a three-judge panel in response to specific credible allegations of executive misconduct. The panel appoints special prosecutors to investigate the allegations. These prosecutors are independent of the Federal Justice Department and unfettered by political obligation. And, they have almost unlimited resources to investigate illegal conduct by the highest officers of government, and to recommend action.

The purpose of the act was to prevent violations of public trust and strengthen public confidence in the integrity of government employees. George Bush, in 1989, added that public employees must avoid creating even the appearance of impropriety, illegal acts, or unethical behavior.

Efforts to control corruption have become so extensive that the government's capacities for service and action have been seriously impaired (Anechiarico & Jacobs, 1996). Public agencies have become layered with policies, procedures, investigative mechanisms, and law enforcement oversight.

What is more, with enactment of independent counsel laws, politicians are too often tempted to resolve political differences by accusing one another of criminal activities. Attorneys selected by the three-judge panel have pursued 17 independent counsel investigations from 1978 to 1997.

Despite more than 20 years of turning the screws in these aggressive ways, the majority of Americans have become even more disillusioned with government. They believe that the moral fiber of government and the political process have deteriorated, corruption is endemic, and that the system no longer works as it should (Gilbert, 1988; Ornstein, 1994).

## HOW CAN TEACHERS ADDRESS DISILLUSIONMENT IN THE STUDY OF U.S. SOCIAL POLICY?

Teachers must help students understand that many U.S. policymakers have sought responsible solutions to pressing issues. Policymakers' efforts have, at times, produced disappointing results.

Furthermore, teachers should inform students that politicians try to recruit advisors and aides who, as policymakers, usually represent the best this country has to offer. Politicians select staff members who studied at the most respected universities and worked in the most successful and prestigious organizations. More often than not, they are sincere in their intentions, preeminent in their fields, and are knowledgeable about substantive issues that face the nation.

Students may test this idea by studying past and present elected officeholders, and political appointees' professional and personal biographies. Although this supports the theory that U.S. policy is controlled by an elite minority, many of these biographies are available in references such as *Who's Who*, in magazine and newspaper articles, and on the Internet.

Students can use a variety criteria, including some they create in class, to evaluate prominent government officials. Patterson and Kim (1994) produced a list of such criteria by surveying a random national sample of 1,000 people. Students may use Patterson and Kim's criteria in assessing the degree to which leaders display the following qualities:

1. Character and integrity.
2. Kindness and compassion.
3. Clear vision and direction for the future.
4. Charisma.
5. Confidence and ability to inspire confidence.
6. Competence and capability.
7. Articulate and communicative manner of speaking.

Students will discover that some politicians appoint staff members for reasons of patronage rather than experience and ability. However, such study will reveal that even though their views share much in common with politicians who appoint them, many other appointees are well qualified to work in government.

Furthermore, students will discover that appointees' work is hard, at times thankless, and its landscape treacherous and insecure. As a result, many leave government proud of their accomplishments, but worn down and disillusioned by the tensions and stresses of public service. This occurs as these often invisible people plan and hammer out policy, and their ideas are presented to the nation by its elected representatives.

Students will find that some leave as scapegoats whose reputations may be unjustly and irreparably damaged. This is most tellingly described by former Reagan White House Chief of Staff Don Regan: "I find some amazing similarities between surviving in WWII jungle battles and surviving in Wash. [ington] political circles" (cited in Darman, 1996a, pp. 171–172).

Regan was one of the casualties of the Iran–Contra scandal along with National Security Advisor Admiral John Poindexter and the infamous Oliver North. According to Darman (1996a), even presidents' wives become embroiled in some political feeding frenzies.

What is worse, students may discover that many capable individuals with valuable skills and experience have begun to refuse to work in government. Since Richard Nixon's forced resignation from the presidency, success in government service has become a matter of keeping one's reputation intact rather than emerging with enhanced prestige and standing. Successful mid-career executives, professionals, and academics who are at the high point of their productivity now see the perils of public service to be too great relative to the rewards.

Because the political process in the United States can be so harsh and exhausting, teachers must be careful to avoid passively or actively encouraging students to "drop out." Anyone may easily criticize the system as unresponsive, ineffective, cannibalistic, or corrupt. Instead, teachers should help students comprehend the forces and the complexity of the process through which drug and other policy initiatives emerge. This is important to substance abuse prevention and drug education.

Teachers should emphasize the importance of the average citizen's active participation, and stress the vacuousness of unreasoned rebellion, self-destructive forms of protest, capitulation to despair, and private withdrawal from community life. Accordingly, teachers should enthusiastically recruit students for student government, school newspaper and yearbook production, and other student organizations, and clubs. Letter writing to office holders and to the editors of newspapers, and joining community organizations have long been among the tactics of grass-roots U.S. politics. Substance abuse prevention is one of many benefits students may derive from activities such as these.

Furthermore, teachers may provide service learning opportunities and field trips to government agencies and the offices of reputable private organizations and advocacy groups. In these ways, teachers help students to "learn the ropes" of the U.S. political system and discover that the policymaking process has an arguable logic. Students also will have opportunities to learn, practice, and apply valuable social and verbal skills.

## HOW SHOULD TEACHERS DESCRIBE
## THE PROCESS OF POLICYMAKING?

Students will find that in most cases, policy does not emerge from evil thoughts and sinister intention. Rather, it begins with sincere and deeply felt dissatisfaction about pressing social conditions and issues. For action to occur, this dissatisfaction must attract the attention of the media and politicians. Solutions proposed by leaders then must be broadly acceptable and in concert with important cultural values. And, the leaders themselves must be reassuring.

Teachers should help their students understand that these precursors to action are just the beginning. They are necessary but insufficient for successful initiation of new policies, and that the "politics" of acceptance then come to play.

Students should learn of politicians' and their staff members' carefully planned efforts. These efforts are a minimum requirement to push initiatives through checks and balances of the U.S. constitutional system. Students should also come to appreciate that leaders make themselves vulnerable to censure, impeachment, and criminal prosecution if they do not carefully play by the rules.

Most important, students will discover, using the criteria described in the preceding paragraph, that appointees possess many admirable personal qualities in addition to their strong professional qualifications. These include credibility, commitment, skills, and tenacity to push, organize, and negotiate despite many obstacles. Not only must the committed energy be present, but such individuals must join together to create strategy and manage the process of negotiation.

Also, teachers should help students learn that policymakers must be flexible, willing to form strange alliances, and join in unlikely partnerships to gather strength. And, students will find that policymakers must avoid expressing misplaced confidence in their own abilities and the rightness of their cause. Clearly, arrogance can be distracting and bring on resistance, accusation, and defeat.

Students can study the moral, ideological, and pragmatic arguments on which policy advocates base their strategies. For example, the concept of a "mandate from the people" exploits politicians' "moral obligations" to do the bidding of their constituencies. So does ideology that proclaims drug use to be the equivalent to moral terrorism, and the pragmatic need to push for unpopular tax increases or reduce services to balance government budgets.

Furthermore, students can discover the various ways in which policymakers bring important individuals and groups who oppose an initiative into line. In most instances, they use negotiations, horse trading, and compromise in which they and opponents split differences between their respective positions. Often, goodwill, statesmanship, and substantive debate bring out the best in all participants. What is particularly important, policy advocates must try to prevent opposing individuals and groups from uniting as a powerful coalition.

Teachers should help students understand that in these negotiations, policymakers address substantive issues. But, they also must be responsive to tensions and sensitivities among socioeconomic classes, races, ethnic minorities, and a host of special interest groups. As a result, a rapprochement between substantive issues and political necessity demands much stretching, reinterpretation, and selective attention. Students should realize that this permits necessary coalitions to form for passage, but, the process may weaken, or distort proposals in unanticipated and counterproductive ways.

Students will discover that, at times, opponents may be coerced with some form of threat. The possibility of a loss of status and credibility with the public, diminished influence and power, and distancing of political friends and allies are levers to which all politicians are vulnerable.

Teachers must help students recognize how policymakers seize opportunity inherent to crises and dramatic events. Such stimuli can mobilize action and generate public support for policy proposals, or at least postpone their erosion. Then, the coalitions who pass on policy initiatives must discern enough political advantage in their agreement to overlook some disagreements and substantive inconsistencies.

As a consequence of these intricacies, U.S. society has been both guilty of and victimized by what Darman (1996b) called "policy corruption." The 200-year history of U.S. social policy reveals much waste, futility, banality, cruelty, avarice, and greed. The United States has had institutionalized indentured service, slavery, witch hangings, child abuse, and persecution of racial, ethnic, religious, and behavioral minority groups to name but a few travesties that have checkered its past.

Teachers should help students understand that, despite policymakers' best efforts, not all policies and the laws that impose them are humane, rational, or good. Like it or not, many policies have been patently unfair, and some continue to maintain inequity, injustice, and malevolence through which some community members seeking wealth, power, and ideological dominance may victimize others.

This discussion of policy is particularly important to teachers because of the schools' place in socialization of the young. Teachers not only transmit art, science, and technology to succeeding generations of children, but they also help to prepare children for complicated social demands that are inherent to community life.

These demands reflect both the splendor and the failings of policies that govern U.S. society. Consequently, teachers must teach about the past and present of social existence in ways that prevent students from becoming disillusioned about the future. Teachers must also work at the leading edge of change that promotes rationality, justice, and benevolence in the community. These goals for change all have profound meaning relative to the U.S. drug problem.

## WHAT RECENT EVENTS HAVE CREATED OPPORTUNITIES FOR CASE STUDY IN THE CLASSROOM?

Teachers should emphasize that the process described in the previous section usually produces moderation and incremental change in U.S. social policy. And, teachers should sensitize students to circumstances that bring about large-scale nonincremental change. One such circumstance is the existence or illusion of broad-based, emotionally driven, popular appeal (Darman, 1996a). In this formula, those ideas and policy solutions that are simple and have panacean allusions are the most seductive.

Nevertheless, radical change emanating from politically extreme positions is rare because the constitutional system of checks and balances presses policy toward the middle of the road. As the failed national experiment with alcohol prohibition revealed so dramatically, when policy does not incorporate the views of the middle, problems follow. For this reason, instances of dramatic change provide good case material for the classroom.

One example is Ronald Reagan's 1981 tax revision that produced the largest tax cut in the history of the nation, rather than an incremental change. Students will find that politicians jumped on the tax-cut bandwagon. They were happy to be identified with such a politically pleasing development, and were afraid not to be.

However, the other side of the initiative required proportionate cutbacks in expenditures, and this was the politically painful side. No one wanted to be identified with reductions in entitlements, especially middle-class entitlements such as social security, Medicare, student loans, farm price supports, veterans benefits, and so on (Darman, 1996a). The same reluctance led to accelerated defense spending rather than reductions. As a result, federal deficits and national indebtedness ballooned and have plagued the nation for more than a decade.

Clinton's 1996 welfare reform legislation provides another case study of large-scale change. Clinton recruited David Ellwood, a Harvard social policy expert, to write new welfare legislation. Ellwood (1988) had authored the book *Poor Support*, an antipoverty classic that called for time limits on welfare.

Ellwood produced data indicating that most welfare recipients left the rolls in less than 2 years. But, he also found that a substantial minority stayed, and enough of these accumulated so that their numbers came to dominate the welfare rolls. At any given time, the average welfare recipient was in the midst of a 10-year spell of dependency (DeParle, 1996).

Ellwood's central principles advocated time-limited support. However, he argued that time limits must be balanced with pledges of health care, child support, child care, wage supplements, and, if necessary, jobs when one's entitlements expired. The original plan incorporated this principle to a reasonable degree, and as late as July 1994, looked as though it might become law.

However, within a few months, the Republicans captured Congress. The plan was shredded to tatters as President Clinton began to accede to conservative congressional demands, and Ellwood resigned in July 1995.

In passing the "Personal Responsibility and Work Opportunities Reconciliation Act of 1996," the president and Congress grabbed the political carrots by imposing time limits on welfare. But, they avoided the political pain of providing financial support for welfare recipients' transition into the world of work. Transitional support was at the heart of Ellwood's thinking, but was not important in the new law.

The reform was broad, sudden, and sweeping, and in no way followed the American tradition of incremental change. As a result of this act, 60 years of welfare policy were swept aside and the federal government will cut its expenditures by about $9 billion per year over the next 6 years.

By the time the act was signed, Ellwood was long gone. As Ellwood's associates had warned him, the politicians hijacked his time limit ideas and forgot about everything else.

Furthermore, one cannot help but wonder if the poor and their children have become scapegoats and been sacrificed once more; this time in the name of deficit reduction. The question is whether or not politicians did so to avoid angering powerful constituencies who resist any tampering with middle-class entitlements and defense spending. Although the number is large, the $54 billion welfare reform saving seems paltry compared to the hundreds of billions to be spent during the next 6 years for middle-class entitlements and defense.

Furthermore, the states are now free to simply cut welfare recipients off the rolls. Although state governments may provide helpful transitional services that approximate Ellwood's plan, there are many incentives for their not doing so (DeParle, 1996).

The recency of the 1996 Welfare Reform Act has not permitted an evaluation. Although there are dire and optimistic predictions, only the test of time will tell whether the 1996 reform improved or worsened an already troubled welfare system. Changes in levels of substance abuse is one of the indicators against which welfare reform may be assessed.

## SUMMARY OF KEY POINTS

The efforts of policymakers are sometimes disappointing and disillusioning for adults and young people. It is important for teachers to help students resist this disillusionment to prevent many forms of antisocial and destructive behavior, including drug abuse.

Helping children comprehend the strengths and weaknesses of the U.S. political system and that most policymakers are sincere and capable is a confirmatory strategy for substance abuse prevention. Teachers can help children understand that for better or worse, policy initiatives must survive an ordeal of checks and balances before government officeholders can enact them as law. In the process of negotiating this system, the intent and spirit of many good ideas are altered by moral struggles, ideological conflict, pragmatic issues, and political concerns. Students should learn about this process so that they do not feel marooned in inscrutable and hopeless disappointment, and may grasp and celebrate the stability and success of the system.

U.S. drug policies are subject to the same difficulties as other social policies. At this time in history, there is increasing evidence that some important social policies have failed and have created many additional problems, too. Drug problems, one by-product of these failures, cling tenaciously to the forefront of U.S. social concerns.

Furthermore, teachers should help students understand the linkages between drug policies and other social policies, particularly those that address tensions created by racial issues, social class, and economics. Such understanding addresses many risk factors associated with substance abuse.

# Substance Abuse Prevention in the Context of Distrust of Politicians and Antigovernment Attitudes

The goal of this chapter is to examine distrust of political leaders and government in order to accomplish the following:

1. Teachers can use the study of political events as a vehicle for substance abuse prevention.
2. Teachers can help their students examine issues of political integrity as these issues relate to drug use.
3. Teachers may understand the impact of political scandal on their role as agents of prevention.
4. Teachers who work in communities that are beset by corruption and scandal may help students find constructive responses to these disillusioning and depressing events.
5. Teachers can help children examine and cope with realizations that political leaders have human frailties just as do others.
6. Teachers may help students understand the processes through which political leaders become embroiled in scandal and recognize that community apathy is a contributing factor.

The history of U.S. social policy contains much to breed distrust, damage credibility, and destroy public confidence in policymakers. Consequently, the political scandal and government corruption that feed Americans' long-standing suspicions of politics and politicians force teachers into an awkward position with students. This is so because, somehow, teachers must acknowledge drug policies that often are tainted by the duplicity of community leaders who formulated and implemented them. Disappointing news about judges, prosecutors, police, and other agents of government only worsen these problems.

Also, juries' recent decisions in several highly publicized criminal cases have attracted negative attention, and further shaken trust in the judicial system, especially the following:

1. The initial acquittal of police who witnesses videotaped brutalizing Rodney King in 1991.
2. O.J. Simpson's criminal acquittal and subsequent civil liability in the 1994 murder of his former wife Nicole Brown and her friend Ron Goldman.
3. Lemrick Nelson's acquittal for the 1991 murder of Hassidic scholar Yankel Rosenbaum and subsequent conviction for violating Rosenbaum's civil rights.

In view of these disturbing events, Tom Wolfe (1987) was prophetic in his novel *Bonfire of the Vanities*. Wolfe satirized politicians, the business interests and behavior of the denizens of Wall Street, public policy, the judicial system, prosecutors, and the police in modern New York. He seems the parallel of Jonathan Swift whose 1725 writing of *Gulliver's Travels* mocked the same human failings of pride, avarice, and dishonesty in England during an earlier time. The degree to which human nature has changed in the 260 years that separates these writers is a question that teachers may pose to students.

The liabilities of human nature are particularly damaging when exposed in government leaders. These leaders not only serve the public trust, they develop huge personal followings, are idealized by young and old alike, and become role models and icons of the American dream (Wines, 1997). For leaders who achieve greatness or heroic images, their followings continue in perpetuity, and their words and actions embroider the tapestry of U.S. history and national pride.

According to ratings by historians (Schlesinger, 1996), George Washington, Thomas Jefferson, Andrew Jackson, and Abraham Lincoln, are prototypes of the great U.S. hero. Teddy Roosevelt, Woodrow Wilson, Franklin Delano Roosevelt, and Harry Truman are their more modern political descendants. All these national leaders left indelible impressions on the U.S. psyche and the ideals of the nation.

Therefore, teachers who address the problem of drug use must be sensitive to children's parental image of adult leaders and powerful wishes for them to be trustworthy. These wishes make visions of greatness seductive to young and old alike. Consequently, important leaders who topple from their pedestals do so with a crash that resounds beyond the personal consequences and dishonor they may suffer

(Patterson & Kim, 1994). The disillusioning impact of their fall from grace is experienced far and wide across the community, and can linger for years among the young and even into future generations of U.S. citizens (Kocieniewski, 1997).

Since Watergate, Americans have found the search for heroic statements and trustworthy heroes to express them to be disappointing. Consequently, social policies that oppose drug use and the fervor of policymakers' pronouncements acquire a hollow and hypocritical ring, especially to those who are at greatest risk. These policies' association with dishonored leaders diminishes their credibility and value.

After all, it was Richard Nixon who in 1973 started the current war on drugs. His criminal acts and forced resignation from the presidency shook the foundations of Americans' trust in their political system and brought shame to the nation. And later, Marion Barry, the Democratic mayor of Washington, DC, was reelected to office despite his arrest for smoking crack cocaine in 1990 and serving 6 months in prison for illegal drug possession.

Because the young need so much to find heroes who genuinely represent the best of U.S. ideals, their crumbling idols cause them to turn all too readily to antiheroes of popular culture. Antiheroes' negativity is made attractive by its simple honesty, and antiheroes themselves seem principled and unwilling to suffer stupidity and hypocrisy. However, as Sales (1996) described so vividly, the antiheroes' messages to the disillusioned advocate nihilism, hedonistic withdrawal, and rebellious self-indulgence. One may too easily pursue these values through drugs.

## HOW MAY TEACHERS ADDRESS DISAPPOINTMENTS WITH LEADERS?

Teachers must respond with caution to public disclosures of government corruption and political scandal. Furthermore, students must come to terms with the anger and disillusionment such events evoke. However, teachers must control their own righteous indignation so that they themselves do not model or advocate antisocial or dangerous behavior, or even appear to do so.

Instead, teachers must strive to counter the allure of the antihero and must offer themselves as replacement heroes to their students. In doing so they need not, and indeed usually cannot, rely on the glamor, drama, and wealth that some antiheroes and other prominent figures ride into the public's consciousness.

However, teachers can capitalize on daily face-to-face contact with children, and on trust they develop between themselves and these children. Teachers establish this trust by being competent, trustworthy, and affirming of their students' dignity.

To be viewed as competent by students, teachers must know their subject area; be skillful in manipulating the processes of teaching and learning; and be effective in creating and managing a positive learning environment. Knowledge of one's teaching subject and correlating issues about drug use to its content are particularly important to the classroom teacher's role in substance abuse prevention.

For students to accept a teacher as trustworthy and affirming of students' dignity and worth, teachers must be:

1. Stable and consistent in word and action.
2. Benevolent, and serve the best interests of students.
3. Flexible and adaptive to the dynamics of the classroom and the special needs of some students.
4. Reasonable and appropriate about the purpose and meaning of education.
5. Calm and thoughtful, especially during crises.

From this moral high ground, teachers can address tensions generated by the negative community events that assault their students. And, teachers can sensitize students to the ways in which community members express their disillusionment.

For example, the recent trend in which voters are deciding increasing numbers of policy issues in referendums rather than through government representatives is clear evidence of the growing loss of confidence in political leadership. The 1996 referendums that legalized medical use of marijuana and some other federally banned drugs in California and Arizona are relevant cases.

Another trend, directly related to the schools, is the increasing number of children whose parents have chosen to educate them at home rather than to send them to school. In 1970, 10,000 to 15,000 children were schooled at home, nationally. Present estimates of the number of U.S. children receiving home schooling range from 500,000 to 2.5 million (Roorbach, 1997). Although these figures represent less than 1% to possibly 3% of the 66 million school-age children in the United States, the rate of growth in home schooling since 1970 is striking.

Many parents who make this choice do not trust the schools. They feel that teachers cannot or will not respond to the special needs of their children, and are unable to protect children from the negative socialization of the peer group. These parents are fearful about violence, teen pregnancy, sexually transmitted disease, and the availability and use of illegal drugs in the schools. Furthermore, some parents argue that traditional education sorts children needlessly into winners and losers and permanently affixes loser status to those whose personal attributes do not fit the standard mold.

The accusations of abuse brought against former physical education teacher and Montana State Senator Casey Emerson certainly do not calm these fears, nor do they inspire confidence in the schools. At least 10 former students, who were 40 years old at the time they voiced their accusations, claimed that Emerson was brutally assaultive to students during his 18 years as a teacher and athletic coach at Bozeman Junior High School (Robbins, 1997). Emerson, a member of the Education Committee of the Montana State Senate, introduced legislation to restore corporal punishment, which was banned in Montana in 1991. Parents may find comfort in the fact that the Education Committee voted down the bill.

These trends and the fact that fewer than 50% of voters vote in most elections reflects the degree to which the American people have lost confidence. Americans' distrust of the people and systems on whom they have traditionally depended to guide community life is painful to observe. Increasingly, they see policymakers and their legal agents to be:

1. Unstable in their attitudes and position on important issues and inconsistent in their actions, as in the case of Bill Clinton and House Speaker Newt Gingrich.
2. Callous, indifferent, and withholding, as in the cases of Richard Nixon, Ronald Reagan, George Bush, and Robert Dole.
3. Punitive and vengeful, as in the instances of Senators Jesse Helms, Strom Thurmond, and Nixon's Vice President Spiro Agnew.
4. Rigid and unyielding, as was Lyndon Johnson in connection with the Vietnam War.
5. Clumsy or ineffectual, as in the case of Gerald Ford.
6. Superficial, inept, and poorly prepared, as in the cases of Dan Quayle and Supreme Court appointee Clarence Thomas.
7. Arrogant, unhealthy in outlook, and conniving, as in the cases of Richard Nixon and Newt Gingrich.
8. Lurching and inept during a seemingly endless series of domestic and foreign policy crises, as seemed Jimmy Carter.

The Watergate scandal and Richard Nixon's resignation from the U.S. presidency were the most serious of the many negative political events that occurred during the last quarter of the 20th century. Senator William Cohen of Maine, then Nixon's Republican party mate and more recently Secretary of Defense in Clinton's presidential cabinet, described Nixon's actions to have "allowed the rule of law and the constitution to slip under the boot of indifference and arrogance and abuse" (Clymer, 1996).

The misdeeds of the Nixon administration created problems of trust and credibility from which the U.S. political system has never recovered. Consequently, in the view of many Americans, the people who run the system, that is "all" the politicians, are crooks, thieves, and liars (Wines, 1997). President Clinton's impeachment and Senate trial has only served to strengthen these perceptions.

Speaker of the House of Representatives Newt Gingrich's congressional reprimand and $300,000 fine is yet another recent negative political event. This penalty was the most severe the House ever imposed on a member and is the only time in its 208-year history that the House of Representatives imposed a sanction against a speaker. Gingrich admitted to misuse of tax-exempt funds for partisan purposes and then lying to the House Ethics Committee inquiry (Clymer, 1996).

The conclusion and penalties are just a dramatic climax to many controversies that have surrounded Speaker Gingrich. Earlier, there were ethics concerns about his readiness to accept $4.5 million from HarperCollins Publishers as an advance on an unwritten book. Gingrich declined the cash advance after others in Congress protested that such a large sum violates House rules. These rules limit outside payments to members of Congress to usual and customary value of services. Earlier, Gingrich had attacked and contributed mightily to the resignation of former Democratic House Speaker Jim Wright for a book contract that earned Wright $55,000.

The book issue is further clouded because Rupert Murdoch has a controlling interest in HarperCollins. Murdoch, a U.S. citizen, controls the Australian media company that has controlling interest in six U.S. television stations of the Fox Network. Because federal law forbids foreign ownership of broadcast stations, Murdoch's company may lose control of Fox. This would happen if the Federal Communications Commission (FCC) rules that his Australian media company is a foreign interest. This agency is investigating the matter, but its dismantling was on Gingrich's political agenda.

As mentioned earlier, corruption and abuse of power by judges, prosecutors, and police continue to erode public confidence in the judicial system and law enforcement. Recently, criminal cases over which corrupt judges presided have made their way to the Supreme Court, even though the cases are unrelated to the corruption for which the judges were convicted (Greenhouse, 1997).

In and around Chicago, juries convicted 18 Cook County judges for corruption in the past 10 years. In late 1996, three Dupage County, Illinois, prosecutors and four sheriff's deputies were indicted for conspiracy, perjury, and obstruction of justice. Investigators accused them of fabricating evidence in the capital murder conviction of two

Hispanic men (Terry, 1996a). The two men were released after serving 3 years on death row.

Also, juries indicted seven Chicago police officers for a scheme to extort and steal money from drug dealers. The courts overturned 50 convictions in which the officers were involved and reviewed hundreds of others (Terry, 1996b). In one case, a 54-year-old grandmother spent 3 years in prison because police planted drugs in her house and lied about it in court. Nicholas Bissel, former prosecutor from Somerset County, New Jersey, fled his home and then killed himself to escape a prison sentence. A jury convicted him for corruption and fraud (Golden, 1996). Abuse of power in connection with drug suspects and threats to plant cocaine in the car of a business associate were among the charges for which Bissel had been sentenced to 10 years in prison. The courts have freed at least one person against whom Bissel had obtained a drug-dealing conviction and a life sentence (Hanley, 1996).

In Philadelphia, corrupt police work in the form of a bribe to a witness led to the overturning of a first-degree murder conviction, there ("Inmate set," 1997). Other cases in Philadelphia cost the city millions of dollars in out-of-court settlements.

In New York City, corruption scandal investigators first exposed in 1994 led to convictions of 33 police officers in just one precinct (Kocieniewski, 1997). Consequently, the courts dismissed 125 criminal cases and cleared 98 defendants. Unlawfully imprisoned individuals have filed at least 25 civil suits against the police department, and the city has paid $1.3 million in awards and settlements. This last figure may swell to more than $10 million because prosecutors have identified 2,000 cases in which corrupt officers' testimony may have tainted evidence.

Recently, corruption has even tarnished the earthy Smokey the Bear image of state police. In rural New York State, investigators found state troopers to have routinely planted false evidence in criminal cases (Perez-Pena, 1997). Troopers had fabricated evidence, usually by planting fingerprints, in 36 cases prosecuted between 1984 and 1992. Troopers may have tainted evidence in 10 other cases, as well.

All such events damage public confidence, but the actions of some leaders, although they themselves may be law abiding, just make things worse. For example, Ronald Reagan was loved by many, but his legacy further inflamed suspicion about politics and politicians.

Reagan had an abiding disdain for government, thought it to be worthless, and had no intention of bringing respect to it (Wills, 1996). The following occurred during Reagan's term as president:

1. The national debt tripled, incurring such a financial burden that the government became paralyzed. This severely compro-

mised government's capacity to sustain existing social programs and initiate new ones the nation may need.

2. The gap between the rich and poor widened precipitously as income of the bottom 10% of the population fell by 10.5% but increased by 24.4% for the top 10% from 1977 to 1987. Income for the top 1% grew by 74.2% during that time.

3. The government failed miserably in its role as a redistributor of wealth. The share of wealth controlled by the top 1% of U.S. families jumped from 22% in 1986 to 42% in 1992.

4. The federal Home Loan Bank Board neglected problems in the savings and loan industry until they became a debacle that cost taxpayers billions of dollars.

5. Oliver North's illegal actions created "Iran–Contra" and produced a constitutional crisis involving the executive branch's subversion of Congress's power to control spending.

6. Allegations were raised that the CIA was involved with cocaine smuggling and sales in the early 1980s. According to these allegations, the CIA did so to raise funds for the Nicaraguan Democratic Force, known as the "Contras," to destabilize the "Sandanista" government of Nicaragua.

7. Deborah Dean of the Department of Housing and Urban Development was convicted of 12 felony counts including accepting payoffs, fraud, and perjury.

8. Rita Lavel was convicted of perjury and obstruction of justice as a result of congressional inquiries into her abuse of office in the hazardous waste division of the Environmental Protection Agency.

9. Thorne Auchter, whose family construction firm had been cited for nearly 50 violations of safety rules, was made head of the Occupational Safety and Health Administration (OSHA). During that time, OSHA had to be forced by court action to perform its duties as mandated by law.

10. During Clarence Thomas' tenure as head of the Equal Employment Opportunity Commission, the commission was so unresponsive to cases of discrimination that the Senate considered investigating its inaction. George Bush later nominated Thomas to the U.S. Supreme Court in a continuation of Reagan's effort to stack the court with conservatives.

Reagan came into office promising to reduce government spending and the deficit, curtail government regulation, and shrink the federal government. Sadly for those who voted him in, he did not deregulate a single industry or eliminate any major government agency (Wills, 1996).

For some critics, the preceding list suggests that Reagan chose a strategy of neglect rather than legislative abolition to dismantle government machinery. The Iran–Contra debacle took the steam out of his second term in office and the media ridiculed Reagan as an absentee president (Darman, 1996a).

Americans, apparently, had enough of the Reagan legacy when they voted his successor and protégé George Bush out of office in 1992. They later denied the presidency to Robert Dole in 1996. The 1992 and 1996 presidential election winner, Bill Clinton, brought a new set of disappointments.

Although Americans seem to view Clinton as a kindly and affable fellow, many question his character, suspect him to be a scoundrel, resent his chameleonlike approach to vote getting, and are put off by his deference to political correctness. The fact that Clinton's wife presented herself as Hillary Clinton during the 1992 election campaign and as Hillary Rodham Clinton after the election caught the attention of many. News of Bill Clinton's extramarital sexual involvement with White House intern Monica Lewinsky was startling confirmation of the suspicions of many Americans.

With regard to drugs, Clinton did not help himself during the 1992 campaign when political adversaries challenged him about smoking marijuana as a university student. His statement that he tried it once, did not inhale, and never tried it again was laughable to many. People were more concerned about his honesty than about whether he may have tried marijuana 30 years previously.

Interestingly, the question of past drug use among politicians has become a sensitive issue because the children of the 1960s drug explosion have now matured into positions of power and influence. By the late 1970s, even famous radical activists of that time had joined the establishment (Darman, 1996a). Tom Hayden had been elected to public office in California and Eldridge Cleaver ran for the U.S. Senate as a Republican. Others had become successful business persons. When political candidates and potential government appointees are questioned about their youthful drug-taking behavior, they appear to walk a fine line between credibility and politically necessary contrition.

The 1990s have much less of the drug- and crime-related hysteria that plagued 1980s. Clinton put an end to drug testing of White House staff, and has reduced the size of the Office of National Drug Control Policy by 83%.

However, presidential candidate Robert Dole sought to re-energize the drug war with his 1996 campaign cry that drug use is the equivalent to moral terrorism. In making this claim, Dole connected the drug issue with the near panic associated with tragic events unrelated to drugs. By tying drugs to terrorism and morality to achieve a political advantage, Dole might have instigated even more futile, wasteful, and inhumane policies, had he become president.

Although Clinton joined the war on drugs, his administration did attempt to infuse rationality into the debate about national drug policy. In 1993, former Attorney General Joycelyn Elders suggested that drug legalization should be studied, and in 1996 Clinton proposed that tobacco should be regulated as a narcotic because of its addictive potential. Later, Elders resigned under criticism for her proposal that children be taught to masturbate as a strategy for preventing teenage pregnancy and the spread of AIDS.

Nevertheless, the Reagan legacy remains on the books in the form of the Anti-Drug Abuse Law of 1988. And, the aura of Nixon's Watergate is on Clinton's Whitewater. The following events that involved Clinton and his wife, Hillary, further heightened smoldering suspicion in connection with the Rose law firm and Whitewater:

1. Irregularities and missing records in the investigation of the death of Clinton advisor Vincent Foster.
2. Hillary Clinton's mysteriously vanished billing records that suddenly reappeared in the White House living quarters 2 years after they were subpoenaed.
3. The conviction of Arkansas Governor Jim Guy Tucker, James McDougal, and Susan McDougal in connection with the Whitewater land deals.

Attorney General Janet Reno's handling of Justice Department enforcement activities not only fanned suspicion, but inflamed anger and fear toward the government. The following events drew powerful public response:

1. The Bureau of Alcohol, Tobacco, and Firearms and the FBI's siege of the Branch Davidian's compound in Waco, Texas in 1993. This resulted in the death of 86 people, including 22 children.

2. The Ruby Ridge tragedy occurred just before Clinton won the 1992 presidential election and Janet Reno became attorney general. However, the killing by federal marshals of Idaho survivalist Randy Weaver's wife and son at Ruby Ridge set the stage for powerful reactions against the events at Waco, Texas.

Scandals about Clinton's personal life have raised still more questions about his character. Voters generally disregard issues raised about the personal lives of candidates for national office. Although the following accusations have little to do with Clinton's ability to govern, they still confront Americans with the specter of their most powerful leader marching on feet of clay:

1. Paula Jones' charges of sexual harassment and $700,000 civil suit.
2. Jennifer Flowers' claim that Clinton had an extramarital affair with her while he was governor of Arkansas.
3. By association in 1996, Clinton campaign advisor Richard Morris' involvement with a prostitute.
4. The scandal surrounding Clinton's admission that he had engaged in improper sexual behavior with White House intern Monica Lewinsky.

The following accusations, investigations, and dismissals of appointees for financial mismanagement and wrongdoing also have attracted negative attention:

1. The sudden firings of employees in the White House travel office.
2. Associate Attorney General Webster Hubbell resigned and was later convicted of various charges.
3. Agriculture Secretary Mike Espy was forced to resign.
4. Housing and Urban Development Secretary Henry Cisneros was forced to resign.
5. Energy Secretary Hazel O'Leary's possible misuse of expense account funds.

The list of disappointments and suspicious goings on seems without end. Nevertheless, teachers must emphasize to students that the system is not beyond repair and that many good people hold office. Teachers must emphasize also that intelligent and active participation in the community's political process is the one way in which citizens may positively influence the selection and actions of officeholders, even if just by going out to register and vote.

Teachers should warn students and further explore the proposal that apathy is the community's worst enemy. If necessary, teachers must badger students to prevent their withdrawn, depressive, and futile surrender to the liabilities of human nature. This is especially important when these liabilities are displayed in the politics of the community.

## HOW SHOULD TEACHERS RESPOND
## TO ANTIGOVERNMENT ATTITUDES?

Teachers must warn students that activism can take many forms, and some of these can be destructive, too. For example, the many disillusioning and costly disappointments have raised Americans' traditional suspicion of politics and politicians to seething contempt for government, itself (Wills, 1996). In the extreme, the militias, the Freemen, and the bombers of the federal building in Oklahoma City have emerged as ominous and frightening caricatures of the anger that many Americans feel about government.

Teachers are at the forefront of those who must act to defuse this explosive potential and redirect the angry energy behind it toward positive action. This is especially important because the destructive behavior of a few can spread quickly and easily among the peer group. When this occurs, there is great risk that extreme and dangerous behavior will become faddish and infuse broadly into youth culture. As is discussed in chapter 12, this was what occurred in the 1960s.

In this preventative effort, teachers should help students contemplate their own feelings about the general and specific concerns that underlie such outrage. And, teachers must help students develop skills and insights to use their fears and anger as sources of energy for constructive exploration and action.

For example, among those who are fearful and angry, approximately 40% of Americans harbor antigovernment anger and believe that "the federal government has become so large and powerful that it poses an immediate threat to the rights and freedoms of ordinary citizens" (Bovard, 1995). People holding this belief fear that they have become imprisoned in bureaucratic regulation and deprived of the right to due process. They see their entitlements and property to be in jeopardy. They feel helpless to pursue justly deserved damages incurred by inept, inefficient, and irresponsible government agents.

However, this general belief is based on a variety of specific concerns, each of which is amenable to study, dialogue, and contemplation in the classroom. One specific concern is about civil rights policies. Although the United States has its fair share of bigots, most Americans support the notion of equal opportunity.

The courts, the political branches of government, and the public approve of the idea that all people must have an equal opportunity to participate and succeed on the basis of merit. Although they are less accepting of gay men and lesbians, mainstream Americans are tolerant of almost everyone, including working mothers, racial minorities, religious minorities, and cultural minorities (Wolfe, 1998). They believe that people have the right to seek the benefits of U.S. community life without hindrance because of race, sex, religion, or other protected status. Participation by racial and ethnic minorities, and other protected groups in mainstream U.S. life has improved dramatically since the 1960s.

Policies such as school busing and affirmative action that go beyond merely forbidding discrimination are causes of great bitterness. Those who are most dissatisfied argue the following:

1. Such policies are forms of reverse discrimination against members of nonprotected groups.
2. They further argue that the value of "merit" is being lost in a system of quotas, set-asides, timetables, political correctness, and other preferential treatment.

Those who support these policies claim the following:

1. Lack of success by members of protected groups is evidence of continuing lack of equal opportunity, and not indication of a lack of merit.
2. Lack of success is indicative of subtle and pervasive forms of bias that cannot be easily eliminated.
3. Past injustice suffered by members of protected groups has handicapped them so that mere elimination of barriers does not assure equal opportunity.

Possibly the greatest anger is about abuse of the system, heavy-handed regulation, and unfair enforcement of civil rights laws. In any group, there will be those who attempt to exploit their benefits beyond the limits of reason. However, opportunism and frivolous claims of discrimination or sexual harassment are serious concerns for people who may be the targets of such actions. Anger and fear associated with these charges are only amplified when there is distrust in those who are responsible for evaluating them.

And, some government bureaucrats have exaggerated views of the purpose and meaning of their position. One issue that has drawn negative attention is the manner in which the federal Housing and Urban Development Department is subsidizing welfare recipients' movement into middle- and upper-class housing. The complaint is that welfare recipients are now enjoying better housing than can be afforded by working people. Undoubtedly, these problems contribute to racial fears and hostility and the deteriorating faith in the system that continue to plague U.S. community life.

Another serious issue is the unbridled use and abuse of police power. This includes brutality, no-knock raids, police confiscation and forfeiture of personal property and assets, use of drunk-driving checkpoints to screen for other law violations, and entrapment through sting operations. Dishonest police who plant false evidence such as weapons and drugs, and offer perjured court testimony to secure convictions and improve performance records are a serious problem. Many of these frightening exercises of police power occur in connection with drug enforcement activities.

Still another concern is environmental regulation. These regulations permit government agencies to suspend private property rights in order to protect wildlife, historic landmarks, and wetlands. Zoning laws permit similar intrusion for other reasons. Furthermore, the Environmental Protection Agency claims the right to extract the entire cost of cleaning a waste site from any single contributor of waste, no matter how minimal that contribution.

A source of fear and anger that has very direct impact on teachers is government intrusion into family privacy, and the exploitation of children against their parents in the enforcement of drug and other laws. Although teachers are mandated reporters, frivolous or patently false allegations of child abuse have become very real threats to parents, teachers, and child-care workers.

The child protection system appears to be biased toward confirming reports of abuse rather than seeking truth. As a result, the courts have sentenced innocent adults to long prison terms solely on the basis of unsubstantiated testimony of 3- and 4-year-old children. Often these children have been harassed and badgered by zealous child protection workers (Ceci & Bruck, 1995). The courts are overturning many such convictions, but after irreparable damage, and great pain and expense to the accused.

Similarly, some police officers who provide service in the broadly disseminated DARE program in the schools follow up inadvertent or indiscreet comments by children (Bovard, 1995). This has led to police raids of children's homes, arrests of parents, and serious family disruption.

One more issue about which there is anger is the Food and Drug Administration's (FDA) increasingly aggressive intrusion into health care. Those problems about which there is strongest reaction are as follows:

1. Delays and inefficiency associated with approval of new medicines and drugs.
2. Regulatory ambiguity and prohibition of health-related devices.

3. Suppression of information about and use of medications and devices for purposes other than those for which they were originally tested.
4. Efforts to control the dietary supplement industry and to suppress advertisements claiming health benefits.

Similar disaffection is apparent about the Drug Enforcement Administration's (DEA) refusal to permit medical use of marijuana for treatment of AIDS, cancer chemotherapy side effects, and glaucoma. Despite the results of the California and Arizona referendums, the DEA reports that it will suspend the license of any physician in these states who prescribes marijuana for medical treatment.

The contempt and rage with which Americans regard their representatives who formulate policy extends all too easily to the agents who implement policy. This means that the public is poised to direct its distrust and anger at police departments, government health agencies, and public school systems. Within the context of drug policy, teachers are very prominent agents, second only to law enforcement personnel.

However, teachers are also at the forefront of those who must turn back the despair and social withdrawal that such destructive beliefs and attitudes portend. Adults and children may all too easily throw up their hands in futile resignation as the foibles of leaders, policymakers, and other public figures are exposed in the media. Such resignation can contribute to many forms of destructive behavior, including substance abuse.

## SUMMARY OF KEY POINTS

Political scandal and corruption in the community are important to teachers committed to substance abuse prevention. Although some of the words and actions of young people seem frivolous and superficial, teachers should not assume that students are oblivious or indifferent to such events. Clearly, the behavior of politicians, judges, prosecutors, police, and other public servants can be disappointing, traumatic, and disillusioning for adults and young people.

Therefore, it is important for teachers to help students examine such events as a means to prevent angry, antisocial, and self-destructive reactions, including drug abuse. This is important when children witness the dangerous and extreme reactions of some adult groups.

Teachers must help children understand that most politicians and other agents of government are sincere and honest. This is especially necessary when widely publicized misdeeds create the appearance that most, if not all, politicians are rotten apples.

Furthermore, teachers must help students recognize that apathy and withdrawal are tantamount to surrender. And, that vigilance and active involvement in the mainstream of community life are viable alternatives to antisocial behavior or self-destructive passivity. This is a confirmatory strategy for substance abuse prevention.

# 10

# Substance Abuse Prevention in the Context of Drug Policy

The goal of this chapter is to describe U.S. drug policy so that the following can be accomplished:

1. Teachers can use the study of drug policy as a vehicle for substance abuse prevention.
2. Teachers can help students examine family values as they relate to the history of U.S. drug policy.
3. Teachers understand the mix of social attitudes that have shaped U.S. drug policies.
4. Teachers can help students examine the conflicts that exist between cherished freedoms, social values, and drug policies.
5. Teachers can help students explore the relation between social class, race, gender, age, and drug policy.
6. Teachers can help students examine the positive and negative outcomes of U.S. drug policy.
7. Teachers can help students examine the problems and side effects produced by drug policy.
8. Teachers will be sensitive to the complicating effects of drug policy failures on their role as agents of prevention.
9. Teachers can assist students in a meaningful examination of alternative policies that might better manage problems associated with drug use.

For the first 100 years of the nation, Americans made drugs a part of life inside and outside the family. People commonly used alcohol, opiates, cannabis, and cocaine for recreational and medicinal purposes and obtained them with and without a doctor's prescription. Also, many unlabeled over-the-counter remedies and some popular beverages contained these drugs.

By the end of that first 100 years, increasing numbers of Whites smoked opium and southern Blacks and other oppressed groups made cocaine their drug of choice. The total absence of drug laws during this period expressed Americans' laissez-faire attitude toward drug use. Consequently, most people had some exposure to drugs when the United States entered the 20th century (Courtwright, Joseph, & De Jarlais, 1989; Kandall, 1996; Musto, 1987).

Then, social, political, and economic pressures to control drug use began to grow. In response, federal, state, and local legislators started to enact the laws and government bureaucrats began to develop the regulations that now govern drug use in the United States. Also, ordinary people passed drug laws as they did in Arizona and California where voters legalized medical use of marijuana in 1996.

In these ways, U.S. communities continue to create and revise the policies that define their ever-changing responses to drugs. These responses include prohibition, taxation, licensing, research, education, propaganda, and other actions.

Teachers and students can examine the obvious and practical issues that underlie drug policies by seeking answers to questions Democratic Congressman Charles Rangel asked in a *Washington Post* article (1988). Rangel's questions, which are particularly germane to dangerous, mind-altering substances that attract recreational users, included:

1. Which psychotropic drugs should be legalized, and which should be banned?
2. How should communities make decisions about drug laws and what criteria should they use in deciding about which drugs to tolerate and which to forbid?
3. Who should have access to psychotropic drugs? Anyone? Adults? People for whom the drugs serve medical purposes? Addicts?
4. Would limits be imposed on supplies?
5. Would the heavily addicted become a public burden, either because their addiction has incapacitated them, or because they may resort to crime to obtain the necessities of living or drugs?
6. Who should provide drugs? Private industry? The government?
7. Where would drugs be available? Pharmacies? Special shops? Clinics? Supermarkets? Mail order houses?

**8.** How would drugs be paid for? Would drugs be provided at cost or for profit? Should drugs be taxed and at what rate?

**9.** What limits would be imposed on drug use in safety-sensitive occupations, and private activities, such as operating an automobile?

**10.** What are the health consequences of drug use? What costs will these consequences add to health insurance rates? What additional financial burdens will drug use impose on the health care system?

Teachers should be aware that policymakers have always provided confusing and ambiguous answers to these questions, even though they have written drug laws that are increasingly restrictive. In part, this is so because lawmakers ignore many realities of drug use, and U.S. mores vacillate between periods of greater and lesser tolerance of drugs.

## HOW HAS U.S. DRUG POLICY EVOLVED?

Teachers and students who examine its history will discover that drug policy is linked with many enduring social problems beyond those posed by drug use. For example, unholy alliances of prohibition-minded reformers, politicians, and members of dominant social classes unduly influenced drug policy. These alliances helped wealthy and powerful members of society to use drug laws and the police to maintain social and economic control. As a result, drug policies are rarely independent of social, political, and economic pressures that haunted policymakers of earlier eras.

This has not changed, and has shaped drug policy so that it invariably has a disproportionately negative impact on society's least powerful and most vulnerable members. In America, these have been racial minorities, marginalized ethnic groups, the poor, immigrants, women, and children.

Although policymakers argue that drugs are a public health problem and a threat to a safe and orderly community, drug policies really attend to moral, political, and social issues. Consequently, teachers must struggle to answer students who ask why supposedly health- and safety-conscious lawmakers do not ban alcohol and tobacco, the most dangerous and addictive drugs of all. The fact that alcohol and tobacco are legal complicates the answer to this simple question because these drugs cause more casualties each year than have all other drugs combined for the whole 20th century.

## HOW HAVE FAMILY VALUES
## INFLUENCED U.S. DRUG POLICY?

Conservative politicians made family values a modern issue during the Reagan and Bush years in the White House. As a result, political concern about family values seems to be a recent development, and associated with the cocaine panic of the 1980s.

However, preservation of the Puritan and Victorian ideals of the family has been at the heart of U.S. drug policy debate since the late 1800s. Policymakers argued then and they argue now that a major goal of drug policy is to preserve the family as a secure haven in which to rear children. They rarely acknowledge that the family has important social meaning beyond its child rearing function. Historical evidence indicates that family wealth and social influence are meanings to which U.S. drug policy has been most responsive.

Teachers and students can examine the intimate connection between drugs and these broader meanings of family life. For example, during the late 1800s, the pharmaceutical industry and the medical profession exploited Victorian social definitions of females as the needier, weaker, and more vulnerable members of U.S. families (Kandall, 1996). The industry targeted women for advertising and endorsements, and uninformed or unscrupulous physicians enthusiastically prescribed addictive drugs to control female symptoms and complaints. No doubt, there was profit to be made from sufferings of wives and mothers whose husbands could pay for their spouses' drugged subservience.

Consequently, by the end of the 1800s, married middle- and upper class White women comprised the largest group of addicts in America. U.S. culture made this possible by identifying female symptoms and complaints with rigidly stereotyped views of femininity, despite protests by early feminists.

Clearly, maternity and childrearing were too important to the economy for society to permit women to pursue their own inclinations and pleasures. Prior to passage of restrictive drug laws and for some time after, communities even pushed unmarried women into child-care roles as schoolteachers and librarians. Women who found other employment could do so only at the smallest wage and lowest level of skill. Community members stigmatized successful single women of good reputation as sad, unfulfilled, and social failures, to some degree. The term *spinster* had many negative connotations, but now has passed into disuse.

Thus, U.S. laws, customs, and religious doctrine exacted numerous duties and responsibilities from women, provided few if any rights, and entrapped women in marriage and the home. U.S. communities just had too many reasons to fear unbridled expression of female sexuality.

Victorian morality controlled female sexuality by keeping women chaste during the bloom of youth and then hidden in the monogamous fidelity of marriage. Furthermore, 19th-century U.S. communities pressed women to be guardians of this morality at home and in the community. Respectable ladies attended Sunday church services and occasionally joined in volunteer activities with other decent women. A woman's place was in the home with her Bible, and then the onrush of the Industrial Revolution made a wife's idleness a status symbol for her husband.

Such pressures enforced women's roles in childrearing, protected paternity and lineage, and sustained the cherished value of family privacy. Most important to the status quo, men of means ensured their influential position in the community, power as lords over the home that was their castle, and retained possession of the living, breathing chattel who resided there.

Communities limited women's freedom in other ways, too. Women had no property rights and their earnings became the property of their husbands, as were the women themselves. Even the welfare system, to some degree, forced women into the Victorian mold of respectability. According to Mezey (1996), state governments often imposed eligibility criteria that denied public assistance to women on the basis of impropriety. Women were denied benefits for working outside the home, having illegitimate children, and in some states, failing to keep a tidy household.

What is more, communities authorized public officials to inspect homes and make judgements about the character of welfare recipients (Giovannoni & Becerra, 1979). Black, Hispanic, and Native American women were excluded from state-provided Mother's Pensions on racial grounds.

Also, U.S. women did not have the right to vote until passage of the Nineteenth Amendment to the Constitution in 1920. This occurred more than 70 years after the Seneca Falls Convention of 1848, at which women began to demand enfranchisement. Elizabeth Cady Stanton, who organized the convention, and Susan B. Anthony, were among the first U.S. feminists prominently involved with women's suffrage.

The town of Seneca Falls, New York, where Stanton and other suffragists held the convention, was in the midst of its own transformation from an agrarian frontier village into an industrial boomtown. This community had begun exploiting its abundance of water power to nourish its burgeoning industry. No doubt, economic change was beginning to drive social change, and the old was giving way to the new at the time of the convention.

Class and race issues divided this movement, even though its leaders were vocal abolitionists vehemently opposed to southern slavery. In 1869, Anthony, Stanton, and others refused to endorse the proposed Fifteenth Amendment, which gave the vote to Black men because it did not also give the vote to women.

Some of the resentment this issue generated during those times still exists. In 1997, the National Congress of Black Women (NCBW) protested about a marble statue honoring Susan B. Anthony, Elizabeth Cady Stanton, and suffragist Lucretia Mott because it did not honor Sojourner Truth, a Black contributor to the cause ("A Black group," 1997). The National Women's Party commissioned the statue, named "The Portrait," and presented it to Congress in 1921. The NCBW opposes its display in the Capitol Rotunda.

Nevertheless, the Seneca Falls Convention revealed that many women found the poor fit between human nature and the corsets, bustles, and girdles of the Victorian feminine role to be too painful. Teachers and students can examine and debate the possibility that drugs became another means to keep these women docile, compliant, and quietly at home.

Some women who used drugs to cope with confinement and vacuousness in their own lives used the same drugs to cope with distressing aspects of pregnancy and childrearing. These women used these drugs to treat childhood illness, but some women used them to quiet crying babies, to calm agitated children, and to slow active youngsters (Kandall, 1996). Mothers, ignorant of unlabeled contents, gave children opiates and cannabis in soothing syrups, paregoric, and laudanum; all sold over the counter. Perhaps some women sought only occasional relief from the onerous responsibilities of motherhood, but others too often refused to subordinate their own needs to those of their children.

Some mothers, whose heavy-drinking spouses were cruel and violent, thought their acts to be a kindly alternative to harsh abuse of their children. This was an age when beliefs that "He who spares the rod hates his son," "Children should be seen and not heard," and "To spare the rod is to spoil the child" justified such assaults on children by drunken husbands.

Teachers and students may explore the origins of these harsh childrearing attitudes, to which some Protestant Christians of the U.S. mainstream adhered. Advocacy of physical punishment appears in Old Testament sayings attributable to King Solomon. However, such punishment is distinctly un-Christian and contradicts New Testament teachings that forbid harsh treatment and abuse of children (Milburn & Conrad, 1996).

In fact, the adage "Spare the rod and spoil the child" does not have biblical origins. It comes instead from a poem written in 1664 by satirist Samuel Butler. The broad literal acceptance of Butler's words indicates that many people missed the humor and sarcasm of his poetry.

Also, this was an era when U.S. communities were just beginning to wake up to the problem of child abuse, although they ignored it for another 100 years. Child protection threatens family privacy, which was, and remains, a cherished value of U.S. communities. This value protects people's right to marry whom they please and bring up their own children, and ensures children's right to live with their own family.

Agents of the community usually must remove neglected or abused children from their family in order to protect them. This, in turn, imposes the expense and inconvenience of childrearing on the community, and subjects children to a troubled foster care system.

The 1874 case of Mary Ellen Wilson exposed the shameful truth that no community agencies existed to protect and advocate for the welfare of children. Mary Ellen had been abandoned by her mother, and a neighborhood church case worker found that her foster parents had beaten and starved her, and chained her to a bed.

The case worker's own efforts to protect Mary Ellen were fruitless so she appealed to Henry Bergh, founder of The American Society for the Prevention of Cruelty to Animals. Bergh got a hearing in New York Supreme Court. The court ordered Mary Ellen removed from her foster parents.

Mary Ellen recovered from her experience, became a successful mother, and lived to the age of 92 (Oates, 1996). What is more important, Bergh and Attorney Elbridge Gerry went on to found the New York Society for the Prevention of Cruelty to Children, the first organization in the United States to promote children's rights, and a model for others that followed.

Clearly, communities used children, drugs, morality, social recrimination, economic pressure, and other assorted mechanisms to keep women firmly in their place. That is, to keep women away from the raucousness of business, politics, the marketplace, and especially the sexual temptations of the world of men.

Therefore, until World War II, when women went to work in factories of the "Arsenal of Democracy," U.S. communities confined most women of good social standing to their place as homemakers and mothers, in marriage. World War II shook the world and was a turning point in the emancipation of U.S. women.

"Rosie the Riveter" symbolized this emancipation. Rose Will Monroe became the real life Rosie of the popular World War II song "Rosie the

Riveter." Hollywood actor Walter Pidgeon discovered her working as a riveter when he filmed an advertisement for war bonds in an aircraft plant. From that point on, Rose Will Monroe was in the movie business and became a metaphor for the dignity, strength, and patriotism of working women.

After the war, Rosie continued to work as a cab driver, beautician, and as the founder of a home construction business she named Rose Builders. She also learned to fly and in 1978 was seriously injured in a flying accident. Herself widowed for 50 years, she died at age 77 on May 31, 1997, leaving 2 daughters, 9 grandchildren, and 13 great-grandchildren.

The plight of women and children in U.S. families during those times demonstrates an important point about the evolution of U.S. drug policy. This point, as Kandall (1996) observed, is that U.S. communities quietly tolerate drug use as long as drugs serve useful purposes among accepted social classes. Such may be the answer to students' nagging question about the legal status of alcohol and tobacco.

## WHAT SOCIAL ATTITUDES UNDERLIE U.S. DRUG POLICIES?

U.S. tolerance of drug use lessened dramatically when members of marginal groups sought social and economic change to better themselves. Interestingly, drug hysteria helped those who wanted to strengthen repressive controls on upstart minority groups after the Civil War and did so again after civil rights victories of the 1960s.

After the Civil War, the public's sympathetic image of respectable wives and mothers sadly victimized by their medically prescribed laudanum gradually eroded. Communities recast the stereotype of the addict as an innocent and harmless female drug habitue into a sinister drug fiend who was poor, urban, male, a member of a feared or despised minority group, and a criminal. Furthermore, society redefined addiction from a pathetic iatrogenic illness to a self-inflicted, immoral, and stigmatized condition (Courtwright, Joseph, & De Jarlais, 1989).

Then, national tolerance of drug use and denial of drug problems became strained. Prejudice against Blacks, Chinese, Mexicans, immigrants, and White poor fueled disdain for drug users. As U.S. communities more closely identified drug use with these groups, prohibition and increasingly harsh measures to enforce prohibition followed soon after.

This happened in part because of sensationalized news reporting about women. As America entered the 20th century, print media portrayed White women to be targets of drug-toting men of color and as sexual victims who were vulnerable to marauding drug-crazed men from racial and ethnic minorities. The government promulgated rumors (Kandall, 1996) that these men prowled parks, movie theaters, and dance halls armed with drugs and hypodermic needles. The film industry of the silent era capitalized on Americans' fear and fascination with these possibilities by producing more than 200 movies featuring drug addicts, peddlers, and smugglers.

Panic spread that these villains used drugs to ensnare and make prostitutes of innocent White women. In this way, the government, dramatic exaggerations by the press, and the film industry propagated a terrifying myth that Black, Chinese, and other dark-skinned men threatened White women with "violence, seduction, rape, and enslavement" (Kandall, 1996, p. 73). Consequently, fears of a drug-fueled "white slave trade" led federal lawmakers to pass the Mann Act of 1910, which prohibited interstate transportation of women and girls for immoral purposes.

During the 1980s cocaine panic, the media generated hysteria about minority women. However, this time reporters painted the women as the villains. Sensational news stories propagated a terrifying myth of an epidemic of cocaine-damaged babies. These babies had been produced by mothers who used crack cocaine during pregnancy. People saw crack users and crack babies in press photos and on television screens, and almost all the images were of Black or Hispanic women who were poor, single parents, and inner-city ghetto dwellers.

Teachers and students who examine events such as these will find that the dramatic intrusion of Americans' social attitudes into drug policies is not surprising. History indicates that American attitudes toward drug use have been ambivalent since colonial times, even though drug policy was laissez-faire (Resnik, 1990).

For example, American colonists used opium for its narcotic effects and to treat a variety of gastrointestinal ailments, as did the colonial militias during the American Revolution (Kandall, 1996). Colonists made opium available in medical prescriptions, in laudanum, which contained alcohol, and black drop, which contained no alcohol (Musto, 1987).

At the same time, colonists regaled its habitual use as producing tremors, paralysis, emaciation, and stupidity. Recreational drug use was tinged with immorality and users most often hid these activities from public scrutiny. Never did the act of taking a drug approach the boisterous displays of drinking in colonial taverns, saloons of pioneering communities, and modern American bars and nightclubs. Despite fears and moral reservations, communities quietly integrated drug and alcohol production and use into the larger economy for profit and utility.

However, the Puritans enshrined the community as a repository of morality (Gitlin, 1990). This is important because Americans historically have viewed drug use to be primarily a moral issue, and continue to do so now (Patterson & Kim, 1994). Thus, U.S. social attitudes had sown the seeds of a protracted conflict long before restrictive policies became the law of the land.

In this conflict, reformers argued their position from the seemingly benevolent perspective of public health and continue to do so. However, the negative social and health consequences of nonmedical drug use were never sufficient to prompt the level of criminalization that eventually occurred (Courtwright, Joseph, & Des Jarlais, 1989). Even the medical use of marijuana is framed as a public health dilemma (Wren, 1997a) though no one in America is known to ever have died from medicinal or recreational marijuana use.

Clearly, practical utility and the profit motive are strong incentives for drug use and sales. But, drugs' juxtaposition to powerful moral and social concerns raises interesting questions about U.S. social attitudes as they are expressed in drug policy.

For example, stringent federal controls on the use of methadone, an effective treatment for heroin addiction, have made it far more difficult and costly for addicts to obtain than heroin (Wren, 1997b). Despite methadone's known effectiveness, it is so stigmatized by its association with illicit drugs and false rumors that its greatest success stories go untold (Wren, 1997f).

Worse yet, policymakers such as New York City Mayor Rudolf Giuliani energetically resist its use in drug treatment (Massing, 1998). Giuliani described methadone as "a chemical that's used to enslave people" despite strong evidence that methadone works. It reduces addicts' craving for heroin, thus enabling them to restore normalcy to their lives, return to work, reduce the risk of contracting and spreading AIDS, and stop criminal behavior. Nevertheless, eight states including Idaho, Mississippi, Montana, North Dakota, South Dakota, West Virginia, Vermont, and New Hampshire refuse to permit methadone clinics within their borders.

Similarly, communities remain resistant to needle exchange programs since public health advocates proposed them as a prevention strategy for AIDS and hepatitis B. This resistance continues despite evidence indicating that needle exchange programs can yield a 30% decrease in new infections and are not associated with increases in drug use ("Drug and," 1997). As of March 1997, the U.S. had just 100 needle exchange programs, as compared to 2,000 in Australia, which has one tenth the U.S. population.

The 1996 referendums in California and Arizona pushed these social attitudes to the forefront by making marijuana legal for medical purposes in those states. Proponents argue that marijuana is useful in treating the following illnesses:

1. **Glaucoma:** a progressive condition that causes blindness due to increased pressure, inside the eyeball. Smoked marijuana reduces this pressure but may also reduce blood flow to the optic nerve, worsening vision.
2. **AIDS:** AIDS causes loss of appetite, loss of muscle tissue, and other wasting. Proponents argue that marijuana improves appetite.
3. **Epilepsy and multiple sclerosis:** Supposedly, marijuana reduces muscle spasms, urinary and digestive incontinence, and emotional depression.
4. **Cancer:** Proponents claim that marijuana relieves nausea and vomiting caused by chemotherapy.

Furthermore, Arizona's initiative rejects punishment for people who are first- and second-time offenders of drug possession laws. The new law requires that the courts sentence these individuals to probation and mandatory drug treatment (Golden, 1997). Connecticut's State Legislature is considering a similar change and an overhaul of its drug laws that would emphasize treatment instead of punishment, too (Wren, 1997d).

In a slightly different vein, opinion polls of residents of Vermont ("Vermon survey," 1997) reveal that they, too, favor legalizing production of hemp, the plant from which marijuana is derived. Hemp fibers are commercially useful in fabrics and cordage, although the plant's psychoactive agent is found in its leaves and buds.

Accordingly, teachers and their students can debate and contemplate the following questions as significant social issues:

1. Will national policymakers legalize marijuana because of its harmlessness relative to legal drugs such as alcohol and tobacco?
2. Will they do so because marijuana may be America's largest cash crop, is valued at more than $10 billion (Pollan, 1995), and currently is untaxed?
3. Is the campaign to legalize marijuana for medical use really part of a strategy to legalize its recreational use? Or, does it have value as a medicine?
4. Do present federal restrictions on marijuana represent nothing more than a translation of morality into law?

The federal government gave this dilemma new prominence because officials promised reprisals against physicians and others who violate federal controls that conflict with the new California and Arizona laws. The Department of Justice vows to revoke the prescription licenses of physicians who prescribe or recommend marijuana to their patients, and the Internal Revenue Service has declared the costs of medicinal marijuana not to be a tax-deductible medical expense (Rosenbaum, 1997).

The DEA has already begun to harass and intimidate some California physicians ("A doctor," 1997). And, in accordance with federal law requiring random drug testing, transportation workers in California and Arizona who use marijuana for medicinal purposes are still subject to dismissal (Janofsky, 1997).

However, in early 1997, the federal government set aside $1 million in federal funds to study marijuana's medical uses. General Barry McCaffrey, head of the White House Office of National Drug Control Policy for the Clinton administration, oversaw these funds. But, proponents of medical use saw McCaffrey to be closed-minded and untrustworthy. Steve Michael, a spokesman for an AIDS advocacy and protest group, claimed that "Putting McCaffrey in charge of this research is like putting Nixon in charge of the Watergate files" ("Government to," 1997). Surely, the resolution to this two-headed national dilemma of practicality and money versus morals and politics will be an important statement about the character of U.S. drug policy.

## WHAT SOCIAL VALUES CONFLICT
## WITH U.S. DRUG POLICIES?

U.S. leaders gave these and other problems serious meaning when they instituted the first major national drug policy initiatives early in the 20th century. The new laws were the Pure Food and Drug Act of 1906 and the Harrison Act of 1914. The first required manufacturers to list narcotic substances on labels of patent medicines that contain opiates, cocaine, and cannabis, and the Harrison Act prohibited use of narcotics without a medical prescription.

In the 1920s, the U.S. Supreme Court ruled that doctors' prescriptions for narcotics to maintain addicts violated the Harrison Act. Consequently, 30,000 physicians were arrested for dispensing drugs and 3,000 served prison sentences during those times.

The current war on drugs, started by Richard Nixon during his presidency (Musto, 1987), seeks to impose the consistency and stability of action that policymakers deemed necessary to effective prohibition. Efforts by Nixon and other national leaders to mobilize consistent response across all segments of the community have made drug policy increasingly punitive. However, these efforts to impose a homogeneous response on a heterogeneous society run afoul of many cultural ambiguities, and collide with important issues of personal freedom.

Consequently, critics claim that U.S. drug policy falls tragically short of important social values. These critics are diverse in background and perspective, and include Nobel Prize-winning economist Milton Friedman, Nobel Peace and Chemistry Prize winner Linus Pauling, former Baltimore Mayor and Rhodes Scholar Kurt Schmoke, and psychiatrist Thomas Szasz. Teachers may read and refer their students to Evans and Berent (1992), whose edited volume presents these and other informed observers' observations of U.S. drug policy as well as the views of many who support current policy.

Billionaire financier and philanthropist George Soros concurs with the critics, and has put his money where his mouth is. Since 1994, he has committed $15 million of his own funds to U.S. drug research programs. He contributed another $1 million in support of the successful 1996 California and Arizona ballot initiatives to legalize medical marijuana.

Soros, who was born in Hungary, survived both the Nazis and the communists and has firsthand experience with tyranny. According to Soros, U.S. policymakers are in blind denial that the war on drugs is doing more harm than the drugs themselves (Fineman, 1997). He also supports critics' claims that U.S. drug laws are only succeeding to fill the prisons with nonviolent drug users, and are sustaining the criminal underground who profit from the drug trade.

Moreover, if the two-to-one vote for passage of the provisions of the 1996 Arizona referendum is representative, the general public is unhappy with government drug controls, too. Arizona is one of the most politically conservative states in the nation, but its citizens voted to pass one of the nation's most liberal state drug laws (Golden, 1997).

Members of the U.S. literary community express most eloquently the concerns many people have about U.S. drug policy. Some did so from the perspective of their own life experience. For example, Claude Brown, African American author of the autobiographical novel, *Manchild in the Promised Land* (1965), and later, *The Children of Ham* (1976) candidly described the grim living conditions of the Black ghetto of his childhood. For teachers and students, these writings provide insight into conditions that place children at risk of drug use, and are worthy of study for their literary value.

According to Brown (1989), U.S. social history reveals much about the moral corruption and hypocrisy of American legislators' and administrative policymakers' responses to drug use. Brown concluded that practically all antidrug laws and administrative decrees have been rooted in prejudice and emerged from a successful campaign to promote public hysteria. Therefore, agreed medical historian David Musto (1987), actions and regulative decisions against drug abuse lack any true regard for the realities of drug use.

So, too, claimed William S. Burroughs, whose novel *Naked Lunch* (1959), a compilation of sketches about various forms of addiction, brought him fame and a landmark anticensorship ruling by the 1962 U.S. Supreme court (Shattuck, 1996). Burroughs, who died in 1997 at age 83, and himself a former morphine addict, long advocated drug legalization and argued that prohibition has generated a vast and troublesome criminal underground of pushers, wholesalers, and money launderers. In Burroughs' view, drug prohibition has wasted billions of dollars and is a transparent, but successful, pretext to create a police state.

Cooper (1996) provided some evidence supporting Burroughs', Soros' and others' concerns that U.S. drug policies are turning the United States into a police state. He reported that "quality of life" arrests in New York City rose by 21% to nearly 250,000 during 1996. Writing on this same issue just 9 months later, Purdy (1997) wrote that arrests jumped to 345,000. This is equivalent to more than 3% of the city's population. Police arrest people for sleeping on park benches and urinating in public places, but they also apprehend people for drinking alcoholic beverages in public, smoking marijuana, and possession of small quantities of illegal drugs.

In these cases, police seize legally obtained prescription drugs, and there is no way for arrested persons to get needed medication without a trip to the hospital. Although police and the courts have recently speeded up the arraignment process, those arrested may spend from 20 to 60 hours in confinement for minor, nonviolent offenses, many of which are for violation of drug laws (Cooper, 1996; Purdy, 1997).

These observations suggest, as Musto (1987) stated, that U.S. concern about narcotics may be most meaningfully viewed as a political problem rather than a medical or legal issue. As in all political struggles, adversaries exaggerate the scope and consequences of a problem to influence the political process. This has long been and continues to be so for claims about the dangers of drug use and the numbers of drug users (Wren, 1997e).

## HOW HAS SOCIAL PREJUDICE
## INFLUENCED U.S. DRUG POLICY?

Issues of social class, race, generational tensions, and to a lesser degree, the attraction and consequences of some drugs have driven drug control and prohibition. Consequently, support for drug prohibition has been associated with passion and fear about a given drug's effect on a specific minority group (Musto, 1987). To enforce drug laws, policymakers and the courts gradually reduced the restraints on federal police powers and increased the prerogatives of local and state police with regard to these minority groups.

According to Musto, drug laws expressed the following racist fears at times when crises with specific groups were at a peak:

1. Prohibitionist and racist propaganda claimed that cocaine permitted Blacks to withstand bullets and stimulated them to sexual assault of White women.

At the turn of the century, drug reformers and southern politicians made cocaine part of the battle for political control of freed Blacks. Cocaine was popular among Whites and Blacks in the north and south, but prohibitionists associated it with Black expression of hostility toward Whites. To promote their drug policies, prohibitionists joined with southern politicians who advocated regressive social policies toward Blacks. These politicians sought to sustain racial segregation, black political disenfranchisement, and some advocated violence and lynching.

2. Opium fostered sexual contact between Chinese men and White U.S. women in the far west.

U.S. labor targeted the Chinese and opium smoking during the economic depression of the late 1800s. At that time, the Chinese were low-paid competitors for scarce U.S. jobs. As a result, U.S. communities' bias against Chinese involvement with opium intensified, as did other forms of anti-Chinese discrimination during this period. Then, business people in China organized a boycott of U.S. goods when they heard of U.S. prejudice against Chinese immigrants and travelers.

In response, drug reformers joined with U.S. business interests to reopen the seemingly unlimited Chinese market. They lobbied President Theodore Roosevelt to help China's increasingly nationalistic government deal with its "opium problem." In this way, they argued, the United States might ingratiate itself to the Dowager Empress, who ruled China at that time. The Dowager blamed opium use for her nation's backwardness.

However, U.S. offers to help the Dowager seemed empty and hypocritical because the United States had no drug laws of its own. Therefore, economic opportunism and anti-Chinese racism all seem to have been part of the morality play that generated America's first antinarcotic laws.

**3.** Marijuana incited Chicanos to violence in the southwest.

During the Great Depression of the 1930s, the Chicanos were a visible and unemployed minority who would work for low wages just as the Chinese did, earlier. Largely as a result of Harry Anslinger's large-scale propaganda campaign of the mid-1930s, legislators made marijuana illegal in 1937. The narcissistic and power-hungry Anslinger became head of the federal Bureau of Narcotics immediately after repeal of alcohol prohibition. Anslinger used marijuana prohibition to solidify his self-proclaimed status as the nations's greatest expert on drug use.

**4.** Heroin was linked in the 1920s with urban gangs of adolescents and young adults.

Heroin was part of the reckless and promiscuous behavior of young people during the Roaring 20s. Consequently, policymakers first recognized the connection between popular culture and drug use. Just as today, U.S. communities identified the glitz and the glamor of the young and suddenly rich and famous with hedonism, self-indulgence, and drugs.

Drug-related scandal and intrigue, and deaths due to overdose, murder, and suicide amid the glamor of Hollywood movie studios heightened these fears (Anger, 1984; Jonnes, 1996). Denunciations from the press and the pulpit besieged Hollywood as news of such events spread. Threats of boycotts by Women's clubs, church organizations, and community anti-vice committees were a serious concern for the entrepreneurs of the film industry.

These problems began with the heroin-implicated death of silent screen star and erstwhile "Ideal American Girl" Olive Thomas in 1920 at age 20. This energized the Watch and Ward societies of U.S. cities (Anger, 1975). These groups and others who offered themselves as the voice of a dominant Victorian morality warned that the depravity of filmland was a new menace to U.S. maidenhood.

Then, Keystone comedies star Fatty Arbuckle's criminal trial created a huge scandal for Hollywood and ruined his career in 1921. Police accused Arbuckle of killing 25-year-old starlet Virginia Rappe by rupturing her bladder with a bottle in a drunken sexual assault. Although a jury acquitted Arbuckle after three trials, his heavy drinking worsened following his banishment from Hollywood, and he died 12 years later at age 46.

Silent screen star Mabel Normand's cocaine use had a part in Paramount Studios director William Desmond Taylor's murder in 1922. Although police never solved the case, it took on a dope angle because the killer shot Taylor to death soon after Taylor tried to protect Norman in a confrontation with drug dealers and blackmailers.

However, even the chivalry and martyrdom of Taylor was sullied. Taylor turned out to be William Dean-Tanner, who in 1908 had abandoned his wife and daughter in New York (Anger, 1975). And, news reporters claimed that they had seen him in meeting places where hosts served their patrons opium, morphine, and marijuana on wheeled tea carts.

The death of Wallace Reid, a morphine- and heroin-addicted matinee idol created another huge Hollywood scandal in 1923. Reid's demise in a padded room of a sanitarium at age 31 was the last straw (Jonnes, 1996). Reid was an intravenous drug user and descriptions of the 3-year illness that eventually killed him seem remarkably similar to the illness of AIDS patients, today. Although AIDS was unknown when Reid died, he had high fevers, suffered weight loss of more than 60 pounds, grew too weak to walk, and had failing lungs and kidneys (Jonnes, 1996). Medical tests of those times were unable to identify the cause of his progressively worsening condition.

In response to these scandals, movie magnates offered Will Hays the position of movie czar and moral watchdog to protect their market. Hays became president of the hastily formed Motion Picture Producers and Distributors of America, Inc., in 1922; a position he held until 1945. He ordered that films be cleaned up; no sex, no drugs or booze, morals clauses in film contracts, and banishment for scandalous off-screen behavior.

With Hays' approval, movie moguls hired detectives to investigate the private lives of performers and others in the industry. These detectives used all the dirty tricks of their trade to produce a list of 117 Hollywood names who Hays and others declared unsafe to the film industry.

Those interested in film as an art form protested vehemently against these stern acts of personal and artistic censorship. Many successful actors and actresses simply used wealth to hide their personal lives behind the locked and guarded gates of lavish estates. Actress Barbara La Marr became Hollywood's most glamorous junkie until she died of a drug overdose in 1926 at age 26. Later, dramatic actress Alma Rubens died of an unspecified morphine- and heroin-induced illness in 1931 at age 33. Neither of these stars were on the infamous list of 117.

Interestingly, Anger (1975) described Hays as a corrupt political chiseler who was active in Republican politics and was implicated in corruption that racked the administration of President Warren Harding in 1923. Harding had appointed Hays to his soon-to-be scandal-ridden cabinet as postmaster general.

In 1928, investigators of the Teapot Dome scandal found that Hays had received $260,000 from oil man Harry Sinclair. As chairman of the Republican National Committee, Hays used his position to tilt the 1920 Republican nomination toward Harding, and Sinclair profited. But, in 1927, Sinclair served a 9-month prison sentence for contempt of court and contempt of Congress for his role as a key figure in the Teapot Dome scandal of 1923. In that major scandal, Secretary of Interior Albert Fall served 1 year in prison for accepting a $100,000 bribe to permit private development of federal oil reserves.

Similarly suspected of accepting a bribe, Hays claimed that the monies Sinclair gave him were a $75,000 gift and a $185,000 loan and wriggled out of trouble. However in 1930, Hays was caught red-handed bribing moral leaders. These leaders were supposed to pass impartial judgment for various religious and civic organizations on the moral acceptability of films (Anger, 1975).

    **5.** Alcohol was associated with immigrants crowding into the confined areas of large and corrupt cities.

In 1907, Congress created the Immigration Commission to study the impact of immigrants on U.S. industry and social institutions. The Commission soon characterized immigrants as an alien colony on U.S. soil with their own standards, and systems of control, and portrayed immigrants to be living in isolation from the mainstream of U.S. life (Rumbarger, 1989). Employers described immigrant workers to be more unreliable and insubordinate than U.S. workers, and claimed that immigrants' work habits made them poor candidates for permanent positions and job promotion.

In the view of the Immigration Commission, immigrants' drinking behavior made them the most serious moral problem of the community. These declarations, along with monies provided by industrial capitalists, added to the political momentum behind passage of the Volstead Act of 1917. Subsequently, alcohol prohibition became the Eighteenth Amendment of the U.S. Constitution.

## WHAT ARE THE OUTCOMES OF DRUG PROHIBITION?

Despite these and many other serious questions about U.S. drug policies, evidence does suggest that prohibition may prevent some drug abuse (Sandor, 1995). For example, alcohol prohibition sharply reduced per capita alcohol consumption from preprohibition levels of 2.4 gallons to approximately 0.9 gallons per year during the 1920–1933 prohibition period (Connor & Burns, 1995, p. 49).

Concurrently, death rates for liver cirrhosis among men declined by 66%, hospitalizations for alcoholic psychosis dropped by more than 50%, and arrests for drunk and disorderly conduct declined between 30% to 50% (Moore, 1989). Even after repeal of alcohol prohibition, per capita alcohol consumption did not reach pre-prohibition levels for nearly 40 years.

Also, the problem of drug addiction almost vanished during the 30-year period between the beginning of World War I and the end of World War II. By the mid-1940s, fewer than 40,000 addicts existed in the United States as compared to approximately 300,000 in the late 1890s and prior to passage of restrictive legislation in 1906 and 1914.

However, restrictive legislation may not have produced the declines reported here. For example, during those 30 years, World War I and World War II seriously hampered smuggling activities and restricted illicit drug producers access to materials. Also, this was a period when Americans suffered through the great depression but had more faith in U.S. institutions and leaders.

And most important, it was a time when drug profiteers had just begun to develop the tricks of illicit drug production, smuggling, and distribution. Gangsters, opportunists, shady characters, and unscrupulous pharmaceutical companies from the United States, Canada, France, Italy, Greece, Turkey, and other nations of Europe, Asia, the Middle East, and South America were all involved. As Jonnes (1996) and Musto (1987) described, members of many different ethnic groups, nationalities, races, and political persuasions jumped at the windfalls offered by drug prohibition.

Arnold Rothstein, a Jewish gangster from Brooklyn, New York, was one of the more creative. In the 1920s, he devised systems for smuggling and distributing illegal drugs that are still used to this day. In 1928, Rothstein was murdered in gangland fashion supposedly by Legs Diamond, although police never solved the case (Jonnes, 1996).

Consequently, beyond the 30-year period following passage of the Harrison Act, national drug prohibition has had almost no impact on harm associated with illegal drugs. The wars had ended, the smugglers had polished their trade, and U.S. drug policymakers had begun to lose their shine due to a multitude of political scandals.

Although estimates about the number of U.S. addicts prior to drug prohibition vary, the rate of addiction began to surpass even those levels after that initial 30-year period. This happened despite increasingly strenuous efforts to prohibit drug use.

Just prior to antinarcotic laws, in the 1890s to early 1900s, credible estimates range from a low of about 250,000 addicts (Musto, 1987) to highs of 1.9 million to 2.5 million (King, 1972; Lewis & Zinberg, 1964). Courtwright's (1982) analysis of a variety of sources of historical evidence suggests that the high point of U.S. addiction to opiates in 1890s was about 313,000 addicts.

The credibility of such estimates is uncertain because prohibition advocates often exaggerated the dangers of drug use and the numbers of drug users. However, Musto's (1987) and Courtwright's (1982) estimates of 250,000 to just over 300,000 addicts seem most realistic because of the manner in which they examined historical evidence. These estimates put the addiction rate at about one third to one half of 1% of the population. During the 1890s, the total U.S. population was 75 to 80 million people.

It is important to note that the pre-drug prohibition era was one in which opiates and cocaine were legally available, and were hidden ingredients in patent medicines. Users had easy access to them in grocery stores, at soda fountains, and through mail order houses.

Physicians and lay persons were just beginning to understand the addictive qualities of morphine, and especially heroin, then a relatively new drug. As people learned of the dangers of addiction, use of these drugs declined by 30% to 50% prior to any prohibitive legislation. This decline occurred because of increasing public awareness of the dangers of addiction and physicians' growing reluctance to prescribe opiates for medical purposes.

In contrast, the current rate of addiction is about 1.3% with 3.6 million Americans who are abusers or dependent on heroin or cocaine (Massing, 1998). This group consumes about 75% of the cocaine and heroin that is used, but contains only 20% of the users. This estimate does not include those who abuse or are dependent on alcohol, but represents a threefold increase since pre-drug prohibition times.

Furthermore, approximately, 35 to 40 million nonaddicted Americans use illegal drugs from time to time, including about 15 million who use cocaine and heroin. According to White House Office of National Drug Control Policy estimates, drug users spend between $55 and $95 billion a year; 65% to 70% to buy cocaine, 15% to 20% to buy heroin, and 10% to 15% to purchase marijuana ("Illegal drugs," 1997).

These figures indicate that government expenditure of many billions of dollars on drug interdiction, especially since the late 1980s, has produced little social benefit. Worldwide production of cocaine, opium, and other illegal drugs increases and importation of illegal drugs into the United States continues unabated.

Furthermore, the illegal drug trade unrelentingly improves its technology for production and transport. It is now more efficient, difficult to detect, and responsive to market trends then ever before (Pollan, 1995). The Argonne National Laboratory in Illinois dramatically highlighted this with its discovery that roughly 75% of the $1 and $2 bills in circulation in the Chicago suburbs, Miami, and Houston contain traces of cocaine (Browne, 1997). According to one laboratory spokes-man, the level of cocaine contamination is presumably about the same in all large U.S. cities. Drug dealers wrap chunks of solid cocaine in pa-per money because the ink does not transfer to the cocaine as it does from newsprint or magazine pages.

Even present-day moonshiners who evade liquor taxes by illegally producing and distributing whiskey are a far cry from their alcohol prohibition forerunners. Old time moonshiners usually produced whiskey in a 20-gallon copper still they kept behind an outhouse on their farms. In contrast, modern moonshiners operate a multimil-lion-dollar business, produce huge volumes of liquor in large ferment-ing tanks, and are likely to be felons, murderers, gun runners, and dealers of other drugs (Verde, 1998).

DEA authorities even accuse some in the Miami drug trade to have been negotiating a $5.5 million purchase of a Russian submarine. Drug smugglers planned to use the submarine to transport cocaine be-tween Columbia and North America (Navarro, 1997).

Therefore, it is no wonder that police seizures of nearly 100 tons of illicit drugs in 1996 alone seemed to have little effect on street sup-plies. In fact, drug dealers continually struggle with the problem of storing their excess inventory. Despite losses due to police seizures of drugs, the costs to drug dealers remain low while profits are high (Wren, 1996b).

Furthermore, U.S. marijuana growers have expanded domestic pro-duction since the 1980s in Florida, California, Oregon, and Washing-ton State. Indoor cultivation now makes marijuana production more hidden, and indoor cultivation and plant breeding have raised the 1996 level of delta-9 tetrahydrocannabinol (THC), marijuana's active agent, to 12% to 14% from 3% to 7% in 1991 (Navarro, 1996).

As a result, many teenagers report that marijuana is easier to get than beer or cigarettes and that they can buy marijuana within a day of having decided to do so (Gabriel, 1996). This is true for adolescents in impoverished ghetto neighborhoods and in the elite private schools and communities of the wealthy (Sales, 1996).

The availability and purity of street heroin have increased, too. Film star Courtney Love, the widow of rock star, heroin addict, and suicide victim Kurt Cobain described the availability of the drug in Seattle to be "like apples in an orchard. Its falling off the ... trees" (Thompson, 1994, p. 3). And, the purity of heroin has jumped from less than 5% to 35% to 40% since the early 1990s (Kennedy, 1996). Consequently, us-ers need to purchase, carry, and consume less for any given level of ef-fect, just as with marijuana.

Heroin users now can "snort" (inhale heroin powder) or smoke her-oin to achieve the same effect as was available only through intravenous injection in the past. Users may avoid the recently developed stigma associated with "shooting up" (injecting heroin directly into a vein with a hypodermic needle). Users also may eliminate the risk of contracting AIDS, hepatitis, bacterial infections that damage heart valves, damaged veins, and any other health hazards associated with unclean hypodermic needles. However, physicians recently linked heroin smoking with leukoencephalopathy, a paralyzing neurological ailment for which there is no cure and that can lead to death (Wren, 1996a).

Nevertheless, heroin has become increasingly popular and has recently replaced cocaine as the "hard" drug of choice in popular culture. Although the number of cocaine users in the U.S. dropped from 5.7 million to about 1.5 million since the late 1980s (Wren, 1997c), heroin-related emergency room episodes increased 68% during the period from 1988 to 1994 (Kennedy, 1996).

Just as "yuppies" and "beautiful people" of the 1980s favored cocaine, people in the arts, fashion, and the financial world have now made heroin "chic" (Chase, 1996). An epidemic of deaths, near tragedies, arrests, and court imposed rehabilitation orders have struck the entertainment and music industries particularly hard.

These and other serious drug problems appear to wax and wane over time despite the most vigorous enforcement of drug laws. The numbers of drug related deaths and drug dealers in America remain unchanged (Clifford & Nicholson, 1996).

## WHAT SIDE EFFECTS ARE ASSOCIATED WITH DRUG PROHIBITION?

Much evidence argues that the damage wrought by the treatment is worse than the illness. Police and government corruption, encroachments on personal freedom, and the spread of disease are problems to which drug prohibition has made major contributions.

As occurs for most troublesome social policies, the brunt of problems is borne unfairly by the poor, inner city dwellers, and racial and ethnic minorities (Clifford, 1992). Consequently, U.S. drug policies have placed in double jeopardy those with fewest resources and the greatest economic and social difficulties. Those who are twice victimized must carry on despite the drug problems that ravage their neighborhoods and they must struggle with the destructive consequences of drug prohibition.

As these problems reveal, welfare reform and health care for the poor are pressing drug-related social issues of the day. Such issues are, in large part, raised by gang violence, family disintegration, crime, and drug trafficking. These problems, in turn, have caused entrepreneurs and business leaders to abandon urban centers of commerce and industry. Consequently, reduced economic opportunity for those who need work most, and increased joblessness worsen crime, violence, and drug problems in a downward spiral of accelerating social disorganization (Wilson, 1996).

These circumstances are particularly damaging to Black and Hispanic residents of impoverished inner-city areas. Not only do they suffer isolation from the benefits of mainstream U.S. life, but their circumstances perpetuate a culture of poverty and hopelessness in these neighborhoods. Consequently, many poor families receive public assistance interminably as they pass this culture from generation to generation.

Because of this debilitating malaise, employers who might offer Black and Hispanic inner city residents jobs have become less willing to do so. Employers see poor, inner-city Blacks in particular to be lazy, dishonest, undependable, lacking in language skills, and are therefore reluctant to hire them (Wilson, 1996). Apart from questions about their work ethic, employers also see inner-city Blacks as subscribing to cultural definitions of acceptable public behavior that differ from middle-class definitions that dominate the workplace.

The damage wrought by these conditions is highlighted in rates of incarceration and disenfranchisement among Black adult males (Butterfield, 1997; "Nearly 7%," 1995). Justice Department Statistics reveal that nearly 7% of all adult Black males are in prison and that one in three Black men in their 20s is under the control of the criminal justice system on any given day (Butterfield, 1997). As a result, 1.5 million or 14% of Black men who are either in prison or have been convicted of a felony have lost the right to vote.

Less than 1% of White males are incarcerated. Justice Department statistics indicate that, since the 1980s, the incarceration rate for Whites remained little changed and rates for Blacks climbed steadily. In 1994, the number of Black inmates surpassed the number of White inmates in state or federal prisons for the first time.

The overall number of prison inmates has nearly tripled to 1.6 million since 1980, which gives the United States the highest rate of incarceration of any nation in the world (Milburn & Conrad, 1996). Most observers attribute these increases to more arrests for drug offenses and violent crimes in inner cities, and harsher sentencing laws. However, civil rights advocates claim that repressive federal drug laws and harsh sentencing guidelines have had a disproportionate and biased impact on Blacks. Blacks are more than twice as likely as Whites to receive prison terms for the same offense, and are treated much more harshly than Whites when in prison (Ramirez, 1983; Unnever, 1982).

Clearly, drug prohibition has caused the courts and prisons to be overwhelmed by drug-related crimes. And, those who suffer arrest and imprisonment are not passively disappearing from the community as many who support harsh drug policies would wish.

Outside of the prisons, social workers and family courts place many children in foster homes because a jailed single parent is no longer available to care for them (Hewitt, Nelson, & Velez, 1996). Inside of the prisons, get-tough-on-crime measures have induced a level of rage that has rendered prisons more fearsome places for inmates and corrections officers than ever before (Milburn & Conrad, 1996; Porter, 1995).

Even though the prison population rose 60% between 1988 and 1994, assaults on prison employees increased sevenfold, from about 1,700 incidents to nearly 14,000 per year. This fury is the product of chronic dehumanizing conditions that include beatings, stabbings, and isolation of inmates. Such conditions are only worsened by 290,000 incidents in which male prisoners are raped by fellow inmates each year (Donaldson, 1993).

Furthermore, the prisons are training grounds for criminals, many of whom begin by serving time for nonviolent drug offenses. Not only are these prisoners the most likely victims of attack by other inmates, they often move on to commit crimes against property and then crimes against people as they learn criminal trades in the prison system (Smolowe, 1994).

## HOW DO DRUG POLICY FAILURES
## COMPLICATE THE WORK OF TEACHERS?

In troubled communities and their neighborhood schools, the harsh drug laws of the 1970s and 1980s had an unexpected consequence that amplified youthful violence and children's access to drugs (Canada, 1995). Following the precedent set by "numbers" racketeers (illegal lottery operators) of earlier times, adult dealers began to recruit children into street-level drug trade. Drug dealers did so to avoid long prison sentences that adults now face for drug law violations and to which children are immune.

Clearly, some poor children with austere lives, few job opportunities, and whose tender age provides legal immunity, find quick and plentiful drug money to be an irresistible temptation. The same may be said for more affluent youth who are seeking dangerous thrills and outlets for anger and rebellion.

Criminal activity and weapons possession by students only worsen the teachers' status as drug abuse prevention agents. Teachers can no longer protect their students or themselves (Devine, 1996). Consequently, students who are suspicious of teachers' admonitions about drugs view teachers' helplessness as one more act of abandonment by an uncaring community.

Furthermore, drug policy's association with politics and politicians undergirds this suspicion. Students' chronic lack of confidence in teachers is compounded by drug policy's entanglement with the community's moralistic agendas. As a repository of morality, the community imposes its moral beliefs on young people and uses the schools to do so, in many areas of life. Some such areas include sexual behavior, gambling, pornography, and use of alcohol and other drugs.

For teachers and their students, the entanglement of issues of personal freedom with social policies driven by money and morals creates both problems and opportunities in the classroom. As the preceding paragraph demonstrates, Americans struggle with many such issues including those created by national drug policies. Clearly, teachers must come to terms with their position as agents of policies about which there exists so much controversy, distrust, and emotion.

On the other hand, opportunities abound for study, debate, and contemplation of the forces that drive restrictive social policies in general and drug policies in particular. Such study will reveal to teachers and their students that U.S. society exists in a constant state of tension between forces that promote and others that seek to repress a wide range of behavior. Social policy surrounding drug use makes the drug problem a magnificent case study of the strengths and frailties of U.S. democracy and its mechanisms for managing these unrelenting tensions.

## WHAT ARE THE ALTERNATIVES
## TO UNEQUIVOCAL PROHIBITION OF DRUGS?

In view of the failures, the high costs, and the terrible side effects of our current drug policies, alternatives are sorely needed. These alternative policies occupy a continuum between unequivocal prohibition at one pole and unregulated legalization at the other. Although many thoughtful observers have formulated alternatives and persuasive arguments, policymakers respond to any proposal other than unequivocal prohibition with vigorous resistance at this time.

Consequently, teachers find themselves in a difficult position as agents of policy that is ineffective, causes more problems then it solves, and has become increasingly unyielding and coercive in its implementation. This tension can foster much creative thinking in the classroom. Therefore, teachers can use their own difficult position as a source of inspiration for study and learning by their students.

This opportunity exists because debate about how to define the problem of drug use continues, as it has for 100 years. The voice of the strict and punitive parent is clear in conservative prohibitionists' definitions of the drug problem. Alternatively, the pleas of the permissive and indulgent parent are clear in liberal pro-legalization definitions. And, the voice of the caring and reasonable parent rings in middle-of-the-road calls for moderation and regulated legalization.

This last position describes current policy governing alcohol and tobacco use, and the 1996 referendums in which California and Arizona voters declared medicinal use of marijuana to be legal. Although alcohol and tobacco are legal, they are heavily taxed. Also, policymakers have imposed legal age requirements and limitations on advertising. Laws regulate the use of alcohol and tobacco in the workplace, public and private transportation, and in many public settings.

In fact, rises in alcohol-related traffic deaths since 1994 have stimulated renewed national debate on a national standard for defining drunk driving (Wald, 1998). At issue is the blood-alcohol level at which a driver will be in violation of the law. Currently, 33 states have set the limit at 0.10%, 15 have set it at 0.08%, and 2 have no defined limit, but prosecute drunk drivers on the basis of arresting officers' observations of driving behavior.

This is certainly a debate that can continue in the classroom. The first state blood-alcohol restrictions were set 50 years ago at 0.15%. Other countries, such as Canada and Britain, have limits of 0.08%; France, Holland, and Finland have limits at 0.05%; and Sweden is at 0.02% (Wald, 1998). Among drinking drivers involved in fatal accidents, 70% had blood-alcohol levels at or above 0.12%, and 7.3% had levels at 0.10% or 0.11%. Although only 5.9% had levels between 0.08% and 0.09%, the accident risk of this group is still 11 times higher than for drivers who have had no alcohol.

Still, the challenge for U.S. policymakers is to establish a universal standard that is applicable to a population whose reactions to the effects of alcohol are so varied. In 1995, the U.S. Department of Transportation set a goal reducing alcohol-related traffic fatalities by 35%, to 11,000, by the year 2005.

The fate of the new California and Arizona marijuana laws, and whatever controls are to be imposed on medicinal use in those states, are yet undecided. Opponents to these laws continue to argue that anything less than unequivocal prohibition will convey the "wrong message," and that marijuana is a "gateway" drug that invariably leads to more dangerous and addictive drugs. What is more, opponents claim that a carefully conceived and deceitful campaign aimed at drug legalization has victimized California and Arizona voters.

Policymakers and law enforcement officials report that they will vigorously enforce the restrictive federal laws with which the new California and Arizona laws are in conflict. The Arizona Legislature and the Governor of Arizona have gone so far as to pass laws that overturned the medical use initiative before it could take effect (Golden, 1997).

This debate amplifies the many troubling messages about drug policy and may be confusing to teachers and students. But, the arguments provide rich opportunities for study and discussion in the classroom. The policy debate seeks to resolve the following problems of definition about drug use:

1. Is drug use a legal and moral problem that harms users, makes victims of others, invades and destroys our social institutions, and threatens the nation's most cherished social values? If such is the case, then some argue that drug use is a crime and an act of treason. This is the conservative position.

2. Or, is it a health and social problem symptomatic of disorganization and stress in the community? Are these health and social problems created by the very same values the nation holds sacred? Are these problems a by-product of U.S. values and cultural traditions? If this is the case, then some argue that society is the culprit, and drug use is a disease to be prevented and treated by education and the health care system. This is a position of political moderates.

3. A third disquieting possibility is that drug use is only a problem by legal or regulatory definition. Although many might argue that drug use is undesirable, to what degree is legislating against undesirable behavior consistent with our most cherished value of personal privacy and freedom? This is one position of political liberals.

4. Given the relatively small number of individuals who develop drug abuse problems, and the large numbers of people who emerge unscathed from periodic recreational use of illegal drugs, one might easily wonder what the fuss is all about. If this is the case, then, as some argue, policymakers are confusing drug use with drug abuse. As a result, our effort to control a relatively small problem has turned it into a much larger one. This is a liberal position.

## SUMMARY OF KEY POINTS

Because drug use is entangled with powerful economic, social, and moral concerns, government at all levels has spent 100 years struggling with seemingly insoluble policy issues. Consequently, the study of drug policy provides teachers and students with many insights about the broader social concerns to which the curriculum in history, government, economics, and literature attend.

Americans enjoyed unregulated access to drugs, but policymakers refused to acknowledge drug problems for the first 100 years of the nation. This denial continued so long as policymakers identified the purposes of drug use with acceptable social classes.

Within these social classes, some members used drugs to sustain the wealth and power of their family, and the pharmaceutical industry and the medical profession used drugs to earn profits. Communities extracted the price of these benefits from women and children.

However, when U.S. communities imposed drug prohibition, the price was exacted from racial minorities, immigrants, and marginalized ethnic populations. When U.S. communities identified drug use with groups they feared or despised, drug laws became levers with which to mobilize the police against these groups. Consequently, many observers argue that restrictive drug policy threatens civil rights, womens rights, child protection, and many cherished principles of U.S. democracy.

Although policymakers claim that restrictive drug policies serve public health and other beneficial purposes, the struggle that continually surrounds these policies is political. Therefore, policy emerges out of power and influence rather than wisdom and understanding. Because the first victim in all political struggles is truth, teachers must keep wisdom and understanding at the center of their efforts. Truth will help students grasp the enormity of problems that confront those who formulate drug policy.

U.S. drug policies have failed miserably, and they have created many other problems for which all Americans have paid. The illegal drug trade continues to thrive despite intense and very expensive government efforts to eliminate it. Negative side effects of these efforts include government intrusion into the privacy and freedom of ordinary citizens, corruption, abuses of police power, and the waste of valuable resources. The prisons are bursting at the seams and children are being deprived of the right to be raised by their own family. Drug laws subordinate humanitarian concern about pain and suffering among the sick and dying to political concern about conveying the wrong message to the young.

Teachers can do much to convey the right message to the young. This message is that the true nature of the drug problem in America must be defined in realistic terms, although this task is not an easy one. Furthermore, teachers can help students explore many alternative solutions between restrictive prohibition and outright legalization.

Providing students with a healthy and honest appraisal of drug policy is important to preventing the abuse of drugs and promoting effective and humanitarian solutions to the problem of drug use.

# IV

# Drug Education and Substance Abuse Prevention in Curricular Contexts: Art and Culture

# 11

# Substance Abuse Prevention in the Context of Art and Culture

The goal of this chapter is to describe U.S. culture as it relates to drug use so that teachers can accomplish the following:

1. Use the study of culture as a vehicle for substance abuse prevention.
2. Gain an understanding of U.S. childrearing practices as they relate to culture and drug use.
3. Gain insight into drug use and the culture of child and adolescent society in the schools.
4. Help students examine the impact of political and economic forces on U.S. culture and its response to drug availability.
5. Help students examine the impact of drug use on prominent cultural role models such as artists, writers, and athletes.
6. Refer students to biographical, historical, and fictional writings that illuminate the ethos of drug use in America.
7. Assist students in the exploration of issues of social class, race, ethnicity, and religious doctrine that are entangled with cultural forces that oppose drug use.

Teachers should think of culture as usual ways in which families, groups, organizations, and communities satisfy their members' needs. People create culture when they join with one another and then organize behavior, objects, and implements into repeated patterns of use. These patterns become customary or traditional solutions to problems of living, and address the physical, social, aesthetic, and spiritual necessities of individual and community survival. Culture works best when it satisfies the requirements of living in a stable and consistent manner, and adapts effectively to change and crisis.

Culture not only provides tools for physical survival, but it is also the source through which people find purpose and meaning for their actions. Purpose and meaning are so central to human existence that their flow is prominent in the rise and their ebb equally prominent in the fall of all great civilizations of the past. These civilizations seem to have gone through identical stages (Ruggiero, 1994) as they arose:

1. From enslavement toward spiritual faith.
2. From spiritual faith toward courage, tenacity, and inspiration in the face of adversity.
3. From courageous triumph over adversity into liberty and freedom.
4. From freedom into abundance and prosperity.

And, then amid the erosion of meaning and purpose, they descended:

1. From abundance toward greed and selfishness.
2. From greed and selfishness into complacency and passivity.
3. From complacency to apathy.
4. From apathy into helplessness and dependency.
5. From helplessness and dependency, the cycle is completed with a return to enslavement.

As this history reveals, when culture loses its social and spiritual efficacy, it places the community as a whole and its individual members at risk in many ways. Consequently, culture influences almost every aspect of human existence. And, nowhere is the adage that "There are many ways to skin a cat!" better demonstrated than in the variability of culture.

For example, the simple act of walking is a learned skill rather than an inborn reflex. Consequently, postural habits, locomotor style and gait, footwear, or walking single file or abreast are aspects of human locomotion that exhibit much cultural variation (Devine, 1985). Clearly, people express a variety of culturally promoted beliefs, values, and attitudes about themselves and their world just in the simple act of moving about.

Children vividly demonstrate this in school as they stride the halls and walk about the classroom. Devine's (1996) comments about "stylized sulking" and Canada's (1995) observations about "bopping" describe the provocative posture and gait of some inner-city adolescents. These teenagers use their manner of walking to express mood, warn others, and in some instances to express defiance and hostility toward teachers and classmates.

## HOW DOES CULTURE INFLUENCE
## DRUG USE IN THE COMMUNITY?

All members of the community need trustworthy sources of food, shelter, clothing, means to organize cooperation, and ways of sharing the bounties of their interdependent efforts. However, as discussed previously, the challenge of survival is not limited to the material and practical. People also must cope with growth and change, success and triumph, tragedy and loss, and the inevitability of death. Thus, people use the love and esteem of others and their sense of meaning and purpose to cope successfully with many personal travails.

To satisfy these myriad needs of survival, all cultures devise tools, implements, and technology and attribute social and spiritual meaning to their use. Cultures express social and spiritual meaning in codes of behavior, systems of belief, and rites, rituals, and ceremonies.

Human beings search for social and spiritual peace of mind because communities squander the genius that enables their survival when survival itself is devoid of benevolence and joy. Therefore, they form social bonds in search of companionship, intimacy, and love, and out of their need to make sense of the world. Thus, culture not only provides community members with means to stay alive but also with reasons to do so, and ways to remain together.

For better or worse, drugs have been part of this process in all human cultures since prehistoric times. Because drugs provide such powerful experiences of tension release, pleasure, social disinhibition, and transcendence above mundane aesthetics and consciousness, prehistoric peoples were amazingly thorough in searching them out. As Aldous Huxley observed in 1931, these early humans left almost no natural mind-altering substance undiscovered (Koral, 1995).

Not only does culture influence drug use, but drugs also influence culture. Without doubt, mind-altering drugs changed the cultures, beliefs, attitudes, values, and standards of prehistoric people, ancient and present tribal societies, and ancient and modern civilizations (Rudgley, 1993). This is so for our cigar-smoking, martini-sipping policymakers just as it has been for the shaman whose drug induced visions guide tribal societies.

In examining this idea, teachers should impress on their students that neither prehistoric humans nor tribal peoples of present times fit stereotypes as lumbering oafs or primitives. Prehistoric and present tribal technology may be simpler than our own, but these peoples had and continue to have abundant leisure time. They were and are able to feed themselves in 3 to 5 hours of working effort per day.

Also, teachers should impress on their students that the raw creativity of prehistoric peoples laid the foundation of modern art and craft. Students and teachers should know that prehistoric innovation made possible the later ancient civilizations to which we arbitrarily and exclusively attribute our own technological genesis.

Humans domesticated opium and hemp (marijuana) between 5000 and 6000 BC. These plants grew as weeds around nitrogen-rich neolithic campsites near the Mediterranean. Much evidence suggests that early peoples exploited these plants' intoxicating qualities along with their other useful attributes.

Humans began to purposefully produce and consume alcohol between 3000 BC and 3500 BC around the eastern end of the Mediterranean in Mesopotamia. Siberian cliff drawings indicate that northern Eurasian peoples used hallucinogenic mushrooms (fly-agaric) between 2500 BC and 3000 BC, although some experts speculate that they may have used these mushrooms even earlier. Inhabitants of the Amazon Rain Forests and other areas of the New World have exploited approximately 100 species of hallucinogenic plants for many centuries. These included mushrooms (mescalin, fly-agaric), cacti (peyote), vines (banisteriopsis caapi), snuffs, tobacco, and New World Water Lilies.

This list is far from complete, but prehistoric and present day tribal people derived and used mind-altering drugs to contemplate the same spiritual and existential issues that face modern societies. Furthermore, all such groups appear to have regulated their members' use of these drugs. They forbade children to use them, integrated them into religious and social rituals, and used drugs for purposes other than mere hedonistic experience.

Given this cultural history, it is no wonder that, according to the United Nations, almost 200 million people around the world use mind-altering drugs at this time (Wren, 1997g). About 140 million or nearly 2.5% of the world's population smoke marijuana and hashish. Thirty million use amphetamines, another 13 million use cocaine, and 8 million use heroin. Although cocaine use is greater in the Americas, heroin use tends to be greater in Europe and Asia.

The effort to criminalize international drug trafficking has so far failed to stem the flow of drugs and has created other problems not uncommon to prohibition. Illicit drug businesses generate $400 billion a year in revenues and account for 8% of international trade. This proportion is equivalent to that for trade in textiles.

Probably more than a million acres worldwide have been dedicated to cultivation of drug-producing plants such as opium, coca, and marijuana. Despite the enormity of revenues, less than 3% to 5% of retail sales profit finds its way back to the countries in which these plants are grown and harvested. What is more, widespread money laundering of drug profits has become an important threat to legitimate businesses in many of these and other countries.

## WHAT CULTURAL FORCES PROMOTE
## DRUG USE IN AMERICA?

The family is the centerpiece of culture in all human communities. The family perpetuates culture in its childrearing practices, and in turn the culture that surrounds the family shapes these practices. In fact, every aspect of family life reflects a larger integrated system of culturally derived beliefs about family itself, gender, community, nature, religion, and the supernatural (Lefkerites, 1992).

Because children are the future, the destiny of the community is closely linked to culturally prescribed beliefs and practices about childrearing. Therefore, the customs and traditions of childrearing reflect complex systems of beliefs, attitudes, values, and standards that serve, inevitably, as the glue of community life. For this reason, the community's beliefs about childrearing are central to teachers' concerns about cultural influences on drug use.

Culture is important because the customary and traditional treatment of children may either predispose the young to resist or accede to pressures to use drugs. Unfortunately, childrearing practices in America include much that predisposes the young to use alcohol and other drugs, and, what is worse, to deny risks associated with cavalier and intemperate drinking and drug taking (Milburn & Conrad, 1996).

Underlying these practices are long-standing cultural beliefs and an ideology that identify parent–child relations to be essentially a power struggle, a contest of wills, and a battle to establish control (Dobson, 1992). Quoting from childrearing manuals, Miller (1983) demonstrated that for the last 200 years, Western culture has assumed that children are guilefully and maliciously willful, even in infancy.

Furthermore, Western culture has identified such willfulness as insulting to adults, dangerously antisocial, and inevitably damaging to healthy maturation. According to this thinking, parents must relentlessly, strenuously, and if necessary, ruthlessly quell childish willfulness and teach unquestioning obedience to the will of adults. And, Western culture urges parents to do so as early as possible when children are too young to understand what is happening to them.

As a result, society long ago became desensitized to the abuse and humiliation of children, and accepted a rationalization that such treatment is necessary to good childrearing. Public opinion polls regarding the use of corporal punishment and rates of child abuse indicate that such behavior toward children "is so common that it has become invisible" (Milburn & Conrad, 1996, p. 5).

Not only do Western childrearing practices subject children to harsh treatment, the treatment itself is culturally supported by a system of beliefs that is both subtle and obvious. These beliefs permit parents to

rationalize and deny the selfishness and destructiveness of their actions. Furthermore, they force children to deny their own mistreatment, and restrict young victims' freedom to express feelings of anger,
disappointment, and grief about their own victimization.

Miller (1983) and Milburn and Conrad (1996) summarized these
beliefs as follows:

1. A sense of duty begets love expressed as: "You'll do it and
like it."

2. Anger, rage, and hatred can be eliminated by forbidding
them: "You do not hate your brother, father, Aunt Millie or whom-
ever, no matter how miserably they treat you."

3. Parents, teachers, and other adults deserve respect simply
because of rank based on role and age: "I'm your father and you
can't speak to me in that way, and as long as you live under this
roof ..."

4. Children, because of age, role, and rank are undeserving of
respect, as expressed in the question: "Just who do you think you
are (to express your own wishes, opinions, and judgments)?"

5. Obedience is a source of strength: "If you don't learn to do as
your parents tell you, just what do you think is going to happen in
the real world where people in charge don't even care about you?"

6. High levels of confidence and self-esteem produce arrogance and hubris: "You will get your comeuppance when you fall
off that high horse."

7. Low self-esteem and a lack of self-confidence produce benevolence, tolerance, and altruism: "You are not so perfect and
wonderful that you have a right to criticize others, no matter how
troubling and unreasonable you find their actions to be."

8. Tenderness and doting are bad: "You're spoiling that child
rotten!"

9. Compliance with a child's demands, needs, and wishes is
always bad: "You are going to create a monster if you jump every
time that kid calls!"

10. Severe, withholding, and emotionally cold parents provide children with better preparation for life in the real world:
"When you're out their on your own, nobody will give a hoot about
what you want or need."

11. It is better to hide disappointment and displeasure behind
a false smile than to let people know they were somehow obnox-
ious, insensitive, or irresponsible: "Can't you at least pretend to
appreciate Aunt Millie's wet sloppy kisses on the cheek? After all,
she is nearly ninety years old and has no teeth."

12. Parents, teachers, and other adults are always right: "Because I said so, that's why!"

Inevitably, teachers and students interested in substance abuse prevention must acknowledge that U.S. childrearing practices contribute in grand fashion to its being a drug-using society. In many instances, the teacher's primary task is to assist students to cope in constructive ways with the ebb and flow of these cultural forces that have such powerful impact on growing up.

What is more, U.S. culture surrounds its children with the technology to produce potent drugs and assaults them with the economic rewards of producing drugs and promoting drug use. Not only do the tobacco, liquor, and pharmaceutical industries push their products through the media, children learn of prominent role models and opinion leaders who use and advocate using licit and illicit drugs. U.S. culture also offers children social incentives to use drugs. Some of these incentives are a by-product of cultural values that support risk taking and individualism.

Furthermore, U.S. social policy puts frosting on the cake with a prohibitionist system against which the young may rebel by using drugs. Many Americans regard violation of drug laws to be justifiable, a personal declaration of independence, and an assertion of free spirit. In response to drug laws, some who would otherwise have no interest in drugs regard drug use to be socially correct and a duty as well as a pleasure.

Antidrug hysteria and misinformation compound these reactions, evoke distrust and heighten young people's interest in experimentation with drugs. In this way, society has made drugs a "forbidden fruit" with which counterculture or outlaw groups identify (Sandor, 1995, p. 518). Just as "Banned in Boston" was a sure way of stimulating book sales, so too does prohibition stimulate interest in drugs.

Also, many communities in which teachers work are beset by such disorganization and stress that drug use ranks high as a need-meeting activity. More than 100 years of study by sociologists and anthropologists reveals the following cultural and social conditions to be associated with increased drug use.

These conditions fall within four broad categories, all of which have profound impact on the work of teachers in the schools. The first of these is *community disorganization*, which includes:

1. Poorly defined social structure and controls in the community.
2. Vague expectations about parents' executive role and authoritative position in childrearing in the family.
3. Ambiguous gender role definitions.

**4.** Availability of drugs in the community.
**5.** High levels of stress.

The second category is *absence of cultural support* as indicated by:

**1.** Poverty and material insecurity.
**2.** Absence of resources and opportunity for alternative activities that would satisfy needs met by drug use.

The third is *social abandonment* as experienced in:

**1.** Social pressures for individual achievement.
**2.** Cultural valuing of independence and self-reliance.
**3.** Cultural antipathy toward vulnerability and dependency.

And, the fourth is the *attribution of positive meanings and values to drugs and drug use,* which refers to:

**1.** Cultural assignment of positive and even grandiose symbolism to drugs and drug use.
**2.** Drug use as a prominent cultural standard that community members use for positive self-evaluation, and assigning social status to others.
**3.** Cultural attribution of positive value and an important role to drugs as a "social lubricant" or disinhibiting mechanism in social interaction.
**4.** Social support for individuals to use drugs to "get high" (instrumental use) independent of social or religious purpose.

Given the childrearing attitudes and the conditions of many communities, it is no wonder that adolescence is so dangerous a time with regard to drug use in U.S. culture. For better or worse, much of the transition to maturity that occurs during this developmental stage happens within the culture of schools and classrooms.

In the schools, adult authority and time-honored traditions of U.S. education define school and classroom culture. Classroom culture includes the curriculum, goals and objectives, and management tools such as policies, rules, and procedures. These identify purpose, provide and regulate the use of resources, and prescribe rites, rituals, and ceremonies of social interaction. Such are the devices through which the formal elements of school culture promote valued behavior. These devices press for conformity and achievement, impose sanctions on social deviance and prohibited behavior, and mark stages of passage through the educative process.

However, within the educative process, adolescent society engages in its own process of cultural definition. In this process, peers sort themselves into small friendship groups, larger cliques, and still larger crowds with whom members identify, although they may not personally interact. Steinberg (1996) studied this process among 20,000 high school students over a period of 3 years during the late 1980s. He described how the peer group assigns its members to social groups, labels them, and identifies behavior through which status is achieved in each group. His descriptions offer important insights about substance abuse prevention and the effects of students' identification with a "crowd."

According to Steinberg, about 20% of students become "populars" who enjoy success in the peer group and status as a member of a school's social elite. They maintain this status by socializing, dating, and doing whatever peer culture requires to sustain their position among friends, including moderate illicit drug use and some delinquent behavior.

Some students whose success on the athletic field affords them status as heroes, become known as "jocks." They enjoy status similar to that of populars, but are less academically oriented. The jocks often drink excessively, although they are not as involved in illicit drug use as are the populars (Steinberg, 1996).

About 20% of students belong to alienated crowds. These students are labeled by others as "druggies," "greasers," or "burnouts." To maintain this status among their like-minded crowd, they exhibit heavy involvement with drugs, delinquent behavior, and defiant hostility toward teachers.

Another 30% belong to an amorphous crowd that defines itself as average and has no clearly distinguishing characteristic to make its members stand out. And, another 10% to 15% belong to groups defined by ethnicity.

For about 5% of all students, their success in the classroom affords them status as "brains." This crowd defines itself by doing well in school. Other crowds of adolescents heap scorn on them and demean their academic success. The brains relate well and closely to teachers, and avoid drugs and deviant behavior.

## HOW DO ECONOMIC MOTIVATIONS
## PROMOTE DRUG USE IN U.S. CULTURE?

The means to produce powerful drugs has been available for a long time. Because producers and distributers of drugs can earn impressive economic rewards, they continue to make illicit drugs available to the community despite much police effort to stop them. In turn, communities create drug markets by providing direct and indirect social supports for drug use, and exposing their members to cultural conditions that create needs for drugs. As a result, a market of nearly 40 million Americans who use drugs sustain the drug trade in America.

This started during colonial times when people used cocaine, opium, and marijuana for recreation and as medicines. Although U.S. communities were concerned about alcohol abuse, the principles of individual freedom expressed in the Magna Carta (1215) guided community life in the new world (Fishbein & Pease, 1996).

Therefore, rather than regulating individual drug use as is the current practice, colonists attempted to control public intoxication. They sought to discourage drunken disorderly behavior and to promote productive economic contribution. The Puritans advocated temperance and moderation, and they regarded rum as "God's good creature." Using this strategy, the Puritans were successful in establishing a rapprochement between the money-versus-morals poles of the drug dilemma.

This was important because trade in rum, molasses, and slaves was vital to New England economy (Levin, 1995). On the first leg of an infamous trading triangle, sailors brought rum and other goods manufactured in New England to Africa. There, they exchanged them for slaves and exotic treasures of the Middle East. On the second leg, they sailed to the Carribean islands of the West Indies where they traded slaves for sugar. They then returned to New England where treasure was converted to wealth and sugar was made into molasses and rum. Sailors would then repeat the trading cycle.

Interestingly, a tariff was extracted by pirates of the Caribbean who raided the traders' ships and stole treasure. Pirates freed many slaves on the condition that they would join their pirate crews. In some instances, 25% to 30% of the members of pirate crews were freed slaves (Broad, 1997a).

No doubt some pirates, such as Edward Teach, the infamous Blackbeard, were brutal and murderous during the period from 1650 to 1725 (Broad, 1997b). However, many were not, and their crews were adherents to admirable democratic and charitable ideals (Broad, 1997a). New evidence indicates that ships captained by notorious pirates such as Black Sam Belamy were floating commonwealths in which crews shared their booty and treated captives humanely.

The drug of American choice, alcohol, was at the center of their activities. However, Blackbeard blockaded the harbor of Charleston, South Carolina, and ransomed hostages in exchange for a chest full of other drugs and medicines. The drug Blackbeard sought was unguent of mercury to treat syphilis that plagued pirate crews of the time.

Robert Lewis Stevenson's tales of adventure and piracy during this era, *Kidnapped* and *Treasure Island*, are great literary fare for late-elementary school children as are the *Seahawk* and other novels by Rafael Sabatini. James Barrie's *Peter Pan* has the villainous pirate, Captain Hook, and Gilbert and Sullivan present the *Pirates of Penzance* as zestful ner-do-wells. For teachers and older students, David Cordingly's *Under the Black Flag: The Romance and the Reality of Life Among the Pirates* (1995) provides a more realistic look at life on the high seas during those times.

In contrast to the moral issues raised by slavery and slave trading, those associated with drug use seem to pale. Teachers can challenge young readers of the fictional classics and older students of history about the moral difference between pirates and the slave traders on whom they preyed. Students also can examine the place of rum, the manufacture of alcoholic beverages, and the use of other drugs during those times. They will find that this long-past era is a source of fantasy and tales of adventure, but its traditions perpetuated Americans' personal choice about drug use.

In fact, drugs, and particularly alcohol, were so important to the economy that free choice about drug use continued throughout the 1800s until the early 20th century. During that 100- to 120-year period, the medical and pharmaceutical industries were unregulated and pharmacists unlicenced. Therefore, the United States had no mechanisms through which to control production, distribution, or use of drugs.

However, a series of cultural innovations, societal events, and social changes set the stage for increasingly stringent drug control. The earliest of these cultural innovations was the derivation of morphine, and later codeine, from opium during the period from 1806 to 1832. A German pharmacist's assistant developed morphine in 1806 and then in the 1890s, a German pharmaceutical company made heroin commercially available (Fishbein & Pease, 1996). The company marketed heroin as a cough suppressant and as a cure for morphine addiction. The medical community's acceptance of morphine and codeine during the early 1830s led to their widespread use to treat pain, anxiety, and intestinal ailments.

These opium derivatives are analogous to the distilled spirits people learned how to produce about 1,100 years ago (Dweiko, 1993). Distillation is a process through which the amount of alcohol in what would otherwise be beer or wine is increased by evaporating alcohol from its watery medium and condensing it into a more concentrated liquid form. Likewise, morphine and codeine, the active agents in opium, are extracted from opium. The concentration of these active agents makes morphine 10 times more potent than opium and heroin 3 times more powerful than morphine.

The second cultural innovation was Alexander Wood's invention of the hypodermic needle in 1848. Wood was a Scottish physician (Fishbein & Pease, 1996).

Next, the Civil War was a powerful societal event that changed the course of U.S. history with regard to slavery and drug use. The Civil War made slavery illegal and accelerated the use of injectable morphine. Morphine injections provided immediate pain relief for battlefield injuries and controlled the dysentery that was rampant among Union and Confederate troops. Although there is some debate about the extent of use during the Civil War, within 5 years after cessation of hostilities, anyone could purchase a hypodermic needle and injectable morphine from a drugstore.

These and other advances in technical acumen have made production of tobacco, alcoholic beverages, prescription drugs, and over-the-counter medications into global industries. The immense economic power of such industries drives the drug marketplace and influences culture and social policy (Gerbner, 1990; Gitlin, 1990).

Not only does the drug industry generate enormous profits, but, through the media and government lobbying activities, it promotes drug use. This may be particularly so for advertising messages about tobacco, alcohol, and various drugs. However, portrayals of smoking, drinking, and drug use are often prominent in movies and TV drama, too (Chase, 1996; Greenberg, 1984; Greenberg et al., 1984).

In part, the impetus behind drug regulation stems from some reformers' realization that society could not depend on the drug industry, physicians, or pharmacists to safeguard the public interest. Before regulation, the market offered numerous patent medicines and other unlabeled preparations that contained alcohol, cocaine, morphine, codeine, and cannabis. Many physicians and pharmacists prescribed and dispensed these drugs in ways that were, at best, unselective and at worst, unscrupulous.

Such problems continue to emerge in modern times when regulation is extensive. In 1991, former Commissioner David Kessler revitalized a moribund FDA. The FDA staff was overwhelmed and demoralized, and incapable of coping with increased duties and its inadequate budget (Burros, 1996). Kessler went so far as to create an Office of Criminal Investigation to improve enforcement by his agency. He did so to combat food mislabeling, false or inappropriate drug advertising, the proliferation of dangerous food additives, and the marketing abuses of the tobacco industry.

The tobacco companies now stand accused that, to increase profits, they laced cigarettes with added nicotine, thus enhancing their addictive potential. They face the prospect that nicotine, and thus tobacco, will be regulated as an addictive drug. And, health insurance organizations, relatives, and the estates of victims of smoking-related disease are suing tobacco companies for costs and damages (Collins, 1996). In 1999, federal and state governments are negotiating huge financial settlements with the tobacco industry. These settlements are worth hundreds of billions of dollars and may impose strict controls on marketing and production of tobacco products.

Furthermore, since the 1980s, the courts have convicted 50 executives of 14 drug companies of felonies for deceitful product testing and fraudulent reporting of manufacturing processes (Hilts, 1995). More recently, drug companies stand accused of suppressing researchers' negative findings about their products (Altman, 1997; Kolata, 1997), and the U.S. Securities and Exchange Commission (SEC) has cited some drug researchers for insider stock trading crimes ("S.E.C. cites," 1997). The SEC accused these researchers of warning others about negative findings prior to public disclosure. This enabled researchers' friends and associates to sell their stock in affected companies to avoid financial loss. Thus, the economic agenda of the money-versus-morals dilemma is so powerful that even legitimate producers of legal drugs are sorely tempted toward illegal opportunism and exploitation.

## HOW DO PROMINENT PERSONS AND OPINION LEADERS PROMOTE DRUG USE?

U.S. history is replete with individuals whose prominence and social status attracted admiration and emulation, and who advocated drug use in both word and action. As teachers will notice, many of these figures appear prominently in the curriculum of a variety of school subjects.

For example, in 1891, Oliver Wendell Holmes, Sr., physician, writer, and dean of the Harvard School of Medicine, despite his broad condemnation of medicines and drugs, described opium to be a medical prescription from the Creator (Sandor, 1995). Freud and others associated with the early days of psychoanalysis waged their own personal struggles with alcohol, cocaine, morphine, and tobacco addiction (Levin & Weiss, 1994).

Throughout history, prominent musicians, dancers, artists, actors, poets, journalists, and influential writers have achieved as much notoriety for their substance abuse as fame for their artistic and literary achievements. In fact, addiction has been so rampant in the arts, that some observers suspect that a link exists between artistic creativity and substance abuse.

Artists, themselves, have described their experiences with alcohol and drugs as freeing the creative spirit, sweeping aside constrictive inhibition, opening windows to the soul, offering an opening of the mind beyond rationality, and liberating the mind (Charters, 1992; Dardis, 1989; Kirkland & Lawrence, 1992). In 1896, psychologist Havelock Ellis experimented with mescaline and was so impressed with the drug's aesthetic value that he gave some to Irish poet W.B. Yeats (Rudgley, 1993). The Tukano Indians of the Columbian northwest Amazon consider their drug-induced music and art to represent an altered state of consciousness superior to that produced by mundane experience (Rudgley, 1993). As Dardis (1989) noted, the Greek poet Horace's statement that "To the sober I assign a career in business or public affairs; from the grim I withhold the right to write poems" reveals just how ancient and enduring such beliefs are.

These views persist despite the warnings by observers of the lives of famous drug-using artists. In describing the alcoholic damage to the life and career of F. Scott Fitzgerald, biographers reveal that the gift of artistic talent is sorely wasted on drugs and drink (Mellow, 1984), and that alcoholism is the "enemy of art and the curse of Western civilization" (Connolly, 1963).

The French poet Charles Baudelaire described his drug experiences in his 1858 writing The Poem of Hashish. He saw nothing miraculous about the drug's effects and may have been the first observer of amotivational syndrome in describing cannabis to strengthen imagination, but to sap the strength of will to be artistically productive (Rudgley, 1993).

Such warnings are confirmed by self-reports of famous survivors of addiction. These artists' autobiographies describe how damaging substance abuse was to their own lives and artistic careers. Among the autobiographies that may be of interest to teachers of music, dance, drama, or journalism are those of jazz musician Miles Davis (Davis & Troupe, 1989), ballet dancer Gelsey Kirkland (Kirkland & Lawrence, 1992), actress Mariette Hartley (Hartley & Commire, 1990), actress Carrie Fisher (1987), journalist and writer Pete Hamill (1994), and editor and columnist Caroline Knapp (1996).

For teachers of English and literature, the fact that five of seven native-born U.S. Nobel Prize winners in literature were alcoholic is a startling and powerful statement about the artistic allusions held forth by drugs and alcohol. The drunks among Nobel laureates include William Faulkner, Ernest Hemingway, John Steinbeck, Sinclair Lewis, and Eugene O'Neill (Dardis, 1989).

The long list of other prominent writers similarly afflicted suggests that addiction is an epidemic among 20th-century U.S. authors. Others include Jack London, Edna St. Vincent Millay, F. Scott Fitzgerald, Thomas Wolfe, Dashiell Hammett, Dorothy Parker, Ring Lardner, Truman Capote, Robert Lowell, John O'Hara, and Tennessee Williams. And, this list is by no means complete.

Interestingly, alcohol abuse appears to be particular to U.S. authors and occurs far less often among their European and English contemporaries. From Edgar Allan Poe onward, U.S. writers have acquired a well-deserved reputation for heavy drinking.

Poe's chronic alcoholism persisted despite his promises to his wife and mother-in-law that he would reform. He died on October 7, 1849, four days after a drinking binge that left him unconscious outside a Baltimore saloon.

Unlike great European writers, few U.S. writers sustain careers beyond the bloom of their youth and alcoholism is often the major contributor to early decline. Four of the five alcoholic Nobel prize winners were finished as great writers by their late 30s to early 40s. The same is true for other prominent U.S. authors afflicted with alcoholism.

Among alcoholic Nobel laureates, only Eugene O'Neill stopped drinking before losing his powers as a writer. He did so in his mid-30s, and is the one exception who continued to be productive as he approached age 60. His later works included *The Iceman Cometh* and *Long Day's Journey Into Night*, both of which were about addiction (O'Neill, 1955, 1957).

Tragically, Jack London, Hart Crane, John Berryman, and Ernest Hemingway are among the alcoholic writers who eventually committed suicide. The self-inflicted demise of these great authors, and the prematurely exhausted talents and lost creativity of they and others stand in stark contrast to the brilliant beginnings of their careers. Alcoholic writers who continued to write produced increasingly feeble works as they aged and their addiction and the damage wrought by it progressed. They became victims of alcohol's corrosive effects on the clarity of thought and word, sensitivity and consciousness, and recall that are the most important assets of writers (Hamill, 1994).

Interestingly, the Nobel laureates and many of the other writers listed previously matured to greatness during the alcohol prohibition era. They became known as the "lost generation" of U.S. writers of the 1920s, and their hard drinking was at least in part a reaction to prohibition. Prohibition was imposed in 1920 just as these writers began their careers.

Writers such as Hemingway and Fitzgerald are among the many who fled to Paris and London after World War I to escape U.S. philistinism, and President Warren Harding (Charters, 1992) under whose scandal-ridden administration alcohol prohibition became law. According to Dardis (1989), as independent thinkers, many felt a moral duty to violate the law at every opportunity, and that drinking was a matter of principle in the exercise of personal freedom. What is more, prohibition gave drinking new social status, excitement, danger, and mystery.

As the next generation of writers emerged in the 1940s, following World War II, independent thinkers reacted in similar fashion to prohibition of drugs other than alcohol, the Cold War, and the threat of nuclear annihilation. Surprisingly, Herbert Huncke, street hustler, petty thief, chronic drug addict, and sometime writer enthralled and inspired a "galaxy" of these about to be and newly acclaimed authors (Thomas, 1996).

As a living, breathing heretic to a right-thinking, clean-living prohibitionist establishment, Huncke gave the beat generation its name. He introduced Jack Kerouac to the term *beat*, and bragged that he gave William S. Burroughs his first heroin fix. He became a hero to such writers as Burroughs, Allen Ginsberg, Lucien Carr, Jack Kerouac, and John Clellon Holmes. Ginsberg and Carr were 18-year-old Columbia University undergraduates at that time, but they were using marijuana and Benzedrine as sources of inspiration for a new vision of the art of writing.

Burroughs, who became a morphine addict, traveled far and wide in search of new drug experience. He even traveled to the University of Bogota in Columbia so that he might try the exotic Banisteriopsis drug experience.

Despite the intellect and talent of these writers, they were a community of outlaws whose social deviance went beyond drug use (Charters, 1992). They were involved in at least one murder. Kerouac went to jail as a material witness for helping Lucian Carr destroy evidence in a fatal stabbing. Burroughs forged prescriptions for drugs, mugged drunks to support his morphine habit, and consorted with gangsters in Tangier (Miller & Koral, 1995). In Mexico, while drunk, Burroughs shot and killed his wife in a game of William Tell. Allen Ginsberg was expelled from Columbia University and spent time in psychiatric wards after letting Huncke stash stolen goods in his apartment.

Perhaps even more direct in their drug advocacy were Timothy Leary and Aldous Huxley. Both extolled the virtues of psychedelic drugs as paths to enlightenment and altered experience. Huxley wrote of his mescaline experiences in his book *The Doors of Perception* (1954). Harvard University fired Leary from his faculty position for experimenting on himself, his associates, and volunteer subjects with psilocybin. Leary, who later became known as the "High Priest of LSD," then created a magazine called the *Psychedelic Review* in which he published poetic and artistic accounts of drug experiences and papers by eminent scholars.

Although the preceding narrative focuses on writers, other artists have emerged as role models and victims of drug use and abuse, too.

U.S. painters Jackson Pollack, Mark Rothko, and Franz Klein were alcoholics (Dardis, 1989). Musicians Billie Holiday, Charlie Parker, Leonard Bernstein, Elvis Presley, Jerry Garcia, Kurt Cobain, and Janice Joplin were notorious drinkers and drug users. Actors Humphry Bogart, Marilyn Monroe, John Belushi, Robert Downey, Jr., and River Phoenix are but a few of many prominent figures in the performing arts whose actions modeled use of alcohol, heroin, amphetamines, cocaine, barbiturates, and tobacco.

Teachers should note that many of these artists and performers paid for substance abuse with their lives. Those for whom biographies are available are often sources of important disclosures about how drugs became dangerous and malignant for them.

These issues are relevant to physical education teachers and athletic coaches, too, because drug use by collegiate and professional athletes has attracted much attention. These athletes' fame, fortune, free time, and feeling of invincibility enhance their vulnerability to drug use (Wadler & Zemper, 1995). Drug use among athletes is particularly important because of their popularity and potential to be role models to the young (Ackerman, 1995; Lipsyte, 1995).

Nowhere was this better demonstrated than in the growth in sales of androstenedione following media disclosure of its use by home run king Mark McGwire (Derwin, 1998). Androstenedione is a steroid-like drug that increases user's testosterone levels. Sales of this drug increased by 25% following disclosure.

The culture of competitive sports promotes drug use in many ways. For example, some observers suggest that parents' and teachers' overindulgence can cause athletes to think that their extraordinary talent exempts them from usual community obligations. Consequently, some athletes behave as though they have special entitlements and privileges.

This seems to have been the case when members of the U. S. hockey team vandalized their quarters in the athletes' village during the 1998 Olympics in Nagano, Japan. The team was composed of high-profile U.S. stars of the National Hockey League who were seen drinking in local bars on the evening of the incident (Lapointe, 1998).

Furthermore, the media and adoring sports fans all too readily feed the grandiosity and narcissism that have become occupational hazards for famous sports figures. The sports media are quick to dramatize athletes' drug problems when such problems come to light (Sandomir, 1996). Consequently, young admirers may be tempted to emulate athletes' drug-taking behavior when the media expose it.

Furthermore, the pressure to maintain a competitive edge pushes some athletes to use drugs they believe will enhance performance. This has a long history dating back to ancient Greek Olympians who used strychnine and psychoactive mushrooms to prepare for competition.

The first athlete known to die from performance enhancing drugs was a French cyclist in 1886 who had used a mixture of cocaine and heroin. Modern cyclists continue to risk their lives with performance-enhancing but dangerous drugs such as erythropietin (EPO). EPO, which increases the production of oxygen-rich red blood cells, has been linked to the deaths of 20 bicycle racers since the 1980s. Despite the fact that the drug increases the risk of thrombosis and heart attack by thickening the blood, prominent competitors such as Belgian cyclist Eddy Planckaert advocate its use ("Cyclist says," 1998).

By the 1940s, some athletes were using the male hormone testosterone to boost performance. Then in 1953, anabolic steroids were first developed and found to be much more effective as a strength-enhancing agent than anything that had been used previously. Because of their effectiveness, they are very attractive to aspiring athletes. Steroids have many dangerous side effects and are now legally controlled substances.

Despite government regulation, annual black market sales of anabolic steroids are more than $400 million. In the United States, approximately 1 million people use steroids and half of these are adolescents. More than one third of steroid users have no intention of participating in competitive sports (Public Health Reports, 1992; Telander, 1993).

This suggests strongly that the grandiosity and narcissism at times associated with high-level competitive athletics have found their way into the world of nonathletes, too. For nonathletes, personal appearance, status in the peer group, and conformity to the media-promoted muscular image of the modern heroic male are driving forces (Mosse, 1996). Such individuals turn to steroids as a quick route to a culturally promoted form of social success.

In some circumstances, athletes may use drugs such as codeine or Demerol in order to perform while injured as in the case of Brett Favre, the Green Bay Packer football star. During the football seasons of the early to mid 1990s Favre risked addiction to painkillers so that he could continue to play despite his numerous injuries. Although he played in the greatest number of consecutive games of any quarterback in professional football during that period, he did become addicted.

In professional football alone, as many as 10% of more than 1,500 players in the National Football League have serious addiction problems with painkillers (Freeman, 1997). Others, too, have jeopardized their athletic careers and their health by using dangerously high dosages of these painkillers, anti-inflammatory medications, and even anesthetics such as Novocaine or Xylocaine as substitutes for rest and proper healing (Green, 1996).

However, as former player Tim Green (1996) wrote, the financial stakes are so large, and the expectation to play with pain so strong, that at least the moderate use of some drugs is necessary at the highest levels of professional football. Team physicians get caught in a conflict of interest and quiet conspiracy. They, too, are pressured by players, management, and team owners to make risky diagnoses and prescribe quick fixes for athletes' speedy return to the playing field.

And, some athletes use drugs for recreational purposes just as do other people. Most recently, the withdrawal of the Gold Medal won by Canadian snowboarder Ross Rebagliati in the 1998 Winter Olympics for a positive marijuana test is a case in point. Although Rebegliati's medal was reinstated because of flaws in the test, two other Olympic competitors tested positive, as well.

The sports media all too regularly announce the suspension or banning of various athletes when drug tests reveal that they have been using cocaine, heroin, marijuana, or other illegal substances. Some athletes, such as professional football players Bam Morris of the Pittsburgh Steelers and Michael Irvin of the Dallas Cowboys, faced criminal charges because police caught them in possession of illegal drugs. So too, did Green Bay Packers running back Travis Jervey who was arrested for marijuana possession.

Police arrests for drunk driving, domestic violence, or other dangerous and illegal behavior exposes others with alcohol problems. In professional football and baseball, heavy drinking appears to be a strongly reinforced social norm that raises the risks to players and their families in the name of old fashioned camaraderie and celebration (Green, 1996).

Drug use in the sports world has produced tragedies. Professional football player Lyle Alzado attributed the brain tumor that eventually killed him to steroid abuse, and Mickey Mantle's fatal liver cancer was clearly a product of alcoholism. Cocaine overdose caused the sudden death of basketball player Len Bias and football player Don Rogers.

## WHAT CULTURALLY PROMOTED
## SOCIAL VALUES ENCOURAGE DRUG USE?

Despite these and other frightening events, many cherished values of U.S. culture promote drug use. These values include inalienable individual rights, pursuit of private happiness, individualism, and private withdrawal from larger society (Gitlin, 1990). The Bill of Rights and the Constitution present clear evidence that Americans dedicated themselves to establishing and preserving these values from the very beginning of the nation.

In fact, "beat culture" of the 1950s and early 1960s, with which Huncke so closely identified himself, was a caricature of these values. The beatniks who were notorious boozers and drug users prized personal freedom and self-liberation above all else (Pinchbeck, 1995).

That U.S. culture has become one of comfort and convenience, drama and high impact sensation, and is abhorrent to delayed pleasure is the modern translation of these values (Ray, 1972). Play, fashion, travel, and frivolity are their behavioral expression. Although many people challenge the moral integrity of such expressions of personal freedom, the freedom they represent is the most prized of U.S. values.

## WHAT CULTURAL FORCES OPPOSE DRUG USE IN U.S. SOCIETY?

Although many pro-drug use forces are long-standing elements of U.S. culture, powerful forces in opposition to drug use have always existed, too. These forces in opposition to drug use are themselves tainted and evoke much suspicion and distrust, although this was not always the case.

As teachers of history and social studies may observe, from the very beginning, Puritan values advocated hard work, sacrifice, and good character. Colonial Americans condemned drunkenness and punished drunks, despite the fact that taverns were centers of community activity during pre-revolutionary times. Early American cultural standards regarding alcohol consumption advocated temperance and moderation, and were tolerant of drug use, but public policy gradually shifted toward advocacy of total abstinence and prohibition.

In part, this shift occurred because of urban upheaval that occurred in American cities following the Civil War. Many young men began moving away from their families and other sources of moral control. This alarmed those who derived wealth, power, and status from positions of moral leadership. These leaders included clergymen and conservative politicians of the time (Noble, 1990).

Reason exists to suspect that the swing toward increasingly restrictive drug policies was influenced more strongly by economic and political expedience than by moral or health issues. Evidence and circumstance now provide strong arguments that prohibitionist forces were energized by political ambition, greed, zealotry, racism, bigotry, and fear rather than benevolent concern.

As Musto (1987) recognized in the mid-1970s, U.S. concern with drugs is a political problem that goes far beyond the medical or legal issues that surround it. Drug control and prohibition are driven by powerful tensions among social classes, economic groups, ethnic and racial groups, and the attraction and effects of drugs, themselves.

When one examines them closely, community reactions against drug use appear to be more attentive to the social position of drug users than the dangers of using drugs. Consequently, many observers suspect drug laws to be a weapon against people rather than a tool of social progress. The fact that alcohol, which kills 150,000 people annually, and tobacco, that kills 400,000 each year, are the most dangerous of drugs, but are legally available, serves to strengthen such suspicion.

History reveals that drug policy often has been a virulent form of hostility, oppression, and exploitation directed at various segments of society. Distortion, stereotyping, and misrepresentations that associate racial and ethnic groups with drugs are too closely linked with drug policy. For example, the notion that Blacks were especially heavy cocaine users, and under its influence would commit acts of violence against Whites was a frightening, if false, pretext for making cocaine possession a crime (Ashley, 1975). Thus, prohibition not only gave vent to discriminatory antipathy and outrage at antisocial behavior, but also offered a simple and direct solution to racist fears.

That the dangers of substance abuse and the well being of the population appear to have been secondary concerns of policymakers has soured the attitudes of many observers. What is worse, for those who are targets of drug laws, powerful suspicion turns very easily to distrust, contempt, and rebelliousness.

Evidence now suggests that the alcohol prohibition movement's power was derived from support by industrial capitalists who stood to profit greatly from a sober workforce (Rumbarger, 1989). Furthermore, U.S. leaders used drug control as a lever in the negotiation of international arrangements favorable to U.S. political and economic interests.

For example, the Volstead Act that Congress passed in 1917 was motivated to some degree by anti-German sentiment associated with World War I. Also, U.S. merchants' interest in the vast Chinese market for U.S. goods, and U.S. seizure of the Philippine Islands, where opium use was common, greatly energized drug prohibition advocates at the turn of the century.

Furthermore, economic competition with foreign workers stimulated many U.S. communities to ban drugs brought in and preferred by these immigrants. European immigrants, Chinese railroad builders, and Mexican farm laborers each experienced discrimination with regard to their respective preferences for alcohol, opium, and marijuana.

Also, the urban poor became a target as the sons of impoverished immigrants and Black laborers contributed still another population of addicts. As their poverty led to increased involvement in criminal activity, drugs were implicated by association.

Perhaps U.S. relations with the Chinese during the late 1800s and early 1900s best illustrates these actions. Chinese immigrants, many of whom came to the United States as indentured servants, suffered notoriously brutal treatment at the hands of employers and communities. They took dangerous and humiliating jobs no Americans desired, accepted small pay, and were vehemently resented by American workers of the far west for doing so.

This resentment grew during harsh economic times. As Sandor (1995) pointed out, in 1878, San Francisco banned opium-smoking establishments despite the fact that opium and cocaine were legally available in patent medicines and beverages until the eve of World War I. This was clearly prejudicial to the Chinese whose intoxication, gambling, and whoring in their opium dens was not different from the behavior of U.S. Whites in whiskey saloons (Sandor, 1995).

In China, knowledge of the abuses suffered by Chinese immigrants and travelers in America evoked strong protests and a voluntary embargo against U.S. goods by Chinese merchants. Because U.S. traders feared losing the Chinese market, actions were sought that would reduce tensions between the United States and China.

A solution was proposed by U.S. missionary Charles Henry Brent, who was the first Episcopal bishop of the Philippines. Brent had become an international leader in the opium prohibition movement. He suggested that the United States ingratiate itself with the fervently nationalistic Chinese government by helping it in its struggle against opium.

According to British investigators, the effects of opium use in China were probably no more abhorrent than the effects of alcohol in Western countries. Nevertheless, the Chinese government blamed opium as the cause of their nation's lag in education, science, technology, and military power.

President Theodore Roosevelt responded favorably to Brent's idea. In Roosevelt's view, such an action would reduce Chinese resentment against the United States, cast a bad light on the British who were profiting from India's opium sales in China, and give Americans leverage in their competition with Europeans for the Chinese market. Thus, to strengthen control of the Chinese market, Americans sought to exploit the growing Chinese nationalism that had selected opium as the scapegoat for a multitude of humiliations.

To achieve these goals, the United States planned and organized an international conference. At this conference, the United states was to secure agreements for controlling production and distribution of opium from participating countries. These efforts produced the Shanghai Opium Conference of 1909.

The one fly in the ointment was that the United States, as the convening nation, had no laws of its own to control domestic opium use. For Americans to demand strict controls by other nations and to have no exemplary laws of its own was at least awkward, if not embarrassing. Thus, the first laws regulating narcotics in the United States were a face-saving device for a strategy to pursue the imagined riches of the Chinese marketplace.

Just as Bishop Brent's religious zeal fueled his efforts to prohibit opium, such zeal was a driving force in the prohibition of other drugs, too. For example, the Women's Christian Temperance Movement's birth in 1872 eventually led to the Anti-Saloon League in 1893. The Anti-Saloon League applied direct political pressure on lawmakers and candidates for public office to legalize alcohol prohibition.

Their actions displayed the same fervor as some religious leaders of modern anti-abortion groups. These more recent groups seek to reimpose prohibition of abortion despite the fact that its prohibition is unconstitutional and a majority of Americans favor personal choice on this matter. Recent events have demonstrated that some individuals on the prohibition side of the abortion issue have murder in their hearts, and recognize no limits in their attempts to reimpose prohibition of abortion.

As the analogy to the abortion struggle illustrates, U.S. culture and social policy have a long history of competing agendas, mixed messages, honorable and dishonorable intentions, values conflicts, and extreme reactions around many issues. This is especially so regarding drug prohibition. In such an environment, teachers, parents, their children, and other thoughtful community members have difficulty discerning the meanings of the multitude of claims about drugs and drug use.

Truth appears to be inextricably entangled with folkways, values, fears, politics, and economics. Consequently, the teacher's task of identifying truth, discerning its meaning, and teaching these in believable fashion to children is a formidable one. To maintain credibility in the midst of so much that is incredible is daunting, indeed.

Nevertheless, the intent of the previous summary is not to provide a detailed chronology and critique of American culture. Because culture sets the stage for teaching in the present, the intent is to capture the flavor and ethos of U.S. culture as it relates to drug use. An appreciation of culture is necessary so that teachers may better understand the abyss into which the unwary may fall in drug education and substance abuse prevention.

Because culture is not static, this abyss is, in large part, a product of a clash between waves of cultural change and the needs of the established mainstream of U.S. society. At some times this conflict escalates and at others it lays dormant, depending on the power of pressures for change and the strength of reactions against change.

Following World War II, legislators made drug policies increasingly punitive and inclusive of drugs and drug-related activities. Then, in the 1960s, the United States Supreme Court ruled that such policies violated constitutional protection against cruel and unusual punishment. Following that decision, policies became less punitive and more supportive of treatment and rehabilitation of addicts.

Implicit within this change was a glimmer of hope that policymakers were finally recognizing a difference between drug use and drug abuse. Eight states decriminalized marijuana with the endorsement of the American Bar Association, the National Council of Churches, and the Governing Board of the American Medical Association (Grinspoon, 1977). This loosening of prohibition reached its zenith when the State Supreme Court of Alaska made home cultivation of marijuana for personal use legal in Alaska (Bakalar & Grinspoon, 1984).

However, the cocaine panic of the 1980s pushed the drug policy pendulum back in the direction of repressiveness with passage of the Anti-Drug Abuse Act of 1988. Policymakers' motivations are suspect again as some observers claim that the punitive swing served political needs and expediencies rather than the public interest.

The regressive shift in drug policy is consistent with other aspects of the 1980s. President Ronald Reagan cast the Cold War struggle with the Soviet Union as a moral encounter (Wills, 1996), and he used his wife Nancy's "Just say no!" antidrug campaign to do the same in his approach to drug use. This is risky business because moral absolutes unleash fanaticism. Both Reagan's talk of the Soviet Union as an Evil Empire and the Anti-Drug Abuse Act of 1988 were extreme to the point of social irresponsibility.

Nevertheless, Reagan's moral arguments more forcefully sustained the political efforts of his conservative constituency than rational appeals to practical advantage or self-interest ever could have. As Wills (1996) observed, "People will sacrifice for what they are persuaded is deeply right" (p. 37). This is especially so if the sacrifice is to be the rights, interests, and well-being of others, and particularly if those others have been labeled as misfits, traitors, and evildoers. So, Reagan branded Russian communists in righteous indignation over their godlessness, and branded drug users for their treasonous immorality.

This is important to teachers because, as discussed in earlier chapters, substance abuse prevention in the schools is an expression of cultural ambivalence, although it is an extension of social policy in the community. Social policy often exploits cultural ambivalence, and is more a reflection of "political possibilities" for policymakers than sincere efforts at social progress.

## SUMMARY OF KEY POINTS

Drugs have been an integral part of the culture of prehistoric peoples, tribal communities, ancient civilizations, and modern societies. Not only have drugs served medicinal purposes, but throughout the millennia, they have been useful in meeting aesthetic, spiritual, and social needs of diverse peoples around the world. Consequently, all communities have had to assign a proper cultural place to drugs so that community members might enjoy a satisfactory balance of benefits and risks for their use.

Generally, human communities have assigned drugs to religious rites and rituals, and social events and ceremonies, rather than the pursuit of hedonistic experience. The breath of the cultural rapprochement between the risks and benefits of drugs is evidenced in estimates that nearly 200 hundred million people around the world presently use mind-altering drugs.

However, in the United States, drug use is entangled with many powerful cultural issues that are economic and political as well as social and spiritual. Cultural responses to drug use express the multitude of tensions between practical concerns about money, power, and physical survival; social issues about family, childrearing, and perpetuation of community; and spiritual concerns about morality and religion.

For example, Americans approach childrearing as a relentless power struggle between adult family members and children. Adult family members then support an immense industry of drug suppliers by using alcohol, cigarettes, and other drugs in the presence of their children. Consequently, children find drugs to be both a sign of maturity and a convenient way to rebel.

Children then integrate drug use into the partitioning and culture of adolescent society. Not only do children become the next market for drug producers, parents, prominent community members, and a variety of idealized role models such as artists, writers, and athletes promote sales.

Abundant biographical writings are available that describe the devastating impact of addiction on many of these role models. Such writings also describe cultures of the arts, literature, and athletics. These cultures appear to aid and abet drug use among their members in many ways. The prominence and popularity of members of these elite communities puts them in a position to unduly influence the behavior of others.

Nevertheless, the very foundation of cultural values that portrays America as a bulwark of freedom also supports drug use. Individuality, private withdrawal from community life, and a spirit of adventure are among these values. In fact, many observers suspect much drug use to be an act of rebellion against threats to these freedoms.

Despite aspects of American culture that support drug use, there are many that oppose it, too. These include Puritan beliefs in good character, hard work, and frugality. Guardians of these beliefs often entangle themselves in avarice and hypocrisy so that even their most benevolent intentions are suspect.

# 12

# Substance Abuse Prevention in the Context of Popular Culture

The goals for this chapter are to help teachers accomplish the following:

1. Recognize manifestations of popular culture in the behavior of their students.
2. Understand the developmental issues that underlie youthful adherence to trends, fads, and social movements of the young.
3. Grasp the importance of drugs as a defining aspect of popular cultural movements and a lightening rod for community opposition.
4. Trace the evolution of popular culture in the 20th century and the link between its art, music, and literature and current trends in drug use.
5. Identify and challenge basic assumptions that underlie students' adherence to the edicts of the trends, fads, and movements of popular culture.
6. Develop strategies and tactics to help students protect themselves from dangerous aspects of popular culture.

Adults of the Western world have tried for eons to understand the phenomenon of youth. An anthology of papers by European scholars (Levi & Schmitt, 1997) describes this ongoing struggle that has produced an evolving perception of children and adolescents.

Early perceptions declared children merely to be miniature adults, but this changed by the late 1700s. According to Levi and Schmitt's anthology, at the time of the French Revolution and the American Revolution, people began to both admire and fear youth. Adults of those times viewed children to be different from themselves, and to associate youth

**211**

with revolution. Therefore, youth was fearsome because it was rebellious, but admired because of its potential to sweep away an imperfect
world distorted by errors of the past.

Now, adults fear that young people will generate a culture that diminishes the importance of adult rationality and influence, and over-
shadows adults' position as role models and leaders in community life
(Cross, 1997). Consequently, youthful struggles for separation from
parents and individual identity have inflamed many cultural, moral,
and political battles (Weinstein, 1995b). In these struggles, adults fear
abandonment and imagine that young peoples' nihilism and hedonism
will shake the foundations of society.

The tide of youthful behavior about which adults are so fearful man-
ifests itself in popular culture. Teachers, parents, and other adults witness popular culture in fads, trends, and social movements among the
young. Fads are behavioral elements of popular culture that emerge
suddenly and explosively and vanish just as quickly. Other behavioral
elements may develop slowly and persist, or ebb and flow over time as
in the case of trends.

In contrast to trends and fads, youthful social movements have elements of forethought and organization to them. They are actions
against restrictions, demands, and ingenuousness of existing norms
and social policies. Social movements, too, may wax and wane. Some
participants outgrow them and withdraw, new participants join, old issues lose salience, or new concerns achieve prominence. In some instances, adherents to popular culture simply choose new directions
for their energies.

Fads, trends, and social movements emerge when young people
adopt innovations from within U.S. culture, assimilate novel ideas from
other cultures, and imitate the actions of charismatic figures. Such people usually display behavior or personal attributes that make them attractive as representations or symbols of social issues or concerns.

Teachers can observe popular culture in the classroom in students'
clothing, hairstyles, speech, music, labels assigned to social groupings
(hippies, beatniks, punk rockers, etc.), and expressions of peer pressure for or against conformity and nonconformity. Hula hoops,
rollerblades, rap music, baseball caps worn backward, baggy cloths,
purple hair, surfing the Internet, and tatoos and skin piercing are but a
few old and new examples.

In a recent instance, the school uniforms of New York parochial
schools are a target of a youthful fad. Students are pushing limits by
raising hemlines of plaid skirts, making trousers baggy, and wearing
sagging neckties (Hamilton, 1998). In this way, resistance to the dress
code has become a youthful fashion statement and an intrusion of popular culture into the conservative traditions of parochial education.

Usually, youthful participation in popular culture is stimulated by internal pressures inherent to growing up. Physical growth and psychological development generate these pressures as children mature, separate from family, establish themselves in their peer groups, and enter adulthood. For better or worse, popular culture often contains fads, trends, and movements that oppose some unjust or oppressive decree of mainstream culture and social policy (Roberts & Kloss, 1974).

Disappointing and traumatic experiences with parents, teachers, and other adult figures increase young peoples' attraction to popular culture's more rebellious and dangerous options. These options usually appeal to alienated crowds of young people and place teachers and others who represent the mainstream of social norms and policy in a precarious position. Consequently, adult resistance to popular culture ultimately destroys some young people's confidence in those who are agents of policy. This loss of confidence is worsened by real or imagined weaknesses, betrayals, and other disappointments by community leaders, teachers, and parents.

## HOW IS POPULAR CULTURE
## IMPLICATED IN DRUG USE?

Many manifestations of popular culture are benign or have positive social and genuine artistic value. Some forms can be harmful.

Sexual acting out, gang participation, weapons possession and violence, shoplifting, food and diet fads, self-mutilation, youthful drinking and smoking, and drug use are more dangerous manifestations. In fact, waves of change regarding drug use often are a defining aspect of popular culture, and have stimulated or served as a pretext for suppression by the community.

Young people and adults usually associate drug use and other potentially harmful forms of popular culture with social status, glamor, danger, mystery, and alienation. Furthermore, prominent artists, writers, musicians, intellectuals, and other charismatic figures may be at the forefront of such dangerous activity. In this way, various expressions of popular culture became attractive.

Among the alienated, drug use and other risky activities are acts of rebellion against a world that popular culture's proponents characterize as vapid and bourgeois, and dominated by dull routine, bigotry, and wage slavery. Furthermore, otherwise unappealing followers, "groupies," and hangers on to popular culture's creative initiators often acquire a charismatic aura themselves.

They, too, become models for emulation by impressionable and naive admirers. Many of these secondary role models and advocates of popular culture often emerge from an itinerant underworld whose values, morals, and behavior are questionable, if not repugnant. Some young observers are so blinded by the illusion of fame and notoriety that at times surrounds these secondary role models that they will behave in extreme ways to win favor from them.

In fact, punk rock musician Richard Lloyd who was wearing a teeshirt with the words "Please Kill Me" on it, claimed that youths attending a show asked him if he was serious about the request printed on the shirt. They then offered to oblige if that was what he really wanted because "we're such big fans" (McNeil & McCain, 1996, p. 173). Lloyd never wore the shirt again.

Rebelliousness, alienation, and antisocial attitudes and behavior permeate popular culture because charismatic figures to whom popular culture is most responsive are often the "outlaws and madmen of the generation before." This is how F. Scott Fitzgerald characterized the shaping of the post-World War II literary movement of Beat writers (Charters, 1992). The secret heroes of the early Beat writers were models such as heroin-addicted jazz virtuoso Charlie Parker, Welsh alcoholic poet Dylan Thomas, and French poet, drunk, and gun runner Arthur Rimbaud. All of these models were outside traditional Anglo-American ideals and had come to symbolize the "alienated genius" that Beat writers coveted as a self-definition.

Our history and language are checkered with the names of such individuals and groups, and descriptive labels associated with various epochs of popular culture. For example, in the late 1860s, opium smoking first became the rage among a raucous demimonde of gamblers, prostitutes, con men, and theatrical types (Jonnes, 1996). People referred to these groups as the "sporting class" throughout the late 1800s into the early 20th century. Later editions of the sporting class came to be known as "hipsters" (1920s), "hep-cats" (1930s), "bohemians" (1940s) "beats" (1950s), "hippies" (1960s), "punks" (1970s), and "yuppies" (1980s).

Interestingly, each of these eras was an extension of the era that preceded it. However, the punk era of the 1970s was a popular cultural backlash against the hippies' repudiation of materialism and "Peace and love, and feel good" ideals. Punk rockers claimed that the hippie cult of Charles Manson and Tate–LaBianca murders exposed the fraudulence of the hippie movement and caused its demise (McNeil & McCain, 1996). The punk rockers opposed mass movements and advocated individual expression in art and music, and raw and nihilistic hedonism through sex, drugs, art, and particularly rock and roll music.

Each of the generations in which these editions of the sporting class became prominent named itself accordingly. Writers of the 1920s to 1930s referred to themselves as the "Lost Generation," those following

World War II accepted the label of "Beat Generation," the hippies were the "Love Generation," the punks called themselves the "Blank Generation," the yuppies were the "Me Generation," and "Generation X" appeared in the early 1990s. Each edition of the sporting class had drugs with which it primarily identified.

The hipsters emerged in the 1920s from Black urban communities of northern U.S. cities (Jonnes, 1996). Marijuana, which was legal at that time, was their drug of choice. Interestingly, a White Jewish jazz musician named Milton Mezzerow introduced marijuana to Black hipsters of Harlem in 1929. Mezzerow, a car thief and reform school graduate from Chicago, became "a minor luminary of the jazz world whose fame in Harlem was not based on his musical talents" (Jonnes, 1996, p. 122). By the mid-1930s, Mezzerow's sales activities had woven marijuana into the fabric of the hipster lifestyle.

The hep-cats used heroin and the bohemians used alcohol and amphetamines. The beats were noted for drinking cheap wine, using amphetamines, and smoking marijuana. The hippies used marijuana, LSD, and assorted hallucinogens. And, the punks and yuppies were identified with cocaine. Generation X appears to have resurrected heroin, but methamphetamine is also among their drugs of choice.

Never was the process underlying these developments more visible than in the "Counterculture Era" of 1960–1980 (Connor & Burns, 1995). By 1950, bohemians and beatniks had begun to assimilate into popular culture the fads and trends of small cadres of U.S. intellectuals, writers, and artists. Drug use and sexual liberation were dominant themes of these trends and fads. This started during the post-World War II 1940s and continued into the 1950s. By 1960, youthful fascination with bohemians and beatniks took hold and gained momentum.

From their beginnings, bohemians and beatniks were drawn to jazz and folk music. Jazz musicians, who used marijuana and heroin when almost no one else did, caught bohemian and beatnik fancy, and provided inspiration to experiment. In this way, the initial sparks were struck in the 1940s that set the counterculture era ablaze with drugs in the 1960s.

As can be surmised, music has been powerful among the many forces that drive popular culture. The linkage of jazz with drug use provides fascinating evidence of this as does the more recent connection between rock and roll and drugs.

From 1930 to 1945, the "swing" jazz style of the big band era dominated American jazz (Schuller, 1989). Performers such as Benny Goodman, Duke Ellington, Louie Armstrong, Count Basie, Lionel Hampton, Billie Holiday, Glen Miller, Harry James and many others are prominently associated with this musical epoch. What is impor-

tant about this era is that these performers, particularly Benny Goodman (Schuller, 1989) raised popular attention to their music to a level
never achieved by jazz before or since.

This music was dance-oriented and typically played in ballrooms by
large ensembles of 14 or more musicians. The U.S. public was familiar
and comfortable with and liked big band swing (Owens, 1995). Consequently, swing music set the stage for jazz to attract larger audiences
from the many elements of society. This extended the fame of jazz performers beyond the small communities of musicians, jazz aficionados,
and people drawn to musical esoterica who had been its principle en-
thusiasts.

However, World War II drew heavily on the jazz community as military service pulled many musicians away during the period from
1941–1945. While these musicians were overseas, Charlie Parker, one
of the greatest jazz geniuses, ever, revolutionized jazz, in the
mid-1940s.

To be sure, other great musicians made important contributions.
However, musicians and music scholars regard Charlie Parker as the
greatest proponent and leading performer of the "modern jazz" style,
at the time of its inception. The new style replaced swing in 1945, and
later came to be called "bebop" by journalists of the time.

Parker's talent as a jazz musician in his era rivaled that of Bach, Bee-
thoven, and Mozart as classical musicians of their own eras. Parker became an idol of the jazz world.

Audiences and many other jazz musicians heard and described the
new music as "radical, chaotic, and bewildering" (Owens, 1995, p. 3).
No doubt, bebop was a drastic departure from the music of the swing
era that preceded it. Because of its esoteric and exotic quality, it never
achieved the broad popularity of swing. Therefore, gradually, it attracted smaller and less mainstream audiences.

Nevertheless, older musicians returning from military service and
young players seeking entry into the jazz performance community
were astounded by what they heard. Not only did they want to play this
new music, they wanted to play it as well as and sound like Charlie
Parker. Because Parker was such an immense talent, the latter was an
impossible goal for most of these jazz musicians. So, in their effort to
approach his greatness, many asked the same question: "How does he
do it?"

The fact that Charlie Parker was a heroin addict, an alcoholic, and
used amphetamines led some to think drugs, especially heroin, were
the key to Parker's musical greatness. Consequently, many aspiring
Jazz musicians began to use heroin and other drugs in hopes of tap-
ping some imagined reservoir of their own musical ability (Davis,
1989).

In emulating Parker's drug-using behavior, these musicians integrated drug use into the culture of the Jazz community. Not only did users think they would make better music, but they attributed social status to heroin as it became "hip" to be a user. Among the other Jazz luminaries of that era who became heroin addicts were Miles Davis, Sonny Stitt, Bud Powell, Fats Navarro, Art Blakey, Sonny Rollins, Billie Holiday, Stan Getz, Gerry Mulligan, Red Rodney, and Chet Baker (Davis, 1989).

It is this culture to which the bohemians and beatniks of the 1940s and 1950s were drawn, and how the jazz community became a reservoir and its unusual audiences a vector for transmission of drug addiction. During this time, the center of jazz performance was New York City. This history identifies Charlie Parker as the person who, in the 1940s, started the drug explosion of the 1960s.

In the beginning, the best and most intense activity occurred before predominantly Black audiences in Harlem. But soon, 52nd Street and Greenwich Village became centers of intense jazz activity in New York City, too.

Greenwich Village jazz clubs such as Cafe Bohemia, Village Vanguard, and the Blue Note attracted audiences of established and aspiring intellectuals, artists, filmmakers, dancers, actors, poets, and writers who formed bohemian and beatnik enclaves (Davis, 1989). Similar circumstances developed in Los Angeles, which became the west coast center for such activity.

These people were ardent jazz fans, and they attended live jazz performed by small ensembles. Throughout this period, jazz musicians played bebop in small and intimate surroundings of coffeehouses and tiny nightclubs. These settings imposed physical closeness and promoted social interaction between performers and their admirers.

Also, the sales opportunities attracted drug dealers and hustlers to jazz clubs. Dealers sold to drug using jazz musicians and to new customers from among the audience. Musicians and friends in the audience would absent themselves to washrooms and other private spaces to buy and take drugs. New recruits to the world of drug taking were unaware of the damage being wrought by heroin addiction and alcoholism among jazz performers.

Jazz musicians came to New York from all over the United States. They were young, often in their late teens or early 1920s, wide-eyed, and highly impressionable. Most were dedicated artists, from decent families, with great hopes for success as musicians.

As increasing numbers followed Charlie Parker's lead into heroin addiction and drunkenness, the bonds that make a community a cohesive and valuable resource to its members, especially its younger members, were severely strained. Addicted musicians stole from, used, and alienated each other in the most reprehensible ways. And, many had promising careers shortened by illness and death. This continued despite Parker's own untimely death at age 34, in 1955.

However, as Miles Davis (1989) proposed in his autobiography, one can only wonder if these catastrophes were attributable to the evils of heroin addiction or to drug prohibition. Music teachers may raise the following questions with their students:

1. If addicted musicians had legal access to the drugs that would satisfy their incredible, albeit drug-induced, need, would they have behaved so irresponsibly and abusively toward each other?

2. If these drugs were available under medical supervision, would the drug-taking behavior of artists such as Charlie Parker and Billie Holiday, who died in 1959, have compromised their health to the extent that it did?

Both Charlie Parker and Billie Holiday succumbed to pneumonia. Ironically, alcohol abuse was the major, if not deciding, factor in the death of each, and alcohol is legally available.

As these events were taking place in the Jazz community, and among American artists, writers, intellectuals, and at bohemian and beatnik gathering places, other developments were occurring in larger society. These developments, in the late 1940s and early 1950s, made a college education increasingly available to young people.

One such development was the G.I. Bill that paid college tuition for returning military veterans. Another was the booming post-World War II economy that was further stimulated by the Cold War and the Korean War. Also, new automated technologies demanded a more educated and better trained workforce. This required a repudiation of elitism if U.S. colleges and universities were to prepare this workforce.

Menand (1996) described this expansion and asserts that U.S. universities were probably second only to the arms industry as a great beneficiary of the Cold War. After 1945, an expanding Federal government pumped millions of dollars into university research programs and continued to do so for the next 50 years. Research funding to universities became 25 times larger then it was prior to World War II.

This helped to subsidize the education of millions of people who otherwise would have been unable to pursue higher education (Menand, 1996). During the 50 years following World War II, university enrollments increased by a factor of 10 over what they were in the 1930s. The percentage of college-age Americans attending college increased from 16% to 40%.

Clearly, these developments were predicated on beliefs that a college education would be increasingly important to future economic security and success for the individual and the nation. Consequently, young people emerged from military service, the shops and stores of the bourgeoisie, the working classes, and the farm communities of America to pursue educational dreams in the ivory tower.

Therefore, newcomers to U.S. college campuses of the 1950s and 1960s were truly newcomers, and many would be the first of their family to seek higher education. They were young, wide eyed, and impressionable. They idealized and stood in awe of professors, writers, and artists whose liberal and often left-leaning views challenged traditional values and conformity.

To the many naive and innocent among the ranks of new college students, the beatniks and bohemians appeared to be living these challenges and new ideals, and seemed so far ahead. And, the new ideals offered heretofore unimaginable access to a new consciousness, transcendent experience, hedonism, sex, and drugs.

Many young people wanted to catch up with what they thought they had been missing in the shelter of their conservative families and communities. So, they, too, began to experiment with many forbidden fruits that were offered by the liberal avant garde of university life.

Interestingly, of the five decades of expansion, the 1960s was the period of most intense expansion in which enrollments increased by 120%. It was also the time during which the great explosion of 20th-century drug use began. Parents, teachers, and politicians who had denied and withheld these and other gratifications had become suspect. Thus emerged the beginnings of the widespread experimentation with drugs, sexual revolution, and a new music.

Because of their lack of sophistication, and emergence from what was largely the mainstream of U.S. society, modern jazz was too esoteric for most of these young people. American jazz came out of southern Black culture whose art emerged amid slavery, poverty, persecution, and oppression. With the demise of swing, jazz became an increasingly unbridled and exotic art form. Based to a degree on the blues, it expressed a sense of loss about an eminently lamentable past, but also pointed toward freedom and optimism about the possibilities of the future (Hentoff, 1995).

In the late 1950s and early 1960s, new students in our colleges and universities were largely White, upwardly mobile, and were not suffocated by a history of abject misery. These young people had to find other issues to which they could relate more closely, and a music they could understand.Therefore, White middle-class college students found an impetus, an idealism, and, of course, a music to call their own. This music was folk music.

The musicians who wrote and played this uniquely American music converged on Greenwich Village in the early 1940s in parallel with Jazz, the only other uniquely American music. Folk musicians held the first Manhattan "Hootenanies" in Greenwich Village. The inherently political impetus behind this music is apparent in the fact that the term *Hootenany* emerged from a Democratic Party benefit held in Seattle.

What began with then pioneer folk musicians Burl Ives, Josh White, Sonny Terry, and Leadbelly gained momentum with Woody Guthrie, Pete Seeger, Lee Hays, and Millard Lampell (Shelton, 1965). Bob Dylan, Tom Paxton, Phil Ochs, Joan Baez, and Joni Mitchell are among the many who carried this music forward into the 1960s.

Woody Guthrie, in particular, offered music that was inherently appealing to this generation. He knew poverty in his small-town Oklahoma upbringing, knew about life on a farm, distrusted bankers, and identified with working people of all the world. Guthrie would have "poured his fiercest scorn on the criminal fools who sucked America into the Vietnam mess" (Seeger, 1983), had he not succumbed to Huntington's Chorea, in 1967.

Guthrie and other songwriters of his genre were balladeers, philosophers, and poets. Their lyrics protested the inequity, injustice, and the malevolence to which the poor and the downtrodden were subjected at the hands of those with political and economic power. For the folk musicians, the message was the music, and for the Jazz musicians the music was the message. Thus, popular culture of the late 1940s and early 1950s primed a whole generation to listen and march to the iconoclasm, satire, and protest music of Bob Dylan, Tom Paxton, Phil Ochs, Arlo Guthrie, and other folk singers of the 1960s.

Consequently, popular culture once again became synonymous with rebellion. The rebellion began with drug experimentation and sexual emancipation. By the mid- to late 1960s, more and more young people were caught up in popular counterculture and began to stagger to the beat and lyrics of music inspired by hallucinogenic drugs.

The more popular of these drugs were marijuana, hashish, LSD, mescaline, and peyote. American and British musicians such as the Grateful Dead and the Beatles rode to wealth, fame, and popularity on the crest of a psychedelic wave as the themes of folk music crossed over into rock and roll.

The late 19th-century drawings of Aubrey Beardsley, that took 1895 London by storm, again became a craze in the 1960s. Beardsley's art was a symbol of young peoples' pursuit of hallucinogenic experience and spiritual transcendence, although Beardsley died of tuberculosis in 1898 at the young age of 26. An iconoclast who was described by one biographer (Weintraub, 1976) as the "Imp of the perverse," Beardsley had used morphine to ease pain in the later stages of his fatal illness.

Although much was lost in its execution, late-1960s dress and hairstyles emulated the delicacy, taste, and eroticism of Beardsley's art. Thus, with Beardsley as their couturier and Art Nouveau as their decorative style, Timothy Leary in the pulpit, and acid rock as their music, the "hippies" emerged as a new wave of bohemian and beat proselytes.

During this period, drug use became increasingly normalized and actually glamorized in direct opposition to what young people condemned as an untrustworthy political establishment. That which young people claimed to be hypocritical about drug prohibition and politicians' duplicitous attempts to heal the schism between money and morality were core issues.

Young people, in growing numbers, experimented with illicit drugs, seeking transcendent experience, recreation and fun, and tension release (Gitlin, 1990). The frantic and misguided reactions of parents and teachers added to the difficulties of substance abuse prevention, and only succeeded in earning further distrust and ridicule of drug policy. Although the Vietnam War was a principle focus of youthful outrage, much dangerous behavior was rationalized as a reaction against tyranny by an intrusive, materialistic, and prohibitionist establishment.

The behavior of that era, in which "drugs, sex, and rock and Roll" became woven inextricably together, appeared to be a mass enactment of "the myth of the primal horde" (Freud, 1959). In living the myth, the best and brightest of youth challenged and attempted to hold accountable those in authority. Young leaders attacked agents of government at all levels for duplicity, abuse of wealth and power, for continuing the war, racism, police brutality, drug prohibition, and a list of transgressions *ad infinitum*.

Consistent with the myth's spirit of courage and valor, Abbie Hoffman, Jerry Rubin, Angela Davis, Tom Hayden, Bobby Seale, and the Chicago Seven are among those who became heroes of the era. Interestingly, all these names have faded to obscurity as some died and others aged away from youth, rebellion, and drugs into the mainstream of U.S. society. The media demeaned former Harvard University professor Timothy Leary as a "pop scoutmaster" (Mansnerus, 1995). Leary's LSD-inspired call to "Tune in, turn on, drop out" had made him a revered leader of the counterculture.

Now middle-aged people, who were young followers during that era, look back on their own behavior with shame and embarrassment (Gabriel, 1995). They would not have their own children behave as they did.

Although some positive outcomes occurred, and most young participants emerged intact, the nihilism, irresponsibility, and destructiveness of those times continue to haunt the nation. The tragic experience
and lingering grief of families whose student–children were killed during the Kent State University antiwar demonstrations are sad memori-
als. And, the unhappiness of neglected and abandoned but now grown
children of prominent figures of that era are scars of a different kind
(Pinchbeck, 1995).

Still, the distrust of those times remains endemic despite the fact
that cavalier attitudes about using dangerous drugs, such as
crack-cocaine and angel dust, have produced much negative experience. Although prostate cancer recently killed Timothy Leary, he continued as an iconoclast and an apparition of the 1960s right to the end.
At age 75, and after 2 years as a fugitive and 3½ years in prison on drug
charges, Leary used his own imminent demise to defy and taunt the
death establishment of priests, popes, medics, and funeral directors
(Mansnerus, 1995).

Nevertheless, through the 1970s and the 1980s, drug use was on the
decline and attitudes toward recreational use became increasingly
negative and supportive of prohibition. This trend was, at best, attributable in extremely limited ways to efforts at prevention in the schools.
More likely, the decline was a product of economic conditions and
emergent social influence of more conservative elements of popular
culture.

For example, social policy and public sentiment are more tolerant of
drug use during periods of economic strength, and less so during periods of hardship such as the 1980s. Also, public health activists have
pressed home the observation that much illness and mortality are attributable to environmental and behavioral factors (Gerbner, 1990).
This realization and the enormous health care costs such problems incur have stimulated considerable regulatory activity and cultural
change. Mandatory seat belt laws, toxic waste disposal regulations,
and restrictions on alcohol and tobacco advertising are but a few of
such developments.

Furthermore, these observations and changes stimulated social
trends among the aggregate of individuals, and have influenced cultural expectations among groups, and communities. For individuals,
reduced drinking, smoking, and drug use are consistent with trends
toward better nutrition, more exercise, greater attention to stress
management, and other aspects of preventive health care.

In communities, increasing awareness that users are not the sole
victims of intemperate drinking, smoking, and drug use has evoked
parallel responses. For example, smoke-free workplaces, restaurants,
and public transportation facilities represent cultural responses to

new sensitivity to the dangers of secondary smoke. Similarly, many states raised the legal drinking age from 18 to 21, and campaigns against drunk driving have a long history.

What is most important, members of families and other primary groups now are more active and vocal. They are expressing their disapproval and intolerance of the dangers and inconveniences posed by family members and friends who are drinkers, smokers, and drug users.

Thus, just as shifts in popular culture promoted large-scale drug experimentation during the 1960s, the atmosphere of the 1980s and early 1990s pushed the pendulum in the opposite direction. Economic disarray, crime, violence, the AIDS epidemic, and other social problems pressed society to, once more, circle the wagons and batten the hatches in a defensive posture. Although such conditions favor prohibitionist leanings, teachers must exercise great care if their own advocacy of temperance or abstinence is not to be rendered impotent by the taint of suspicion.

## HOW CAN TEACHERS HELP PROTECT STUDENTS FROM DANGEROUS TRENDS, FADS, AND SOCIAL MOVEMENTS OF POPULAR CULTURE?

Perhaps the classroom is the best place to equip students to manage pressures associated with sweeping youthful acceptance of new norms of popular culture. This is so because many young people are sincere and idealistic as they join in fads, trends, and movements, but these same young people often embrace popular culture and its accompanying beliefs without questioning the assumptions that underlie them. Teachers can initiate and guide this questioning.

However, most meaningful evaluation occurs within the peer group whose pressure to conform can be formidable. For, as C. S. Lewis observed, every age has its defining illusions, and they "are likliest to lurk in those widespread assumptions which are so ingrained in the age that no one dares to attack or feels it necessary to defend them" (Ruggiero, 1994, p. 21). One dares to attack such assumptions by confronting the peer group. And, this must be done in the face of defensiveness that perpetuates the unsupportable and supposedly self-evident truths of the peer group's illusions. No doubt, such questioning can be a terrifying undertaking. The peer group may fight vindictively and tenaciously if adults or some of its own members threaten gratifications that emerge from an absence of accountability.

In initiating such exploration, teachers should help students examine the following assumptions, which undergird popular culture's adherents' cries of alienation:

1. Parents, teachers, and other adults are responsible for the problems and frustrations of young people. A teacher should challenge students about the degree to which they must be responsible for their own destiny.

2. Each individual's personal construction of truth and reality is inherently valid independent of the reality of others or any objective assessment. A teacher should challenge students about the degree to which they must be responsible for actions emanating from unconfirmed and self-serving notions about themselves and their world.

3. Truth must be constructed to protect self-esteem and unconditional self-acceptance. Teachers should challenge students about the degree to which people should be truthfully confronted about behavior and attitudes that are dangerous, destructive, or repugnant.

4. Artistic–intuitive approaches to living are superior to conscious monitoring and reasoned deliberation about truth, reality, and important life decisions. Teachers should challenge students about the degree to which young people should trust their impulses and feelings as guides to action.

5. Morality is purely a subjective matter to be decided on individually by each person. Teachers should challenge students to determine the degree to which people are accountable for their moral principles and judgments.

6. Each culture determines its own moral systems and members of other cultures may not criticize these systems. Teachers should challenge students about whether emergent cultural subgroups (such as those that may form as adherents to a popular cultural movement) must abide by moral principles that transcend culture.

The questioning of these assumptions challenges popular culture's connection with drug use. Perhaps, through such a challenge, teachers may examine the moral side of the drug use issue without moralizing, and manage in a more considered and deliberate manner the social pressures through which popular culture gains its momentum. This is especially important to students who are at risk of being overwhelmed and swept along by the periodically rising tide of such pressure.

## SUMMARY OF KEY POINTS

Teachers should be alert to the fact that youth and popular culture are profoundly intertwined. The appeal of popular culture to young people is rooted in developmental needs and processes of growing up. Teachers must accept the possibility that in the eyes of children, adults represent the past rather than the future. Therefore, teachers should be acutely sensitive to the link between popular culture and healthy growth and development.

Teachers can assist young people in the process of growth and development and help them separate from the past of their elders. Teachers do this by challenging young people to question and examine the assumptions, purpose, and meanings that underlie youthful fads, trends, and social movements of popular culture. Furthermore, the history of popular culture provides rich material from which to draw in examining the effects of drug use on many prominent persons. These people were proponents and adherents of the various phases of popular culture from the 1860s to the present. The challenge for teachers is to creatively integrate such opportunities and content with ongoing learning activities in the classroom. Popular culture offers teachers much opportunity to integrate the study of drug-related issues with their teaching specialty.

# 13

# Substance Abuse Prevention in the Context of Cross-Cultural and International Comparison

The goals of this chapter are to prepare teachers for the following:

1. Integration of international and cross-cultural comparisons into the study of drug use.
2. Use of these comparisons to teach about links between social conditions and drug use.
3. Helping students understand how other nations address social problems related to substance abuse.
4. Helping students study links between culture, policy, and the creation of a conspicuous underclass.
5. Helping students understand the difficulties members of the social underclass face in all nations.

Clearly, drug use is more prevalent in the United States than in other countries, but more people use drugs generally in nations that have a conspicuous underclass. Therefore, teachers and students should understand that problems related to drug use in the United States often illuminate the plight of the U.S. underclass, even though substance abuse respects no social boundaries.

Teachers and students may examine the struggles of children in the U.S. underclass and the problems our culture creates for socially abandoned and economically disenfranchised citizens. Inevitably, this examination will reveal social issues that have made drug use a particularly "American disease" (Musto, 1987). Students will find that U.S. character, culture, and social policies have caused our drug problems to be much worse than those of the many other nations that also have drug problems.

## ARE U.S. DRUG PROBLEMS WORSE
## THAN THOSE OF OTHER NATIONS?

From the earliest days of the nation, Americans' affinity for alcohol astonished foreign visitors, including Charles Dickens and Alexis de Tocqueville (Dardis, 1989). In the 19th century, Europeans jokingly referred to the United States as the "Alcoholic Republic."

Also, the exceptional pain-killing and calming qualities of morphine led to its use by battlefield physicians during the Civil War and in U.S. medical practice after the war. Some writers claimed that this trend explained increases in addiction in the United States during the late 1800s (Musto, 1987, p. 1). However, European nations such as France, Germany, Great Britain, Russia, and Italy fought wars during the last half of the 19th century and used morphine to treat pain, too. The European experience produced no increases in numbers of addicts.

Attitudes toward the poor are an important consideration when examining differences between the U.S. and European experience with addiction. Social policies in the United States reflect the long history of hostility and contempt with which Americans have viewed the poor, and especially welfare recipients. This negativity toward the poor emerged out of the social welfare policies of Elizabethan England. In her 1601 "Poor Laws," Queen Elizabeth transferred welfare assistance from churches and other charitable organizations to local governments. These laws established the public welfare system in England and colonial America. The system remained largely unchanged for more than 300 years.

English poor law identified poverty as a sign of moral and personal deficiency, and paupers were treated as sinners. Communities provided grudging assistance under humiliating and onerous conditions. Often, recipients only sought assistance in utter desperation.

Charles Dicken's *The Adventures of Oliver Twist* provides a substantially accurate, although fictional account of early 1800s poverty under Elizabethan poor laws. Oliver Twist was born in a workhouse and orphaned at birth. Students may gain valuable insights about the harshness of community response to the poor during this era by examining Oliver Twist's early years of life.

As the ebb and flow of welfare debate indicates, the poor have long been at the center of U.S. policy concerns. The Great Depression of the early 1930s generated large numbers of poor people and stimulated 60 years of humanitarian change. However, the 1996 welfare reforms clearly indicate that old attitudes persist and welfare provisions remain cloaked in stigma. Consequently, the poor have powerful incentives to resist a social system that deprives them of material necessities and assaults their dignity.

The welfare debate may continue in the classroom. Modern American arguments reflect much of the thinking of Elizabethan England:

1. The poor are "slackers," and "gold bricks," who have no intention of bettering themselves.
2. The poor have discovered that welfare pays more than working.
3. The poor have learned to exploit the system by having babies to increase their welfare benefits.
4. The poor are entitled only to temporary and brief assistance, and must earn more extended benefits by work.

However, others argue that:

1. The poor are unfortunates who seek to rise above their circumstances.
2. Social inequity and injustice have deprived the poor of opportunities to better their circumstances.
3. To rectify these problems, society should provide financial assistance, especially for children, and create opportunities for education, job training, and employment for adults.

These arguments reveal community support for the poor to be a powerfully divisive social issue. Its divisiveness is amplified by racism, gang violence, family disintegration, crime, and drug trafficking. Worse yet, these problems have caused American business leaders to abandon urban centers of commerce and industry where the poor reside. Consequently, reduced economic opportunity for those who need work most, and increased joblessness intensify crime, violence, and drug problems in a downward spiral of accelerating social disorganization (Wilson, 1996).

U.S. Blacks have disproportionately borne the negative consequences of this process of urban decay. For Blacks, the Civil Rights Movement yielded a dual outcome rather than broad equality. The Black upper and middle class have grown and benefited greatly, but the distress and the size of the Black underclass have grown, too. The problems of the Black underclass are undermining the gains of the Black middle class (Patterson & Kim, 1994).

Clearly, U.S. antipathy toward the poor and reluctance to provide welfare support, even for children, is not shared by most Western European democracies. Working and middle-class citizens of these democracies have firmly resisted efforts to cut back assistance as joblessness has become a growing problem there, too. Although soaring budget deficits have forced many nations to reduce subsidies and social programs, the European attitude seems to be one of pay now to prevent problems caused by poverty or pay much more, later, to solve them.

## HOW CAN CROSS-CULTURAL COMPARISON EXPLAIN DRUG USE?

Anthropologists have long recognized that one may better understand self by examining the ways of others (Rudgley, 1993). The study of other societies can shed light on our own. Accordingly, teachers may help students examine conditions, social policies, and drug use in other nations. In this way, students can contemplate why drug use is so disproportionate a problem for Americans.

Scotland, Norway, and Japan make wonderful case studies for drug education and substance abuse prevention in the context of social policy. Each has a culture and social policies that are very different from the others and from U.S. culture and policies. These differences are strongly related to poverty, family disruption, crime, violence, health care, and drug use.

For example, in Glasgow, heroin addiction became a serious problem in the late 1970s after Scotland's shipbuilding and manufacturing industries collapsed (Ibrahim, 1996a). This raised unemployment to 40% in some sections of the city.

In Scotland, generally, unemployment is higher than the British average, although newly discovered North Sea petroleum reserves are bringing some wealth to Scottish northern ports. New industries such as plastics, electronics, and consumer goods have begun to replace some of the losses suffered with the collapse of shipbuilding.

Nevertheless, whiskey distilling continues to be an important economic activity. Furthermore, Glasgow has a harm reduction program in which city agencies legally dispense drugs and hypodermic needles to addicts. Now, Possil, a low-income section of Glasgow, is viewed by sociologist Alex Meikle (Ibrahim, 1996a) as "the heroin shooting gallery of the world."

The 1996 film *Train Spotting*, based on Irvine Welsh's (1996) cult novel portrays the life of heroin addicts in Glasgow. The fact that a film critically acclaimed for so effectively presenting the human experience of addiction was made in Scotland confirms Meikle's observation.

What is more, it vividly portrays the social costs of poverty, of highly promoted but unobtainable materialistic ideals, and of escape through drugs.

In contrast to Scotland, Norway is now the preeminent welfare state of the world (Ibrahim, 1996b). Perhaps this occurred because the present generation is the first to emerge from the general poverty that nearly all Norwegians faced in the past (Martinson, 1992). Norway is presently among the wealthiest nations in Europe, thanks in large part to its North Sea oil reserves.

Although tax rates are above 50%, inflation is below 2%, and unemployment is the lowest in Europe. All citizens enjoy a short work week and many generous entitlements. These include general benefits to which all Norwegians are entitled:

1. Stipends for every Norwegian child under age 17.
2. Retirement pay for homemakers equivalent to industrial workers' pensions.
3. Ten months of fully paid maternity leave.
4. Medical reimbursements for all costs above $187 per year per individual.
5. A lifelong learning program providing workers with 1-year leaves to improve work skills at full pay every 10 years.
6. Free education and training in universities and professional schools.

Specific public assistance entitlements to those in need include:

1. State continuation of payments to pension funds during periods of unemployment.
2. Free day care for children.
3. Subsidized housing.
4. Subsidized vacations.
5. Free medical and dental care.

These benefits, financed by off-shore oil exports, reflect social policies that promote equality, resist income disparity, are anti-elitist, and are opposed to materialism. Such policies permit the state to make large investments in workers' health, financial security, and education. The dividends have been social peace, a total absence of poverty, no illiteracy, and no labor unrest or strikes.

For these reasons, Norway has actively resisted adopting British social policies, as are in place in Scotland. In the Norwegian view, the British trend toward government downsizing and worldwide anti-union activity is producing serious dissatisfaction and enormous social strains (Ibrahim, 1996b). Such may be the case in Glasgow.

Norway seems to have come close to Rifkin's (1995) notion of distributing to the common citizen wealth produced by advances in technology and other national resources. In this way, workers displaced by technological advances will enjoy benefits rather than be victimized by progress.

However, the education and technical skill of Norwegian workers places them among the most capable in the world (Ibrahim, 1996b). Few are displaced by technology, there is no illiteracy, and there is no conspicuous underclass in Norway.

Interestingly, Norway's social programs and welfare benefits are matched by its other liberal social policies. Norwegian law protects the rights of homosexuals and grants them marital entitlements that are similar to entitlements of heterosexuals. Media censorship is limited and pornography is freely available.

Despite its earlier national poverty, in the 1890s, Norway became the first country in the Western world to enact a national child-welfare system. However, 60 years passed before Norwegians liberalized the system toward protecting children from abuse and neglect rather than continuing the system's original emphasis of protecting the community from delinquent children (Martinson, 1992).

Nevertheless, conservative religious leanings found their way into child care again when the 1975 act establishing day-care centers was amended in 1981. This amendment stipulated that day-care centers must be founded on basic Christian values and is indication of Norway's blurred boundary between church and state.

Conservative leanings also are evident in Norwegian drug policies. Norwegian drug laws are the most strict of any Scandinavian country. Norway joined the United States and Finland by passing laws for alcohol prohibition just prior to 1920. It also repealed these laws in 1932, just as did the United States. Alcohol and cigarettes are regulated and taxed, but Norway is part of the northern European "vodka belt" where even stuporous drunkenness at parties is socially acceptable.

Whether or not Norway's drug laws work, fewer than one half of 1 percent of a population of 4.1 million are drug users. This rate is considerably lower than the United States and Scotland. Further, family disruption due to alcoholism is lower than in other Scandinavian countries (Martinson, 1992).

Despite their affinity for vodka, Norwegians have not suffered the enormous costs that alcoholism has wrought on Russians. The abuse of vodka has compromised the economy and the health of Russia (Specter, 1997) to a much greater extent than it has for Norway. The average Russian male consumes a bottle of vodka every 2 days and has a life expectancy of 58 years.

The Russian alcohol problem was highlighted in 1997 by Vladimir Yamnikov's ironic death. Yamnikov headed the distillery that produces Stolichnaya vodka. He shared the Russian penchant for his company's product and died of cirrhosis of the liver at age 56 (Lohr, 1997).

The Russian penchant is clear in figure skater Oksana Baiul's explanation of her blood-alcohol level (0.168%) at the time she drove into a high-speed car crash. She said she had only four or five drinks and claimed she was not drunk because "I'm a Russian" (Untitled, 1997).

In contrast to Norway, Japan may be described as a welfare society rather than a welfare state (Johnson, 1996). The government has left welfare to the private sector. The Japanese expect the family, the local community, and private employers to take responsibility for social welfare and health care. As a result, welfare is now primarily a family affair (Kristoff, 1996).

In part, this is attributable to a process of cultural change that began 1,200 to 1,400 years ago. In 1603, the Tokugawa regime unified warring feudal factions into a centralized state. The regime isolated Japan from Western influence in the 1630s by prohibiting the Christian faith.

During these times, Shintoism, the indigenous religion of Japan, started to incorporate Buddhist and Confucian ideology (Kumagai, 1996). Buddhist beliefs in ancestor worship, and Confucian morality with its emphasis on personal virtue, justice, and devotion to family became part of the moral code of Japan. The feudal arrangement of a hierarchical social order, knowing one's place in that order, and the Confucian ideals of benevolent leaders, obedient followers, respect for others, social harmony, and politeness emerged as powerful traditions.

The faltering Tokugawa regime fell from power after Commodore Matthew C. Perry forced a Western presence on the Japanese in 1867. This led to the Meiji restoration in 1868 as a group of feudal lords took control of the Imperial Court in Kyoto and declared an end to the Tokugawa Shogunate. In doing so, they returned power to the Japanese emperor and ended military rule that had governed Japan for nearly 700 years.

So began the next phase of cultural change in which Japan was deeply influenced by Britain, Germany, and France. Realizing that they could not keep Commodore Perry's fleet of warships from entering Tokyo Bay, Japan's leaders were determined to transform their nation into a modern industrial society. They Europeanized many institutions including their governmental, legal, military, and educational systems and even transformed Japanese social etiquette. Thus, Japan began to shape its present policies and practices by intermingling imported, indigenous, and traditional ideas.

During this second phase of change, Japan's traditional devotion to family remained strongly Japanese. In fact, it was strengthened and became a universal to all social classes rather than exclusive to the elite, as it had been in the past.

The last cultural transformation occurred after World War II, when Japan bêcame Americanized. The Japanese undertook political reform, abolished the legal foundation for their traditional system of family, offered equal rights to women, and instituted many other changes under seven years of American occupation.

However, devotion to family never wavered despite the changes that inundated Japanese culture following the war. Along with this tradition, the Japanese have retained trust in their social system and faith in the positive side of human nature (Johnson, 1996). Such trust and faith deter crime and other destructive behavior among the Japanese.

Even now, Japan continues to adapt the modern and the traditional to its needs as a society. For example, the Japanese value participation in community affairs as an expression of older cultural traditions and an accommodation to the demands of modern urban life. Consequently, much of Japanese social service is provided by unpaid volunteers, and private organizations. Further, the Japanese government's policy orientation is to turn to the private sector to handle many functions that government serves in other countries and to keep government bureaucracy small (Johnson, 1996).

The educational system socializes children into this orientation from an early age. There is no janitorial staff in Japanese schools and the students sweep and scrub buildings and facilities, including bathrooms and kitchens (Araton, 1998). In school lunchrooms, students serve each other meals and no one begins to eat until all have been served. School days begin at 8 a.m. and end between 4:30 and 6:30 p.m., depending on the weather during the 11-month school year.

These policy orientations emerged out of Japan's early experience with industrialization. During the 1870s, when industrial development began, there was little private interest. Government was active in starting industries such as mining, communications, transportation, and shipbuilding, but was drained by the financial losses of these unprofitable efforts. Therefore, the government sold its interest in industrial enterprises at bargain prices to private purchasers.

Accordingly, the primary social safety net of Japan is the family rather than the government, too (Kristoff, 1996). As a result, less than 1% of the Japanese population receives government welfare benefits as compared to 5% to 12% who receive some form of public assistance in the United States. And, the Japanese government bureaucracy is among the smallest in the industrialized world.

The success of the Japanese system relative to the United States is attributable to a number of differing social and economic conditions. Among these conditions, Japan has much less unemployment (Kristoff, 1996), and fewer than 1% of children in Japan are born out of wedlock as compared to 30% in the United States.

Most notably, Japan has much less crime and a lower rate of criminal incarceration than the United States (Johnson, 1996). In fact, between 1960 and 1991, the prison population in Japan shrunk by nearly 35%, while numbers of prisoners in the United States increased by 245% during the same period.

The "Yakuza," who are Japan's equivalent to the mafia, are chronic offenders. Drug dealing is a prominent criminal activity of this adult group. The "bosozoku," who form youthful motorcycle and hot rod automobile gangs, are the focus of official concern because of their drug use and "traffic acrobatics" (reckless driving).

Despite the activities of these criminal groups, Japan has far fewer drug addicts than the United States. The Japanese instituted laws against opium use in 1879, against morphine, heroin, and cocaine in 1948, and against amphetamines in 1951. Although drug use does not approach that of the United States, drug arrests as a proportion of all arrests have increased dramatically from less than 1% to more than 28% during the period from 1970 to 1992.

Illicit use of amphetamines and Ecstasy, a hallucinogenic amphetamine derivative, are the dominant drug offenses among these arrests. Cocaine is popular among the Japanese equivalent to U.S. "yuppies," and LSD is popular among Japan's counter culture types, but neither is as popular as amphetamines. Marijuana is readily available but not very popular, and heroin and crack are not popular at all.

Despite generally favorable social conditions and emergence of its miracle economy in the early 1960s, Japan has an underclass numbering about 2% of the population. Called the "Burakumin," this group is similar to welfare recipients in the United States. Although ethnically indistinguishable from other Japanese, they have suffered discrimination for centuries as members of a caste of untouchables. Because their ancestors worked in unclean occupations such as animal skinning and burying the dead, they are targets of discrimination.

About 5% (seven times the national percentage for all Japanese) of Burakumin receive public assistance. Also, they are overrepresented among the Japanese who abuse drugs and alcohol, produce out of wedlock births, and drop out of school.

Despite culturally generated problems of the Burakumin, Japan's social policies promote powerful forces in opposition to joining the welfare rolls for all its people. These are amplified by strong feelings of family obligation. Although the Japanese do not identify neediness with criminality, an abiding sense of shame is associated with accepting welfare. The dominant criteria against which welfare eligibility is assessed are poverty and disability.

## DO U.S. POLICY TRENDS DIFFER
## FROM THOSE OF OTHER NATIONS?

Interesting comparisons may be made between American policies toward the poor and those of the three countries discussed previously. Relative to these countries, trends in the United States reflect increasing opposition to welfare support, diminished regard for the family as a basic unit of the community, and less tolerance for problems associated with drug use.

Since 1994, the U.S. welfare system has methodically reduced assistance, particularly to addicted people. Addicts may no longer receive certain social security benefits, are about to be exempted from health insurance coverage for addiction treatment, and may lose protection from discrimination in the workplace under the Americans With Disabilities Act.

Furthermore, passage of the 1996 U.S. welfare reform act has produced a convergence between welfare and criminal justice sentencing policies for drug related offenses (Bernstein, 1996). New welfare provisions deny permanently cash benefits and food stamps to anyone convicted of a drug felony no matter how poor or disabled.

In the United States, bitter debate rages among policymakers and the courtroom judges who must make painful decisions in such cases. This debate, too, can continue in the classroom. The arguments are as follows:

1. Such policies are unfair to mothers who are convicted of drug charges because welfare is an entitlement granted on the condition of poverty. Women convicted of drug crimes will be punished three times over. They will be denied their freedom, lose a financial entitlement, and possibly lose custody of their children.

2. The new provisions will have harmful consequences for children. They may be denied the right to be reared by members of their own family, will be subjected to a troubled foster care system, and will suffer the loss of benefits needed for healthy maturation to adulthood.

On the other hand, some people make the following arguments:

1. Family obligations cannot be used as a shield from punishment for seriously criminal behavior despite the hardships parents and children may suffer.
2. Children are better off with someone other than a drug offender.
3. A lifetime ban on cash assistance and food stamps is another weapon in the war on drugs.

Interestingly, members of the U.S. Sentencing Commission wrote rules in the mid-1980s to eliminate family ties as a consideration in sentences for drug convictions. Congress sought to bring uniformity to regional differences that were occurring in drug sentencing until that time. Some argue that prior to 1987, family ties served as justification for more lenient sentences for White, middle-class men and women (Bernstein, 1996).

As a result, record numbers of women are now serving sentences for first-time drug offenses. Presently, about 115,000 women are in prison, and more than two thirds of them are mothers of children under the age of 18 (Bernstein, 1996; Hewitt, Nelson, & Velez, 1996; Holmes, 1996).

Many of these women, who are to be deprived of benefits, were driven to criminal activity by their poverty, and were providing sole support for children at the time of their imprisonment (Bernstein, 1996). Although children remain eligible for benefits, new welfare provisions will reduce benefits proportionately for families in which an adult member has been convicted of a drug felony.

## SUMMARY OF KEY POINTS

Teachers can use comparisons with other countries to help students understand the linkages between drug policies and other social policies. Those linkages that address tensions created by poverty, racial issues, social class, and economics are germane. Such understanding addresses risk factors associated with substance abuse.

There is increasing evidence that many U.S. social policies related to poverty and social welfare have failed and may have created additional problems. U.S. drug problems, one by-product of these failures, continue to be worse than those of other nations.

This chapter compares U.S. attitudes and policies toward the poor with those of Scotland, Norway, and Japan. Although many other countries offer meaningful comparisons, these were selected because of their very different attitudes toward the poor. Scotland shares a harsh Elizabethan heritage with England and the United States. Norway is a willing and enthusiastic social service provider, and the social welfare burden has been shouldered by the private sector of the Japanese economy. These comparisons suggest that drug use emerges as a more serious problem in countries whose culture and social policies produce an identifiable underclass.

# References

Ackerman, D. (1995). Drug testing. In R. Combs & D. Ziedonis (Eds.), *Handbook on drug abuse prevention* (pp. 473–489). Needham Heights,_MA: Allyn & Bacon.

Ackerman, R. (1983). *Children of alcoholics: A guide for parents, educators, and therapists*. New York: Simon & Schuster.

Ajzen, I., & Fishbein, M. (1980). *Understanding attitudes and predicting behavior*. Englewood Cliffs, NJ: Prentice-Hall.

Allen, J., & Allen, R. (1990). A sense of community, a shared vision and a positive culture: Core enabling factors in successful culture based change. In R. Patton & S. Cissel (Eds.), *Community organization: Traditional principles and modern applications* (pp. 5–19). Johnson City, TN: Latchpins Press.

Allensworth, D., & Kolbe, L. (1987). The comprehensive school health program: Exploring an expanded concept. *Journal of School Health, 57*(10), 409–412.

Altman, L. (1997, April 16). Drug firm, relenting, allows unflattering study to appear. *The New York Times*, pp. A1, A16.

American School Health Association. (1989). *The national adolescent student health survey: A report on the health of America's youth*. Oakland, CA: Third Party Publishing Company.

Anachiarico, F., & Jacobs, J. (1996). *The pursuit of absolute integrity: How corruption control makes government ineffective*. Chicago: University of Chicago Press.

Anger, K. (1975). *Hollywood Babylon*. New York: Dell.

Anger, K. (1984). *Hollywood Babylon II*. New York: E. P. Dutton.

Anthony, E. (1987). Risk, vulnerability and resilience: an overview. In E. Anthony & B. Cohler (Eds.), *The invulnerable child* (pp. 3–48). New York: Guilford.

Applebome, P. (1996, December). After years of gains, minority students start falling behind. *The New York Times*, p. 12.

Araton, H. (1998, February 22). Japan gives athletes a lesson in respect. *The New York Times*, p. 7.

Ashley, R. (1975). *Cocaine: Its history, uses, and effects*. New York: St. Martin's Press.

Associated Press, (1997a, January 1). Inmate set free after account of corruption. *The New York Times*, p. 13.

Avis, H. (1990). *Drugs and life*. Dubuque, IA: W.C. Brown.

Bakalar, J., & Grinspoon, L. (1984). *Drug control in a free society*. New York: Cambridge University Press.

Bandura, A. (1977). *Social learning theory.* Englewood Cliffs, NJ: Prentice-Hall.

Becker, M. (1974). The health belief model and personal health behavior. *Health Education Monographs, 2,* 404–419.

Bernstein, N. (1996, August 20). Criminal and welfare rules raise new issues of fairness. *The New York Times,* pp. A1, A17.

Beyerstein, B., & Hadaway, P. (1990). On avoiding folly. *Journal of Drug Issues, 20,*(4), 689–700.

Blachly, P. (1970). *Seduction.* Springfield, IL: Charles C. Thomas.

A Black group assails statue of suffragists. (1997, March, 9). *The New York Times,* p. 27.

Bloom, B. (Ed.). (1956). *Taxonomy of educational objectives.* New York: David MacKay.

S.E.C. cites drug researchers in insider trading lawsuits. (1997, April 11). *The New York Times,* p. D13.

Botvin, G. (1987). *Factors inhibiting drug use: Teacher and peer effects.* Rockville, MD: National Institute on Drug Abuse.

Botvin, G. (1995). Principles of prevention. In R. Combs & D. Ziedonis (Eds.), *Handbook on drug abuse prevention* (pp. 19–44). Needham Heights, MA: Allyn & Bacon.

Bovard, J. (1995). *Shakedown.* New York: Viking.

Bragg, R. (1997, December 3). Forgiveness, after 3 die in shootings in Kentucky. *The New York Times,* p. A16.

Broad, W. (1997, March 4). Sea may have yielded a piece of pirate lore. *The New York Times,* p. A14.

Broad, W. (1997, March 11). Archeologists revise portrait of buccaneers as monsters. *The New York Times,* pp. C1, C9.

Brown, B., & Mills, A. (1987). *Youth at high risk for substance abuse* (DHHS Publication No. ADM 87–1537). Rockville, MD: U.S. Alcohol, Drug Abuse, and Mental Health Administration.

Brown, C. (1965). *Manchild in a promised land.* New York: Macmillan.

Brown, C. (1976). *The children of Ham.* New York: Stein and Day.

Brown, C. (1989). Forward. In D. Courtwright, H. Joseph, & D. Des Jarlais, *Addicts who survived* (pp. xi–xiii). Knoxville, TN: University of Tennessee Press.

Browne, M. (1997, September 23). Drug money (in literal sense) is a new legal twist. *The New York Times,* p. F5.

Burros, M. (1996, November 26). F.D.A. commissioner is resigning after 6 stormy years in office. *The New York Times,* pp. A1, A18.

Burroughs, W. (1959). *Naked lunch.* New York: Grove Weidenfeld.

Butler J. (1994). *Principles of health education and health promotion.* Englewood, CO: Morton.

Butterfield, F. (1997, January 30). Many Black men barred from voting. *The New York Times,* p. A12.

Bynum, J., & Thompson, W. (1996). *Juvenile delinquency: A sociological approach.* Needham Heights, MA: Allyn & Bacon.

Canada, G. (1995). *Fist, stick, knife, gun.* Boston: Beacon Press.

Carroll, C. (1985). *Drugs in modern society.* Dubuque, IA: W.C. Brown.

Ceci, S., & Bruck, M. (1995). *Jeopardy in the courtroom.* Washington, DC: American Psychological Association.

Central Park Historical Society. (1989). *Leadership program manual*. New York: Author.

Charters, A. (1992). The best minds of a generation. In A. Charters, (Ed.), *The portable beat reader*. New York: Penguine.

Chase, M. (1996, August 26). Doctors puncture myths to justify growing heroin use. *The Wall Street Journal*, p. B1.

Clifford, P. (1992). Drug use, drug prohibition and minority communities. *Journal of Primary Prevention, 12*(4), 303–316.

Clifford, P., & Nicholson, T. (1996). *Barriers to measuring the effectiveness of drug policy*. Unpublished manuscript.

Clinton orders a survey of school violence. (1997, December 7). *The New York Times*, p. 40.

Clymer, A. (1996, December 6). A bipartisan voice. *The New York Times*, pp. A1, B8.

Coccaro, E. (1995). Biology of aggression. *Science and Medicine, 2*,(1), 38–47.

Collins, G. (1996, November 24). Trial date set in a Florida lawsuit against tobacco companies. *The New York Times*, p. 35.

Conner, R., & Burns, P. (1995). Law enforcement and regulatory agencies. In R. Combs & D. Ziedonis (Eds.), *Handbook on drug abuse prevention* (pp. 47–67). Needham Heights, MA: Allyn & Bacon.

Connolly, C. (1963). *Previous convictions*. London: Hamish Hamilton.

Cooper, M. (1996, December 1). You're under arrest. *The New York Times*, Sec. 13, pp. 1, 12, 13.

Cordingly, D. (1995). *Under the black flag: The romance and the reality of life among the pirates*. New York: Random House.

Cornacchia, H., Smith. D., & Bentel, D. (1978). *Drugs in the classroom: A conceptual model for school programs*. St. Louis, MO: Mosby.

Council of Economic Advisors. (1991). *Economic report to the President*. Washington, DC: U.S. Government Printing Office.

Courtwright, D. (1982). *Dark paradise: Opiate addiction in America before 1940*. Cambridge, MA: Harvard University Press.

Courtwright, D., Joseph, H., & Des Jarlais, D. (1989). *Addicts who survived*. Knoxville, TN: University of Tennessee Press.

Cowell, A. (1998, February 1). Now, teen-agers turn to crime: Europe envies America. *The New York Times*, Sec. 4, pp. 1, 4.

Crawford, J. (1981). *City as history*. New York: Learning Through an Expanded Arts Program, Inc.

Cross, G. (1997). *Kids stuff: Toys and the changing world of American childhood*. Cambridge, MA: Harvard University Press.

Cyclist says drug should be allowed. (1998, January 20). *The New York Times*, p. C7.

Dardis, T. (1989). *The thirsty muse: Alcohol and the American writer*. New York: Ticknor and Fields.

Darman, R. (1996, December 1). Riverboat gambling with government. *The New York Times*, magazine, pp. 116–117.

Darman, R. (1996a). *Who's in control: Polar politics and the sensible center*. New York: Simon & Schuster.

Davis, M., with Troupe, Q. (1989). *Miles: The autobiography*. New York: Touchstone Books.

DeParle, J. (1996, December 8). Mugged by reality. *The New York Times Magazine*, pp. 64–67, 99–100.

Derwin, B. (1998, September 20). A uniform drug policy needed for all sports. *The New York Times*, p. 16.

Devine, J. (1985). The versatility of human locomotion. *American Anthropologist, 87*,(3), 550–570.

Devine, J. (1996). *Maximum security: The culture of violence in inner-city schools*. Chicago: University of Chicago Press.

Dewey, J. (1916). *Democracy and education*. New York: Macmillan.

Digorry, J. (1966). *Self evaluation: Concepts and studies*. New York: Wiley.

Dobson, J. (1992). *The new dare to discipline*. Wheaton, IL: Tyndale House.

A doctor is questioned over marijuana law. (1997, February 17) *The New York Times*, p. 14.

Donaldson, S. (1993, December 29). The rape crisis behind bars. *New York Times*.

Drug and sex programs called effective in fight against AIDS. (1997, February 14). *The New York Times*, p. B10.

Dweiko, H. (1993). *Concepts of chemical dependency*. Pacific Grove, CA: Brooks/Cole.

Education Trust. (1996). *1996 state and national data book*. Washington, DC: Author

Eisman, S., & Eisman, R. (1997). *Decisions: A call to action*. Amityville, NY; Baywood.

Eisman, S., Wingard, J., & Huba, G.(1984). *Drug abuse: Foundation for a psychosocial approach*. Farmingdale, NY: Baywood.

Ellickson, P. (1995). Schools. In R. Combs & D. Ziedonis (Eds.), *Handbook on drug abuse prevention*. Needham Heights, MA: Allyn & Bacon.

Ellwood, D. (1988). *Poor support: Poverty in the American family*. New York: Basic Books.

Ennett, S., Tobler, N., Ringwalt, C., & Flewelling, R. (1994). How effective is drug abuse resistance education? A meta-analysis of Project DARE outcome evaluations. *American Journal of Public Health, 84*(9), 1394–1406.

Evans, R., & Berent, I. (Eds.). (1992). *Drug Legalization: For and against*. LaSalle, IL: Open Court.

Fagan, J. (1993). Interactions among drugs, alcohol, and violence. *Health Affairs, Winter 1993,* 66–78.

Farberow, N. (1980). *The many faces of suicide*. New York: McGraw-Hill.

Ferriera, B. (1997, November 20). Untitled paper presented at the meeting of the American Society of Criminology, Topeka, KS.

Fields, R. (1992). *Drugs and alcohol in perspective*. Bellevue, WA: W.C. Brown.

Fields, R. (1995). *Drugs in perspective* (2nd ed.). Bellevue, WA: W.C. Brown.

Fineman, H. (1997, February 3). The cash machine. *Newsweek*, 24.

Fishbein, D., & Pease, S. (1996). *The dynamics of drug abuse*. Needham Heights, MA: Allyn & Bacon.

Fisher, C. (1987). *Postcards from the edge*. New York: Simon & Schuster.

Fisher, I. (1998, February 2). A new health risk for immigrants. *The New York Times*, pp. B1, B7.

Freeman, M. (1997, April 13). Painkillers and addiction, are prevalent in N.F.L. *The New York Times*, Sec. 8, pp. 1, 4.

Freud, S. (1959). *Group psychology and the analysis of the ego.* (J. Strachy, Trans.). London: International Psychoanalytical Press, 1922; New York: Liveright, p. 112.

Freudenheim, M. (1998, February 17). Psychiatric drugs are now promoted directly to patients. *The New York Times,* pp. A1, D3.

Gabriel, T. (1995, November 30). Boomers: The not as I did parents. *The New York Times,* pp. C1, C4.

Gabriel, T. (1996, September 10). Study ties teen-age drug use to parents' marijuana smoking. *The New York Times,* p. D23.

Garmezy, N., & Masten, M. (1986). Stress, competence and resilience: Common frontiers for therapist and psychopathologist. *Behavioral Therapy, 17,* 500–521.

Garvey, J. (1986). Tolerance limits. *Commonwealth, September 26, 1986,* 487.

Gerbner, G. (1990). *Stories that hurt.* In H. Resnik (Ed.), *Youth and Drugs: Society's mixed messages* (pp. 31–52). Rockville, MD: U.S. Department of Health and Human Services.

Gilbert, D. (1988). *Compendium of American public opinion.* New York: Facts on File Publications.

Giovannoni, J., & Becerra, R. (1979). *Defining child abuse.* New York: The Free Press.

Gitlin, T. (1990). On drugs and mass media in America's consumer society. In H. Resnik (Ed.), *Youth and drugs: Society's mixed messages* (pp. 31–52). Rockville, MD: U.S. Department of Health and Human Services.

Goldberg, R. (1996). Introduction, drugs: Divergent views. In R. Goldberg (Ed.), *Taking sides: Clashing views on controversial issues in drugs and society, 2nd ed.* (pp. xiv–xxi). Guilford, CT: Dushkin.

Golden, T. (1996, November 27). Trapped, fugitive ex-prosecutor kills himself in a Nevada hotel. *The New York Times,* pp. 1, B5.

Golden, T. (1997, April 17). Medical use of marijuana to stay illegal in Arizona. *The New York Times,* p. A16.

Goldstein, P. (1985). The drugs–violence nexus: A tri-partite conceptual framework. *Journal of Drug Issues, 15,* 493–506.

Goode, E. (1993). *Drugs in American society,* (4th ed.). New York: McGraw-Hill.

Goodstadt, M. (1978). Alcohol and drug education. *Health Education Monographs, 6*(3), 263–279.

Government to spend $1 million studying marijuana as medicine. (1997, January 9) *The New York Times,* p. B10.

Green, T. (1996). *The dark side of the game.* New York: Warner Books.

Greenberg, B. (1984). Smoking, drugging and drinking in top rated TV series. In S. Eisman, J. Wingard, & G. Huba (Eds.), *Drug abuse: Foundation for a psychosocial approach* (pp. 198–204). Farmingdale, NY: Baywood.

Greenberg, B., Fernandez-Colado, C., Graef, D., Korzenny, F., & Atkin, C. (1984). Trends in use of alcohol and other substances on television. In S. Eisman, J. Wingard, & G. Huba (Eds.), *Drug abuse: Foundation for a psychosocial approach* (pp. 187–197). Farmingdale, NY: Baywood.

Greenhouse, L. (1997, January 11). Justices hear case of killers tried before corrupt judge. *The New York Times,* p. 8.

Grinspoon, L. (1977). *Marijuana reconsidered* (2nd ed.). Cambridge, MA: Harvard University Press.

Haaga, J., & Reuter, P. (1995). Prevention: The (lauded) orphan of drug policy. In R. Combs & D. Ziedonis (Eds.), *Handbook on drug abuse prevention* (pp. 3–17). Needham Heights, MA: Allyn & Bacon.

Hackett, P. (Ed.). (1989). *The Andy Warhol diaries*. New York: Warner Books.

Hamill, P. (1994). *A drinking life*. New York: Back Bay Books.

Hamilton, W. (1998, February 19). Cracking the dress code. *The New York Times*, pp. B1, B8.

Hanley, R. (1996, December 18). Drug suspect freed in inquiry on trial. *The New York Times*, p. B4.

Hanson, D. (1982). The effectiveness of alcohol and drug education. *Journal of Alcohol and Drug Education, 27*(2), 4.

Harding, J. (1964). Prejudice and ethnic relations. In G. Lindsy (Ed.), *The handbook of social psychology*. Reading, MA: Addison-Wesley.

Hartley, M., & Commire, A. (1990). *Breaking the silence*. New York: Penguin.

Hawkins, D. (1993). Inequality, culture, and interpersonal violence. *Health Affairs, Winter 1993*, 80–95.

Hawkins, J., Lishner, D., Jenson, J., & Catalano, R. (1987). Delinquents and drugs: What the evidence says about prevention and treatment programming. In B. Brown & A. Mills (Eds.), *Youth at high risk for substance abuse* (pp. 81–131). DHHS Publication No. ADM 87–1537). Rockville, MD: U.S. Alcohol, Drug Abuse, and Mental Health Administration.

Heinicke, C., & Vollmer, S. (1995). Children and adolescents. In R. Combs & D. Ziedonis (Eds.), Handbook on drug abuse prevention (pp. 321–336) Needham Heights, MA: Allyn & Bacon.

Hentoff, N. (1995). *Listen to the stories: Nat Hentoff on jazz and country music*. New York: Harper Perennial.

Hepburn, J. (1995). User accountability. In R. Combs & D. Ziedonis (Eds.), *Handbook on drug abuse prevention*. (pp. 491–508). Needham Heights, MA: Allyn & Bacon.

Hewitt, B., Nelson, M., & Velez, E. (1996). Mothers behind bars. *People, November 11, 1996*, pp. 95, 97, 100, 102.

Hilts, P. (1995, November 29). Drug company pleads guilty to deceit in product testing. *The New York Times*, pp. A1, D6.

Hirschi, T. (1969). *Causes of delinquency*. Berkeley, CA: University of California Press.

Holloway, L. (1998, February 15). The fear is real enough. The gangs areanother story. *The New York Times*, Sec. 4, p. 4.

Holmes, S. (1996, December 27). With more women in prison, sexual abuse by guards becomes greater concern. *The New York Times*, p. A18.

Huxley, A. (1954). *The doors of perception*. New York: Harper.

Ibrahim, Y. (1996, August 18). Rethinking harm reduction for Glasgow addicts. *The New York Times*, p. 14.

Ibrahim, Y. (1996, December 13). Welfare's cozy coat eases Norwegian cold. *The New York Times*, pp. A1, A12.

Illegal drugs brought $57 billion in 1995. (1997, November 10). *The New York Times*, p. A24.

Janofsky, M. (1997, March 2). Worker fights dismissal for medical marijuana use. *The New York Times*, p. 18.

Jensen, E., Gerber, J., & Babcock, G. (1991). The new war on drugs: Grass roots movement or political construction? *Journal of Drug Issues, 21*,(3), 651–667.

Jessor, R. (1992). *Risk behavior in adolescence: A psychosocial framework for understanding action.* Boulder, CO: Westview Press.

Jewett, C. L. *Helping children cope with separation and loss.* Harvard, MA: Harvard Common Press, Inc.

Johnson, D. (1996, February 22). Good people go bad in Iowa, and a drug is being blamed. *The New York Times*, pp. A1, A19.

Johnson, E. (1996). *Japanese corrections: Managing convicted offenders in an orderly society.* Carbondale, IL: Southern Illinois University Press.

Jonnes, J. (1996). *Hep-cats, narcs, and pipe dreams.* New York: Scribner.

Kagan, J. (1986). The psychological requirements for human development. In A. Skolnick & J. Skolnick (Eds.), *Family in transition* (pp. 375–376) Boston: Little, Brown.

Kandall, S. (1996). *Substance and shadow: Women and addiction in the United States.* Cambridge, MA: Harvard University Press.

Kennedy, D. (1996). Flirting with disaster. *Entertainment Weekly, August 9, 1996*, 18–23, 26.

Kennedy, J. (1986). *A nation of immigrants.* New York: Harper & Row.

Kilpatrick, W. (1963). *Philosophy of education.* New York: Macmillan.

King, R. (1972). *The drug hang-up: America's fifty year folly.* New York: Norton.

Kirkland, G., & Lawrence, G. (1992). *Dancing on my grave.* New York: Berkley Books.

Knapp, C. (1996). *Drinking: A love story.* New York: Delta Books.

Kobasa, S., Maddi, S., & Kahn, S. (1982). Hardiness and health: A prospective study. *Journal of Personality and Social Psychology, 42*, 168–177.

Kocieniewski, D. (1997, January 5). New York pays a high price for police lies. *The New York Times*, pp. 1, 20.

Kohut, H. (1971). *Analysis of the self.* New York: International Universities Press.

Kohut, H. (1977). *Restoration of the self.* New York: International Universities Press.

Kolata, G. (1997, April 17). Safeguards urged for researchers. *The New York Times*, p. D23.

Koral, R. (1995). Introduction. In J. Miller, & R. Koral, (Eds.), *White rabbit* (pp. xi–xvi). San Francisco: Chronicle Books.

Kristoff, N. (1996, September 10). Welfare as Japan knows it: A family affair. *The New York Times*, pp. A1, A14.

Kumagai, F. (1996). *Unmasking Japan today: The impact of traditional values on modern Japanese society.* Westport, CT: Praeger.

Kumpfer, K. (1987). Special populations: Etiology and prevention of vulnerability to chemical dependency in children of substance abusers. In B. Brown & A. Mills (Eds.), *Youth at high risk for substance abuse* (pp. 1–72). (DHHS Publication No. ADM 87–1537). Rockville, MD: U.S. Alcohol, Drug Abuse, and Mental Health Administration.

Lapointe, J. (1998, February 20). U.S. players vandalize a suite at village. *The New York Times*, pp. C1, C3.

Lefkerites, M. (1992). The sociocultural implications of modernizing childbirth among Greek women on the island of Rhodes. *Medical Anthropology, 13*, pp. 385–412.

Levi, G., & Schmitt, J. (1997). *A history of young people in the west.* Cambridge, MA: Belknap Press.

Levin, J.(1987). *Treatment of alcoholism and other addictions.* Northvale, NJ: Jason Aronson.

Levin, J. (1995). *Introduction to alcoholism counseling, 2nd ed.* Washington, DC: Taylor and Francis.

Levin, J., & Weiss, R. (1994). *The dynamics and treatment of alcoholism: Essential papers.* Northvale, NJ: Jason Aronson.

Lewin, K. (1951). *Field theory in social science.* New York: Harper.

Lewin, T. (1997, December 3). Despite recent carnage, school violence is not on rise. *The New York Times*, p. A16.

Lewis, D., & Zinberg, N. (1964). Narcotic usage, II. A historical perspective on a difficult medical problem. *New England Journal of Medicine, 270*, 1045–1050.

Lindesmith, A. (1947). *Opiate addiction.* Bloomington, IN: Principia Press.

Lipsyte, R. (1995, November 26). The college sport of getting smashed. *The New York Times*, Sec. 8, p. 7.

Lundy, K. (1992). *On the edge: A naturalistic study of a small group of street kids.* Unpublished doctoral dissertation, New York University.

Lohr, S. (1996, December 29). Through upbeat economy, people still fear for their jobs. *The New York Times*, pp. 1, 22.

Lohr, S. (1997, February 3). Vladimir A. Yamnikov, 56, premium Russian vodka maker. *The New York Times Obituaries*, p. B8.

Mansnerus, L. (1995, November 26). At death's door, the message is tune in, turn on, drop in. *The New York Times*, Sec. 4, p. 7.

Martinson, F. (1992). *Growing up in Norway, 800 to 1990.* Carbondale, IL: Southern Illinois University Press.

Massing, M. (1998, September 6). Winning the war on drugs isn't so hard after all. *The New York Times Magazine*, pp. 48–50.

Mathews, W. (1975). A critique of traditional drug education programs. *Journal of Drug Education, 5*,(1), 57–64.

McClelland, D., Davis, W., Kalin, R., & Wanner, E. (1972). *The drinking man: Alcohol and human motivation.* New York: The Free Press.

McGuire, W. (1964). Inducing resistance to persuasion. In L. Berkowitz (Ed.), *Advances in experimental social psychology* (pp. 191–229). New York: Academic Press.

McNeil, L., & McCain, G. (1996). *Please kill me: The uncensored oral history of punk.* New York: Grove Press.

McQuiston, J. (1997, November 8). L. I. teacher fined $39,000 overdrinking by students. *The New York Times*, p. B4.

Mellow, J. (1984). *Invented lives: F. Scott and Zelda Fitzgerald.* Boston: Houghton Mifflin.

Menand, L. (1996, September 22). How to make a Ph.D. matter. *The New York Times Magazine*, Sec. 6, pp. 78–81.

Metcalf, J. (Ed.). (1987). *Drama: Voice of Social History.* New York: Learning through an Expanded Arts Program, Inc.

Mezey, S. (1996). *Children in court*. Albany, NY: State University of New York Press.

Milburn, M., & Conrad, S. (1996). *The politics of denial*. Cambridge, MA: MIT Press.

Miller, A. (1981). *The Drama of the Gifted Child*. New York: Basic Books.

Miller, A. (1983). *For your own good: Hidden cruelty in child-rearing and the roots of violence*. New York: Farrar, Straus & Giroux.

Miller, D., & Telljohan, S. (1992). *Health education in the elementary school*. Dubuque, IA: W.C. Brown.

Miller, J., & Koral, R.(Eds.), (1995). *White rabbit*. San Francisco: Chronicle Books.

Mitchell, W., & Simmons, R. (1994). *Beyond politics: Markets, welfare, and the failure of the bureaucracy*. Boulder, CO: Westview Press.

Moore, M. (1989, October 16). Actually, prohibition was a success. *The New York Times*. (Reprinted from *Drug Legalization: For and against*, pp. 13–15, by R. Evans & I. Berent, Eds., 1992, LaSalle IL: Open Court).

Moore, M. (1996). *Downsize this*. New York: Crown Publishers.

Mosse, G. (1996). *The image of man*. New York: Oxford University Press.

Musto, D. (1987). *The American disease*. New York: Oxford University Press.

National Institute on Drug Abuse. (1984). *Drug abuse and drug abuse research, 43* (DHHS Publication No. ADM 85–1372). Washington, DC: U.S. Government Printing Office.

Navarro, M. (1996, November 24). Marijuana farms are flourishing indoors, producing a more potent drug. *The New York Times*, p. 18.

Navarro, M. (1997, March 7). Russian submarine drifts into center of brazen drug plot. *The New York Times*, p. A22.

Nearly 7% of adult black men were inmates in '94, study says. (1995, December 4). *The New York Times*, p. A15.

Ney, T. (1995). *True and false allegations of child sexual abuse*. New York: Brunner/Mazel.

Noble, W. (1990). *Bookbanning in America*. Middlebury, VT: Paul Eriksson, Publisher.

Oates, R. (1996). *The spectrum of child abuse: Assessment, treatment, and prevention*. New York: Brunner/Mazel.

Office of Educational Research and Improvement. (1988). *Drug prevention curricula*. Washington, DC: U.S. Department of Education.

Office of the Inspector General. (1983). *Runaway and homeless youth: National program inspection*. Washington, DC: Department of Health and Human Services, Region X.

O'Neill, E. (1955). *Long day's journey into night*. New Haven, CT: Yale University Press.

O'Neill, E. (1957). *The iceman cometh*. New York: Random House.

Ornstein, N. (1994). Less seems more: What to do about contemporary political corruption. *Responsive community, Winter, 7*.

Owens, T. (1995). *Bebop: The music and its players*. New York: Oxford University Press.

Patterson, J., & Kim, P. (1994). *The second American revolution*. New York: William Morrow.

Peltason, J. (1967). An approach to the study of public policy. In J. Peltason & J. Burns (Eds.), *Functions and policies of American government* (pp. 1–13) Englewood Cliffs, NJ: Prentice-Hall.

Perez-Pena, R. (1997, February 4). Supervision of troopers faulted in evidence-tampering scandal. *The New York Times*, pp. B1, B4.

Pinchbeck, D. (1995, November 5). Children of the beats. *The New York Times Magazine*, Sec. 6, pp. 38–43.

Pinderhughes, H. (1997). *Race in the hood: Conflict and violence among urban youth*. Minneapolis, MN: University of Minnesota Press.

Polich, J., Ellickson, P., Reuter, P., & Kahan, J. (1984). *Controlling adolescent drug use*. Santa Monica, CA: Rand Corporation.

Pollan, M. (1995, February 19). How pot has grown. *The New York Times Magazine*, Sec. 6, pp. 31–35, 44, 50, 56–57.

Porter, B. (1995, November 24). Terror on an eight hour shift. *New York Times Magazine*, Sec. 6, pp. 42–47, 56, 59, 72, 76, 80, 82.

Public Health Reports (1992). WHO begins research on drugs and sports. *Public Health Reports, 107*(5), 606.

Purdy, M. (1997, August 24). What does it take to get arrested in New York City? Not much. *The New York Times*, pp. 27–28.

Ramirez, J. (1983). Race and the apprehension of inmate misconduct. *Journal of Criminal Justice, 1*, pp. 413–427.

Rangel, C. (1988, June 11). Legalizing drugs: A dangerous idea. *The Washington Post*, (Reprinted from *Drug Legalization: For and against*, pp. 13–15, by R. Evans & I. Berent, Eds., 1992, LaSalle IL: Open Court).

Ray, O. (1972). *Drugs, society, and human behavior*. St. Louis, MO: Mosby.

Resnik, H. (1990). *Youth and drugs: Society's mixed messages*. Rockville, MD: U.S. Department of Health and Human Services.

Rifkin, J. (1995). *The end of work: The decline of the global labor force and the dawn of the post market era*. New York: Putnam.

Roane, K. (1998, January 31). Needle attacks at school leave students fearful. *The New York Times*, p. B4.

Robbins, J. (1997, February 14). Sponsor of Montana school punishment bill accused of abuse. *The New York Times*, p. A15.

Roberts, R., & Kloss, R. (1974). *Social movements: Between the balcony and the barricade*. St. Louis, MO: Mosby.

Rogers, C. (1962). The interpersonal relationship: The core of guidance. *Harvard Educational Review, 32*(4), 416–429.

Roman, P., & Blum, T. (1995). Employers. In R. Combs & D. Ziedonis (Eds.), *Handbook on drug abuse prevention* (pp. 139–158). Needham Heights, MA: Allyn & Bacon.

Roorbach, B. (1997, February 2). Mommy, what's a classroom. *The New York Times Magazine*, pp. 30–37.

Rosenbaum, D. (1997, February 23). I.R.S. bans deducting medical cost of marijuana. *The New York Times*, p. 19.

Rudgley, R. (1993). *Essential substances: A cultural history of intoxicants in society*. New York: Kondasha America.

Ruggiero, V. (1994). *Warning: Nonsense is destroying America*. Nashville, TN: Thomas Nelson Publishers.

Rumbarger, J. (1989). *Power, profits and prohibition*. Albany, NY: State University of New York Press.

Sales, N. (1996, December 16). Teenage gangland. *New York Magazine*, pp. 32–39.

Samuelson, R. (1995). *The good life and its discontents: The American dream in the age of entitlement 1945–1995*. New York: Times Books.

Sandomir, R. (1996, September 13). Shedding light on drug use in pro football. *The New York Times*, p. B15.

Sandor, R. (1995). Legalizing/decriminalizing drug use. In R. Combs & D. Ziedonis (eds.), *Handbook on drug abuse prevention. (pp. 509–526). Needham Heights, MA: Allyn & Bacon*.

Sanger, D. (1997, January 9). 'Parting benediction' by lonely liberal. *The New York Times*, p. B8.

Savage-Supernaw, P. (1991, November 19). *The resilient child in the midst of chaos*. Paper presented at conference on "Urban College Student Survival: Coping with Alcohol and other Drug Issues." City College of New York, NY.

Schlesinger, A. (1992). *The disuniting of America: Reflections on a multicultural society*. New York: Norton.

Schlesinger, A. (1996, December 15). The ultimate approval rating. *The New York Times Magazine*, pp. 46–51.

Schuller, G. (1989). *The swing era: The development of jazz, 1930–45*. New York: Oxford University Press.

Seeger, P. (1983). So long, Woody, it's been good to know ya. In W. Guthrie (Ed.), *Bound for glory*. New York: Plume/Penguin.

Sengupta, S. (1996, December 30). Immigrants in New York pressing drive for dual nationality. *The New York Times*, pp. B1, B4.

Shattuck, F. (1996, November 26). For Burroughs at 82, a legion of fans under the influence. *The New York Times*, p. C11, C15.

Shelton, R. (1965). Introduction. In W. Guthrie (Ed.), *Born to win*. (pp. 11–14) New York: Macmillan.

Singer, M., Anglin, T., Song, L., & Lunghofer, L. (1995). Adolescents' exposure to violence and associated symptoms of psychological trauma. *Journal of the American medical Association, 273*(6), 477–482.

Smolowe, J. (1994) ... and throw away the key. *Time, February 7, 1994*, p. 54.

Specter, M. (1997, January 21). Yeltsin goes after a Russian religion: Vodka. *The New York Times*, p. A3.

Steinberg, L. (1996). *Beyond the classroom*. New York: Simon & Schuster.

Steuart, G. (1969). Planning and evaluation in health education. *International Journal of Health Education, 12*,(2), pp. 65–76.

Student's stepfather gets jail in teacher assault. (1997, November 22). *The New York Times*, p. B5.

Telander, R. (1993, November 22). Mail order muscles. *Sports Illustrated*, p. 56.

Terry, D. (1996, December 13). Ex-prosecutors and deputies in death row case are charged with framing defendant. *The New York Times*, p. A18.

Terry, D. (1996, December 21). 7 Chicago police officers indicted in extortion scheme. *The New York Times*, p. 12.

Thomas, R. (1996, August 9). Herbert Huncke, the hipster who defined 'beat' dies at 81. *The New York Times*, p. B7.

Thompson, D. (1994). *Never fade away: The Kurt Cobain story*. New York: St. Martins's Press.

Thurow, L. (1992). *Head to head*. New York: William Morrow.

Truman, D. (1981). *The governmental process: Political interests and public opinion*. Westport, CT: Greenwood Press.

Unnever, J. (1982). Direct and organizational discrimination in the sentencing of drug offenders. *Social Problems, 30*(2), 212–225.

Untitled. *Newsweek Magazine, February 17, 1997*, p. 23.

U.S. Department of Education. (1992). *What works: Schools without drugs.* Washington, DC: U.S. Department of Education.

Vaillant, G. (1983). *The natural history of alcoholism*. Boston: Harvard University Press.

Verde, T. (1998, February 2). 90's moonshiners add drugs and guns to the recipe. *The New York Times*, p. A12.

Vermont survey finds support for the legalization of hemp. (1997, February 17). *The New York Times*, p. 52.

Wadler, G., & Zemper, E. (1995). Sports organizations. In R. Combs & D. Ziedonis (Eds.), *Handbook on drug abuse prevention* (pp. 197–216). Needham Heights, MA: Allyn & Bacon.

Wald, M. (1998, January 30). Drunken-driving standard may shift. *The New York Times*, p. F1.

Webster, D. (1993, Winter). Commentary: The unconvincing case for school based conflict resolution programs for adolescents. *Health Affairs*, 126–141.

Weinstein, S. (1987). Disciplinary action: Dealing with problem behaviors in nonprofit organizations. In E. Anthes & J. Cronin (Eds.), *Personnel matters in the nonprofit organization* (pp. 259–277). West Memphis: Independent Community Consultants.

Weinstein, S. (1991). Prevention of emotional distress and drug and alcohol abuse among musicians and other arts performers and students. *Canadian Band Journal, 15*(4), 39–40.

Weinstein, S. (1995a). *Family beyond family: The surrogate parent in schools and other community agencies*. Binghamton, NY: Haworth Press.

Weinstein, S. (1995b). Family Stress: Adjustment to crisis and transition. In R. Patton (Ed.), *The American family: life and health* (2nd ed., pp. 567–579). Oakland, CA: Third Party Publishing.

Weinstein, S. (1995c, November). Helping troubled children. *Music Educators Journal*, 17–21.

Weinstein, S. (1996, November 16). *Validation of a violence prevention model for the schools*. Paper presented at the annual meeting of the society for Public Health Education, New York Hilton, NY.

Weinstein, S. (1997a). *Evaluation report: The Leadership Program component of the Extended Day Violence Prevention Program in the Bronx Public High Schools*. Bronx, NY: Office of the Superintendent of Bronx High Schools, Special Education Operations.

Weinstein, S. (1997b). *Evaluation report: The Leadership Program component of the Extended School Day and Violence Prevention program in New York City Public High and Middle Schools*. New York: Central Park Historical Society.

Weintraub, S. (1976). *Aubrey Beardsley: Imp of the perverse*. University Park, PA: Pennsylvania State University Press.

Welsh, I. (1996). *Trainspotting*. New York: Norton.

Wepner, S. (1984). Which way drug education? In S. Eisman, J. Wingard, & G. Huba (Eds.), *Drug abuse: Foundation for a psychosocial approach* (pp. 59–69). Farmingdale, NY: Baywood.

Wills, G. (1996, August 11). Its his party. *The New York Times Magazine*, pp. 30–37, 52. 55–59.

Wills, T. (1991, November 19). *Vulnerability and protective factors for substance abuse among 12–15 year old urban youth.* Paper presented at conference on "Urban College Student Survival: Coping with Alcohol and other Drug Issues." City College of New York, NY.

Wilson, W. (1996, August 19). Work. *The New York Times Magazine*, Sec. 6, pp. 26–31, 40, 48, 52–54.

Wilson-Brewer, R. (1995). Peer violence prevention programs in middle and high schools. *Adolescent Medicine: State of the Art Reviews*, 6(2), pp. 233–249.

Wines, M. (1997, January 12). Corruption lite, democracy's junk food. *The New York Times*, Sec. 4, pp. 1, 5.

Winick, C. (1986). The deviance model of drug taking behavior. In B. Segal (Ed.), *Perspectives on drug use in the United States* (pp. 29–50). New York: Haworth Press.

Wolfe, A. (1998). *One nation, after all.* New York: Viking.

Wolfe, T. (1987). *Bonfire of the vanities.* New York: Farrar, Straus & Giroux.

Wolff, M. (1992). *Where we stand: Can America make it in a global race for wealth, health and happiness.* New York: Bantam.

Wren, C. (1996a, December 1). Smoking heroin is linked to neurological ailment. *The New York Times*, p. 49.

Wren, C. (1996b, Decmeber 15). Why seizing drugs barely dents supply. The *New York Times*, p. 4.

Wren, C. (1997a, January 31). U.S. plans meeting to study issue of medical marijuana. *The New York Times*, p. A14.

Wren, C. (1997, February 2). Ex-addicts find methadone more elusive than heroin. *The New York Times*, p. 12.

Wren, C. (1997, March 4). Keeping cocaine resilient: Low cost and high profit. *The New York Times*, p. 1, A20.

Wren, C. (1997d, April 20). Phantom numbers haunt the war on drugs. *The New York Times*, Sec. 4, p. 4.

Wren, C. (1997e, April 21). Hartford mulls an overhaul of drug laws. *The New York Times*, p. B1.

Wren, C. (1997, June 3). One of medicines best kept secrets: Methadone works. *The New York Times*, p. C3.

Wren, C. (1997g, June 29). U.N. report says tens of millions use illicit drugs. *The New York Times*, p. A12.

Zeese, K. (1989). Drug war forever? In A. Trebach & K. Zeese (Eds.), *Drug policy 1989–1990: A reformer's catalogue.* Washington, DC: The Drug Policy Foundation.

# Author Index

# Subject Index